NASA SP-2002-4524

Deep Space Chronicle
A Chronology of Deep Space and Planetary Probes
1958–2000

ASIF A. SIDDIQI

Monographs in Aerospace History
Number 24
June 2002

National Aeronautics and Space Administration
Office of External Relations
NASA History Office
Washington, DC 20546-0001

Library of Congress Cataloging-in-Publication Data

Siddiqi, Asif A., 1966-
　　Deep space chronicle: a chronology of deep space and planetary probes, 1958-2000 / by Asif A. Siddiqi.
　　p.cm. – (Monographs in aerospace history; no. 24) (NASA SP; 2002-4524)
Includes bibliographical references and index.
1. Space flight—History—20th century. I. Title. II. Series. III. NASA SP; 4524

TL 790.S53 2002
629.4'1'0904—dc21　　　　　　　　　　　　　　　　　　　　　　　　　　　2001044012

Table of Contents

Foreword by Roger D. Launius 1

Introduction 11

1958 17
    1) Able 1 / "Pioneer 0" 17
    2) no name / [Luna] 17
    3) Able 2 / "Pioneer 0" 18
    4) no name / [Luna] 18
    5) Pioneer 2 18
    6) no name / [Luna] 19
    7) Pioneer 3 19

1959 21
    8) Cosmic Rocket 21
    9) Pioneer 4 22
    10) no name / [Luna] 22
    11) Second Cosmic Rocket 23
    12) Automatic Interplanetary Station 23
    13) Able IVB / "Pioneer" 23

1960 25
    14) Pioneer 5 25
    15) no name / [Luna] 25
    16) no name / [Luna] 26
    17) Able VA / "Pioneer" 26
    18) no name / [Mars] 26
    19) no name / [Mars] 27
    20) Able VB / "Pioneer" 27

1961 29
    21) Tyazhelyy Sputnik / [Venera] 29
    22) Venera 29
    23) Ranger 1 31
    24) Ranger 2 31

1962 33
    25) Ranger 3 33
    26) Ranger 4 33
    27) Mariner 1 34
    28) no name / [Venera] 34
    29) Mariner 2 34
    30) no name / [Venera] 35
    31) no name / [Venera] 35
    32) Ranger 5 35
    33) no name / [Mars] 36
    34) Mars 1 36
    35) no name / [Mars] 37

1963 39
    36) no name / [Luna] 39
    37) no name / [Luna] 39
    38) Luna 4 40
    39) Kosmos 21 / [Zond] 40

1964 41
    40) Ranger 6 41
    41) no name / [Zond] 41
    42) no name / [Luna] 42
    43) Kosmos 27 / [Zond] 42
    44) Zond 1 42
    45) no name / [Luna] 43
    46) Ranger 7 43
    47) Mariner 3 43
    48) Mariner 4 44
    49) Zond 2 45

1965 47
    50) Ranger 8 47
    51) "Atlas Centaur 5" 47
    52) Kosmos 60 / [Luna] 48
    53) Ranger 9 48
    54) no name / [Luna] 48
    55) Luna 5 48
    56) Luna 6 49
    57) Zond 3 49
    58) Surveyor Model 1 50
    59) Luna 7 50
    60) Venera 2 50
    61) Venera 3 51
    62) Kosmos 96 / [Venera] 51
    63) Luna 8 51
    64) Pioneer 6 52

1966 53
    65) Luna 9 53
    66) Kosmos 111 / [Luna] 53
    67) Luna 10 54
    68) Surveyor Model 2 54
    69) Surveyor 1 55
    70) Explorer 33 56
    71) Lunar Orbiter 1 56
    72) Pioneer 7 56
    73) Luna 11 57
    74) Surveyor 2 57
    75) Luna 12 58
    76) Lunar Orbiter 2 58
    77) Luna 13 58

1967 61
   78) Lunar Orbiter 3 61
   79) Surveyor 3 61
   80) Lunar Orbiter 4 63
   81) Kosmos 159 / [Luna] 63
   82) Venera 4 64
   83) Mariner 5 64
   84) Kosmos 167 / [Venera] 65
   85) Surveyor 4 65
   86) Explorer 35 65
   87) Lunar Orbiter 5 66
   88) Surveyor 5 67
   89) no name / [Zond] 67
   90) Surveyor 6 67
   91) no name / [Zond] 68
   92) Pioneer 8 68

1968 69
   93) Surveyor 7 69
   94) no name / [Luna] 69
   95) Zond 4 70
   96) Luna 14 70
   97) no name / [Zond] 70
   98) Zond 5 70
   99) Pioneer 9 71
   100) Zond 6 71

1969 73
   101) Venera 5 73
   102) Venera 6 74
   103) no name / [Zond] 74
   104) no name / [Luna] 74
   105) no name / [N1 launch test] 75
   106) Mariner 6 75
   107) no name / [Mars] 76
   108) Mariner 7 76
   109) no name / [Mars] 77
   110) no name / [Luna] 77
   111) no name / [N1 test flight] 78
   112) Luna 15 78
   113) Zond 7 78
   114) Pioneer 79
   115) Kosmos 300 / [Luna] 79
   116) Kosmos 305 / [Luna] 79

1970 81
   117) no name / [Luna] 81
   118) Venera 7 81
   119) Kosmos 359 / [Venera] 82
   120) Luna 16 82
   121) Zond 8 83
   122) Luna 17 83

1971 85
- 123) Mariner 8 85
- 124) Kosmos 419 / [Mars] 85
- 125) Mars 2 86
- 126) Mars 3 87
- 127) Mariner 9 88
- 128) Apollo 15 Particle and Fields Subsatellite 90
- 129) Luna 18 90
- 130) Luna 19 90

1972 93
- 131) Luna 20 93
- 132) Pioneer 10 93
- 133) Venera 8 97
- 134) Kosmos 482 / [Venera] 98
- 135) Apollo 16 Particles and Fields Subsatellite 98
- 136) no name / [N1 launch test] 98

1973 101
- 137) Luna 21 101
- 138) Pioneer 11 102
- 139) Explorer 49 102
- 140) Mars 4 103
- 141) Mars 5 104
- 142) Mars 6 104
- 143) Mars 7 105
- 144) Mariner 10 105

1974 107
- 145) Luna 22 107
- 146) Luna 23 107
- 147) Helios 1 108

1975 109
- 148) Venera 9 109
- 149) Venera 10 110
- 150) Viking 1 110
- 151) Viking 2 111
- 152) no name / [Luna] 112

1976 115
- 153) Helios 2 115
- 154) Luna 24 115

1977 117
- 155) Voyager 2 117
- 156) Voyager 1 120

1978

- 157) Pioneer Venus 1 123
- 158) Pioneer Venus 2 124
- 159) ISEE-3 125
- 160) Venera 11 125
- 161) Venera 12 126

1981

- 162) Venera 13 129
- 163) Venera 14 130

1983

- 164) Venera 15 131
- 165) Venera 16 131

1984

- 166) Vega 1 133
- 167) Vega 2 134

1985

- 168) Sakigake 137
- 169) Giotto 137
- 170) Suisei 138

1988

- 171) Fobos 1 141
- 172) Fobos 2 142

1989

- 173) Magellan 143
- 174) Galileo 145

1990

- 175) Hiten/Hagomoro 149
- 176) Ulysses 149

1992

- 177) Mars Observer 153

1994

- 178) Clementine 155
- 179) Wind 157

1995

- 180) SOHO 159

1996 161
- 181) NEAR 161
- 182) Mars Global Surveyor 163
- 183) Mars 8 164
- 184) Mars Pathfinder 165

1997 169
- 185) ACE 169
- 186) Cassini/Huygens 169
- 187) Asiasat 3 170

1998 173
- 188) Lunar Prospector 173
- 189) Nozomi 173
- 190) Deep Space 1 174
- 191) Mars Climate Orbiter 176

1999 177
- 192) Mars Polar Lander/Deep Space 2 177
- 193) Stardust 178

Master Table of All Deep Space, Lunar, and Planetary Probes, 1958–2000 179
- 1958 181
- 1959 181
- 1960 181
- 1961 182
- 1962 182
- 1963 182
- 1964 183
- 1965 183
- 1966 184
- 1967 184
- 1968 185
- 1969 186
- 1970 186
- 1971 187
- 1972 187
- 1973 188
- 1974 188
- 1975 188
- 1976 188
- 1977 189
- 1978 189
- 1981 189
- 1983 189
- 1984 189
- 1985 190
- 1988 190
- 1989 190
- 1990 190
- 1992 190
- 1994 190
- 1995 191

1996	191
1997	191
1998	191
1999	192
Program Tables	193
Appendices	207
Bibliography	217
About the Author	223
The NASA History Series	227
Index	237

Deep Space Chronicle:
Foreword

Foreword

From the 1950s to the present, to some Americans, space has represented prestige and a positive image for the United States on the world stage. To others, it has signified the quest for national security. Some view it as a place to station telecommunications satellites and little else. To still others, space is, or should be, about gaining greater knowledge of the universe. It represents, for them, pure science and the exploration of the unknown. Even so, the history of space science and technology is one of the largely neglected aspects in the history of the space program. This important monograph by Asif A. Siddiqi chronicles the many space probes that have been sent from Earth to explore other bodies of the solar system. It provides a chronological discussion of all space probes, both those developed by the United States and those developed by the Soviet Union/Russia and other nations; basic data about them; their findings; and their status over time. As such, this monograph is a handy reference work that will provide fundamental data for all missions undertaken during the twentieth century.

Since the first flights discussed here, every planet of the solar system has been explored in a modest way at least once (save Pluto), and several of the moons of planetary bodies (including our own), as well as some comets and asteroids, have been visited. We have placed spacecraft in orbit around our Moon and the planets Venus, Mars, and Jupiter; we have landed on Venus, Mars, and our Moon. NASA's stunning missions to explore the outer Solar System have yielded a treasure of knowledge about our universe, how it originated, and how it works. NASA's exploration of Mars—coupled with the efforts of the Soviet Union/Russia—has powerfully shown the prospect of past life on the Red Planet. Missions to Venus (including some that landed on it) and Mercury have increased our understanding of the inner planets. Lunar exploration has exponentially advanced human knowledge about the origins and evolution of the solar system. Most importantly, we have learned that, like Goldilocks and the three bears, Earth is a place in which everything necessary to sustain life is "just right," while all the other planets of our system seem exceptionally hostile.

Planetary exploration has not taken place by magic. It required visionary leadership, strong-willed management, and persevering execution. Like NASA and other aspects of the space program, it began as a race between the United States and the Soviet Union to see who would be the first to get some sort of spacecraft near the Moon. It expanded in the 1960s when space science first became a major field of study. During that decade, both the United States and the Soviet Union began an impressive effort to gather information on the planets of the solar system using ground-, air-, and space-based equipment. Especially important was the creation of two types of spacecraft, one a probe that was sent toward a heavenly body, and the second an Earth-orbiting observatory that could gain the clearest resolution available in telescopes because it did not have to contend with the atmosphere.

The studies resulting from this new data have revolutionized humanity's understanding of Earth's immediate planetary neighbors. These studies of the planets, perhaps as much even as Project Apollo, captured the imagination of people from all backgrounds and perspectives. Photographs of the planets and theories about the origins of the solar system appealed to a very broad cross section of the public. As a result, NASA had little difficulty in capturing and holding a widespread interest in this aspect of the space science program.

Exploration of the Terrestrial (Inner) Planets

During the 1960s, NASA space science focused much of its efforts on lunar missions with projects Ranger, Surveyor, and Lunar Orbiter. Even so, a centerpiece of NASA's planetary exploration effort in that era was the Mariner program, originated by NASA in the early part of the decade to investigate the nearby planets. Built by Jet Propulsion Laboratory (JPL) scientists and technicians, satellites of this program proved enormously productive in visiting both Mars and Venus.

Mariner made a huge impact in the early 1960s as part of a race between the United States and the Soviet Union to see who would be the first to reach Venus. This goal was more than just an opportunity to beat the rival in the Cold War; scientists in both the United States and the Soviet Union recognized the attraction of Venus for the furtherance of planetary studies. Both the evening and the morning star, Venus had long enchanted humans, and it has done so all the more since astronomers realized that it was shrouded in a mysterious cloak of clouds permanently hiding the surface from view. As a further attraction, it was also the closest planet to Earth and a near twin to this planet in terms of size, mass, and gravitation.

After ground-based efforts in 1961 to view the planet using radar, which could see through the clouds, and after learning, among other things, that Venus rotated in a retrograde motion opposite from the direction of orbital motion, both the Soviet Union and the United States began a race to the planet with several robotic spacecraft. The United States claimed the first success in planetary exploration during the summer of 1962, when Mariner 1 and Mariner 2 were launched toward Venus. Although Mariner 1 was lost during a launch failure, Mariner 2 flew by Venus on 14 December 1962 at a distance of 34,827 kilometers. It probed the clouds, estimated planetary temperatures, measured the charged particle environment, and looked for a magnetic field similar to Earth's magnetosphere (but found none). After this encounter, Mariner 2 sped inside the orbit of Venus and eventually ceased operations on 3 January 1963, when it overheated. In 1967, the United States sent Mariner 5 to Venus to investigate the atmosphere. Both spacecraft demonstrated that Venus was a very inhospitable place for life to exist and determined that the entire planet's surface was a fairly uniform 425 degrees Celsius. This discovery refuted the probability that life—at least as humans understood it—existed on Venus.

The most significant mission to Venus began in 1989 when the Magellan spacecraft set out for Venus to map the surface from orbit with imaging radar. This mission followed the Pioneer Venus 1 spacecraft that had been orbiting the planet for more than a decade and had completed a low-resolution radar topographic map, and Pioneer Venus 2, which had dispatched heat-resisting probes to penetrate the atmosphere and communicate information about the surface, Venus's dense clouds, and the 425°C temperature. It also built on the work of the Soviet Union, which had compiled radar images of the northern part of Venus and had deployed balloons into the Venusian atmosphere. Magellan arrived at Venus in September 1990 and mapped 99 percent of the surface at high resolution, parts of it in stereo. The amount of digital imaging data the spacecraft returned was more than twice the sum of all returns from previous missions. This data provided some surprises, among them the discovery that plate tectonics was at work on Venus and that lava flows clearly showed the evidence of volcanic activity. In 1993, at the end of the mission, NASA's Jet Propulsion Laboratory shut down the major functions of the Magellan spacecraft and scientists turned their attention to a detailed analysis of its data.

Mars has attracted significant attention from the beginning of the space age. An attraction yet to be relinquished by most planetary scientists, Mars prompted many missions. In July 1965, Mariner 4 flew by Mars and took 21 close-up pictures. Mariners 6 and 7, launched in February and March 1969, respectively, each passed Mars in August 1969, studying its atmosphere and surface to lay the groundwork for an eventual landing on the planet. Their pictures verified the Moon-like appearance of Mars and gave no hint that Mars had ever been able to support life. Among other discoveries, these probes found that much of Mars was cratered almost like the Moon, that volcanoes had once been active on the planet, that the frost observed seasonally on the poles was made of carbon dioxide, and that huge plates indicated considerable tectonic activity. Mariner 9, scheduled to enter Martian orbit in November 1971, detected a chilling dust storm spreading across Mars; by mid-October dust obscured almost all of Mars. Mariner 9's first pictures showed a featureless disk, marred only by a group of black spots in a region known as Nix Olympia (Snows of Olympus). As the dust storm subsided, the four spots emerged out of the dust cloud to become the remains of giant extinct volcanoes dwarfing anything on Earth. Olympus Mons, the largest of the four, was 483 kilometers across at the base with a 72-kilometer-wide crater in the top. Rising 32 kilometers from the surrounding plane, Olympus Mons was three times the height of Mt. Everest. Later pictures showed a canyon, Valles Marineris, 4,000 kilometers long and 5.6 kilometers deep. As the dust settled, meandering "rivers" appeared, indicating that, at some time in the past, fluid flowed on Mars. Suddenly, Mars fascinated scientists, reporters, and the public.

Project Viking represented the culmination of a series of missions to explore Mars that had begun in 1964. The Viking mission used two identical spacecraft, each consisting of a lander and an orbiter. Launched on 20 August 1975 from the Kennedy Space Center (KSC), Florida, Viking 1 spent nearly a year cruising to Mars, placed an orbiter in operation around the planet, and landed on 20 July 1976 on the Chryse Planitia (Golden Plains). Viking 2 was launched on 9 September 1975 and landed on 3 September 1976. The primary mission of the Viking project ended on 15 November 1976, eleven days before Mars's superior conjunction (its passage behind the Sun), although the Viking spacecraft continued to operate for six years after first reaching Mars. The last transmission from the planet reached Earth on 11 November 1982.

Since the Viking landings, there have been several missions to Mars seeking to further unlock its mysteries. These were energized in 1996 when a team of NASA and Stanford University scientists announced that a Mars meteorite found in Antarctica contained possible evidence of ancient Martian life. When the 1.9-kilogram, potato-sized rock, labeled ALH84001, was formed as an igneous rock about 4.5 billion years ago, Mars was much warmer and probably contained oceans hospitable to life. Then, about 15 million years ago, a large asteroid hit the Red Planet and jettisoned the rock into space, where it remained until it crashed into Antarctica around 11,000 B.C.E. The scientists presented three compelling, but not conclusive, pieces of evidence that suggest that fossil-like remains of Martian micro-organisms that date back 3.6 billion years are present in ALH84001. These findings electrified the scientific world, but they excited the public just as fully and added support for an aggressive set of missions to Mars by the year 2000 to help discover the truth of these theories.

The United States has undertaken several missions since then, including the hugely popular Mars Pathfinder. After launch in December 1996, it sped to Mars and landed on 4 July 1997. There, a small, 10.4-kilogram robotic rover named Sojourner departed from the main lander and began to record weather patterns, atmospheric opacity, and the chemical composition of rocks washed down into the Ares Vallis flood plain, an ancient outflow channel in Mars's northern hemisphere. Pathfinder returned more than 1.2 gigabits (1.2 billion bits) of data and over 10,000 tantalizing pictures of the Martian landscape. The images from both craft were posted to the Internet, and individuals retrieved information about the mission more than 500 million times through the end of July 1997.

Another mission reached Mars on 11 September 1997, when the Mars Global Surveyor, launched in December 1996, entered orbit. That spacecraft's magnetometer soon detected the existence of a planetary magnetic field. This held important implications for the geological history of Mars and for the possible development and continued existence of life there. Planets like Earth, Jupiter, and Saturn generate their magnetic fields by means of a dynamo made up of moving molten metal at the core. A molten interior suggests the existence of internal heat sources that could give rise to volcanoes and a flowing crust responsible for moving continents over geologic time periods.

These missions, coupled with others, began to create a new portrait of the Martian environment through the analysis of data relating to weather patterns, atmospheric opacity, and the chemical composition of rocks washed down into the Ares Vallis flood plain. Despite significant setbacks to the Mars exploration program with the failure of two missions in 1999, scientific returns from the Mars Global Surveyor reenergized interest in the planet. In what may prove a landmark discovery, scientists announced on 22 June 2000 that features observed on the planet suggested that there may be sources of liquid water at or near the surface. The new images showed the smallest features ever observed from Martian orbit—the size of an SUV. NASA scientists compared those features to those left by flash floods on Earth.

Everyone agreed that the presence of liquid water on Mars would have profound implications for the question of life on Mars. NASA's Associate Administrator for Space Science, Ed Weiler, commented, "If life ever did develop there, and if it survives to the present time, then these landforms would be great places to look." The gullies observed in the images were on cliffs—usually in crater or valley walls—and showed a deep channel with a collapsed region at its upper end and at the other end an area of accumulated debris that appeared to have been transported down the slope. Relative to the rest of the Martian surface, the gullies appeared to be extremely young, meaning they may have formed in the recent past. It is possible, scientists said, that water could be about 90 meters to 400 meters below the surface of Mars. Some scientists have been skeptical of these claims, but all agree that the only way to find out what is truly present is to send additional missions to Mars.

Exploration of the Jovian (Outer) Planets

As the heady spaceflight projects of the 1960s—culminating in the lunar exploration effort—suffered from more constrained budgets in the 1970s, NASA's most ambitious planetary science expedition was hatched amongst its leadership. Once every 176 years, the giant planets on the outer reaches of the solar system gather on one side of the Sun, and such a configuration was due to occur in the late 1970s. This geometric line-up made possible close-up observation of all the planets in the outer solar system (with the exception of Pluto) in a single flight, the so-called "Grand Tour." The flyby of each planet would bend the spacecraft's flight path and increase its velocity enough to deliver it to the next destination. This would occur through a complicated process known as "gravity-assist," something like a slingshot effect, whereby the flight time to Neptune could be reduced from thirty to twelve years.

In 1964, to prepare the way for the "Grand Tour," NASA conceived Pioneers 10 and 11 as outer-solar-system probes. Although severe budget constraints prevented the commencement of the project until the fall of 1968 and forced a somewhat less ambitious effort, Pioneer 10 was launched on 3 March 1972. It arrived at Jupiter on the night of 3 December 1973, and while many were concerned that the spacecraft might fall prey to intense radiation discovered in Jupiter's orbital plane, the spacecraft survived, transmitted data about the planet, and continued on its way out of the solar system, away from the center of the Milky Way galaxy. By May 1991, it was about 52 astronomical units (AU) from Earth, roughly twice the distance from Jupiter to the Sun, and still transmitting data.

In 1973, NASA launched Pioneer 11, providing scientists with their closest view of Jupiter, from 42,800 kilometers above the cloud tops in December 1974. The close approach and the spacecraft's speed of 172,800 kph, by far the fastest ever reached by an object from Earth, hurled the Pioneer 11 spacecraft 2.4 billion kilometers across the solar system. In 1979, Pioneer 11 encountered Saturn, closing to within 20,900 kilometers of the planet, where it discovered two new moonlets and a new ring and charted the magnetosphere, its magnetic field, its climate and temperatures, and the general structure of Saturn's interior. In 1990, it officially departed the solar system by passing beyond Pluto and headed into interstellar space toward the center of the Milky Way galaxy. Both Pioneers 10 and 11 were remarkable space probes; they stretched a thirty-month design life cycle into a mission of more than twenty years and returned useful data, not only about the other Jovian planets of the solar system, but also about some of the mysteries of the interstellar universe.

Meanwhile, NASA technicians prepared to launch what became known as Voyager. Although the four-planet mission was known to be possible, it quickly became too expensive to build a spacecraft that could go the distance, carry the instruments needed, and last long enough to accomplish such an extended mission. Thus, the two Voyager spacecraft were funded to conduct intensive flyby studies only of Jupiter and Saturn, in effect repeating on a more elaborate scale the flights of the two Pioneers. Even so, the spacecraft builders designed as much longevity into the two Voyagers as possible with the $865-million budget available. NASA launched these from Cape Canaveral, Florida; Voyager 2 lifted off on 20 August 1977, and Voyager 1 entered space on a faster, shorter trajectory on 5 September 1977.

As the mission progressed, with the successful achievement of all its objectives at Jupiter and Saturn, additional flybys of the two outermost giant planets, Uranus and Neptune, proved possible—and irresistible—to mission scientists. Accordingly, as the spacecraft flew across the solar system, remote-control reprogramming was used to prepare the Voyagers for the greater mission. Eventually, between them, Voyager 1 and Voyager 2 explored all the giant outer planets, forty-eight of their moons, and the unique systems of rings and magnetic fields those planets possess.

The two spacecraft returned information to Earth that revolutionized solar system science, helped to resolve some key questions, and raised intriguing new ones about the origin and evolution of the planets. The two Voyagers took well over 100,000 images of the outer planets, rings, and satellites, as well as millions of magnetic, chemical spectra, and radiation measurements. They discovered rings around Jupiter, volcanoes on Io, shepherded satellites in Saturn's rings, new moons around Uranus and Neptune, and geysers on Triton. The last sequence of images was Voyager 1's portrait of most of the solar system, showing Earth and six other planets as sparks in a dark sky lit by a single bright star, the Sun.

It was nearly two decades after Voyager before any spacecraft ventured to the outer solar system again. In October 1989, NASA's Galileo spacecraft began a gravity-assisted journey to Jupiter and sent a probe into the atmosphere that observed the planet and its satellites for several years beginning in December 1995. Jupiter was of great interest to scientists because it appeared to contain material in its original state left over from the formation of the solar system, and the mission was designed to investigate the chemical composition and physical state of Jupiter's atmosphere and satellites. Because of a unique orbital inclination that sent the probe around the Sun and back on the way to Jupiter, Galileo came back past both Venus and Earth, made the first close flyby of asteroid Gaspra in 1991, and provided scientific data on all. But the mission was star-crossed. Soon after Galileo's deployment from the Space Shuttle, NASA engineers learned that Galileo's umbrella-like high-gain antenna could not be fully deployed. Without this antenna, communication with the spacecraft was both more difficult and more time-consuming, and data transmission was greatly hampered. The engineering team that worked on the project tried a series of cooling exercises designed to shrink the antenna central tower and enable its deployment.

In mid-1995, Galileo deployed the probe that would parachute into Jupiter's dense atmosphere. The two spacecraft then flew in formation the rest of the way to Jupiter, and while the probe began its descent into the atmosphere, the main spacecraft went into a trajectory that placed it in a near-circular orbit. On 7 December 1995, the probe began its descent. Its instruments began relaying data back to the orbiter about chemical composition; the nature of the cloud particles and structure of the cloud layers; the atmosphere's radiative heat balance, pressure, and dynamics; and the ionosphere. The probe lasted for about 45 minutes, during which it stored and returned the data, before the atmosphere and the pressure of the planet destroyed it. For months thereafter, because the high-gain antenna was inoperative, scientists and technicians coaxed the data back to Earth for analysis. Today, Galileo continues to transmit scientific measurements back to Earth. The result has brought a reinterpretation of human understanding about Jupiter and its moons.

Most significant in terms of results has been the discovery of a frozen ocean of water covering Europa, one of the principal moons of Jupiter. On 13 August 1996, data from Galileo revealed that Europa may harbor "warm ice" or even liquid water—a key element in life-sustaining environments. Many scientists and science fiction writers have speculated that Europa—in addition to Mars and Saturn's moon Titan—is one of the three planetary bodies in this solar system that might possess, or may have possessed, an environment where primitive life existed. Galileo's photos of Europa were taken during a flyby of Ganymede some 154,500 kilometers away from Europa. They revealed what appeared to be ice floes similar to those seen on Earth's polar regions. The pictures also revealed giant cracks in Europa's ice where warm-water "environmental niches" may exist. In early 1997, Galileo discovered icebergs on Europa, a discovery that lent credence to the possibility of hidden, subsurface oceans. These findings generated new questions about the possibility of life on Europa. While NASA scientists stressed that the data did not conclusively prove anything, they thought the images exciting, compelling, and suggestive. They called for a concerted effort to send a lander to Europa to burrow through the ice to reach water beneath.

NASA's 2000–01 Near Earth Asteroid Rendezvous (NEAR) mission to the asteroid Eros achieved excellent results. NEAR was the first spacecraft to orbit an asteroid. In one year it met all of its scientific goals while orbiting the asteroid Eros, and then it undertook a controlled descent to the surface of the asteroid on 12 February 2001. The chief goal of the controlled descent was to gather close-up pictures of the boulder-strewn surface of 433 Eros, more than 315.4 million kilometers from Earth. During its five-year, 3.2-billion-kilometer journey, the NEAR mission provided the most detailed profile yet of a small celestial body. It began a yearlong orbit of Eros on 14 February 2000 and collected ten times more data than originally planned. The data include a detailed model culled from more than 11 million laser pulses; radar and laser data on Eros's weak gravity and solid but cracked interior; x-ray, gamma-ray, and infrared readings on its composition and spectral properties; and about 160,000 images covering all of the 34-kilometer bouldered, cratered, dusty-terrain asteroid.

Finally, in 1997, NASA launched the Cassini spacecraft on its voyage to Saturn. In some respects a sister spacecraft to the remarkable Galileo vehicle at Jupiter, this spacecraft will linger for several years collecting all manner of data about Saturn and its moons. Once it arrives in 2003, Cassini is expected to provide a similar level of stunning scientific data about the Saturnine system to the rich harvest that Galileo brought to the human race about Jupiter and its moons.

Conclusion

The Deep Space Chronicle provides a ready reference of deep space missions attempted since the opening of the space age in 1957 and documents the development, testing, and implementation of robotic spacecraft. Here are a few of its features:

- A list of significant "firsts" takes readers from the American Able 1 lunar probe in August 1958, to the Russian Mars 2 spacecraft impact on Mars in November 1971, to the American Sojourner's wheeled touchdown on Mars in 1997, to the American NEAR spacecraft orbit of Eros in February 2000.

- A discussion, with results, of planet flybys introduces attempts on Mars, Jupiter, Saturn, Uranus, and Neptune.

- A detailed bibliography is enclosed, and the author highly recommends Andrew Wilson's *Solar System Log* for more details regarding particular missions.

We are pleased to publish Asif A. Siddiqi's monograph on all planetary missions undertaken during the twentieth century. He is also the author of the recently published pathbreaking book *Challenge to Apollo: The Soviet Union and the Space Race, 1945–1974* (NASA SP-2000-4408). He has created in *Deep Space Chronicle* a factual reference source that will prove useful to all who are interested in planetary exploration.

Roger D. Launius
NASA Chief Historian

Deep Space Chronicle:
Introduction

Introduction

This monograph contains brief descriptions of all robotic deep space missions attempted since the opening of the space age in 1957. The missions are listed strictly chronologically in order of launch date (not by planetary encounter).

Different people have different criteria for which kind of spacecraft to include in a list of "deep space probes." In the list that follows, I have included all robotic spacecraft that satisfied the following guidelines:

1) Any probe that was launched to an "encounter" with a "planetary body."

    Encounters include the following:
    a) flybys,
    b) orbiting,
    c) atmospheric entry and impacts, and
    d) soft-landing.

    Planetary bodies include the following:
    a) Mercury, Venus, Mars, Jupiter, Saturn, Uranus, Neptune, and Pluto;
    b) Earth's Moon;
    c) asteroids;
    d) natural satellites of the planets and asteroids; and
    e) comets.

2) Any probe that was deliberately sent to heliocentric (solar) orbit without a planetary encounter.

3) Any probe that was sent into a halo orbit around the L1 libration point (about 1.5 million kilometers from Earth), where Earth's and the Sun's gravitational forces are exactly equal.

4) Any probe that was launched as part of a lunar or planetary program into deep space (i.e., at least to lunar distance) in order to simulate a deep-space trajectory (such as Zond 4 and a few early Surveyor Model mockups).

I have included probes whether they succeeded in their objectives or not. Thus, some probes never got more than a few meters beyond the launch pad, while others have already left the solar system.

From the launch of Sputnik in 1957 until the late 1980s, the Soviet Union never announced a mission that failed to reach Earth orbit. For deep space payloads that reached Earth orbit but were stranded there, they did not make an announcement of any kind until 1963. Beginning with Kosmos 21 in November 1963, the Soviets assigned Kosmos numbers to deep space payloads that remained stranded in Earth orbit. Since such failed missions had no designation, I thought it useful to provide a quick indication to readers of what these missions were about. For Soviet missions where no name was assigned, the type of mission is bracketed [ ]. The designation inside the bracket denotes the class of the mission, such as Luna, Mars, Venera, Zond, or N1 flight test.

Additionally, some U.S. mission names appear in quotation marks ("Pioneer 0") to indicate unofficial names (that is, not assigned by NASA or assigned retroactively by NASA).

For statistical data on U.S. probes (such as launch vehicle numbers, launch times, list of instruments), I have used, as much as possible, original NASA sources such as press kits and postflight mission reports. Because in many cases there exist wildly contradictory data (even within NASA), I have corroborated statistical data from other nongovernmental published sources. Every attempt has been made to present accurate information, but with a project of this size, there will naturally be errors. Corrections are welcome.

In terms of the mission descriptions, I have kept the focus on mission events rather than scientific results. Mission descriptions have been kept relatively short and to the point; readers interested in learning more details about particular missions are encouraged to search the sources listed in the bibliographies. I would particularly recommend Andrew Wilson's *Solar System Log* for deep space missions up to the mid-1980s.

All spacecraft masses listed in the statistical tables are masses at launch.

Many thanks to Roger D. Launius, NASA's Chief Historian, for his support in facilitating this monograph. I acknowledge, too, the aid of his staff in the History Office at NASA Headquarters, especially Louise Alstork and Stephen Garber. I also thank Lisa Jirousek and Joel Vendette for their attention to detail while proofing, editing, and designing this manuscript. Special thanks go out to Anoo Raman.

Asif A. Siddiqi

Deep Space Chronicle:
1958–2000

1958

1)
Able 1 / "Pioneer 0"
Nation: U.S. (1)
Objective(s): lunar orbit
Spacecraft: Able 1
Spacecraft Mass: 38 kg
Mission Design and Management: USAF / BMD
Launch Vehicle: Thor-Able 1 (Thor no. 127)
Launch Date and Time: 17 August 1958 / 12:18 UT
Launch Site: ETR / launch complex 17A
Scientific Instruments:
   1) magnetometer
   2) micrometeoroid detector
   3) temperature sensors
   4) infrared camera

Results: This mission was the first of two U.S. Air Force (USAF) launches to the Moon and the first attempted deep space launch by any country. The Able 1 spacecraft, a squat, conical, fiberglass structure, carried a crude infrared TV scanner. This device was a simple thermal radiation device comprising a small parabolic mirror for focusing reflected light from the lunar surface onto a cell that would transmit voltage proportional to the light it received. Engineers painted a pattern of dark and light stripes on the spacecraft's outer surface to regulate internal temperature. The spacecraft was also disinfected with ultraviolet light prior to launch. According to the ideal mission profile, Able 1 was designed to reach the Moon 2.6 days after launch; then the TX-8-6 solid propellant motor would fire to insert the vehicle into orbit around the Moon. Altitude would have been 29,000 kilometers with an optimal lifetime of about two weeks. The actual mission, however, lasted only 77 seconds after the Thor first stage exploded at 15.2 kilometers altitude. The upper stages hit the Atlantic about 123 seconds later. Investigators concluded that the accident had been caused by a turbopump gearbox failure. The mission has been retroactively known as "Pioneer 0."

2)
no name / [Luna]
Nation: USSR (1)
Objective(s): lunar impact
Spacecraft: Ye-1 (no. 1)
Spacecraft Mass: c. 360 kg (with upper stage)
Mission Design and Management: OKB-1
Launch Vehicle: 8K72 (no. B1-3)
Launch Date and Time: 23 September 1958 / 09:03:23 UT
Launch Site: NIIP-5 / launch site 1
Scientific Instruments:
   1) three-component magnetometer
   2) two gas discharge counters
   3) piezoelectric detector
   4) scintillation counter
   5) ion traps

Results: The Soviet government approved a modest plan for initial exploration of the

Moon in March 1958. Engineers conceived of four initial probes, the Ye-1 (for lunar impact), Ye-2 (to photograph the far side of the Moon), Ye-3 (to photograph the far side of the Moon), and Ye-4 (for lunar impact with a nuclear explosion). The Ye-1 was a simple probe, a pressurized spherical object made from aluminum-magnesium alloy, approximately the size of the first Sputnik, that carried five scientific instruments. The goals of the mission were to study the gas component of interplanetary matter (using the proton traps), meteoric particles and photons in cosmic radiation (using the piezoelectric detectors), the magnetic fields of the Moon and Earth (using the magnetometer), variations in cosmic ray intensity, and heavy nuclei in primary cosmic radiation. The probe (on its upper stage) also carried one kilogram of natrium to create an artificial comet on the outbound trajectory that could be photographed from Earth. During the first Ye-1 launch, the booster developed longitudinal resonant vibrations on the strap-on boosters of the launch vehicle. The rocket eventually disintegrated at T+93 seconds, destroying its payload.

3)
Able 2 / "Pioneer 1"
Nation: U.S. (2)
Objective(s): lunar orbit
Spacecraft: Able 2
Spacecraft Mass: 38.3 kg
Mission Design and Management: AFBMD / NASA
Launch Vehicle: Thor-Able I (no. 1 / Thor no. 130 / DM-1812-6)
Launch Date and Time: 11 October 1958 / 08 42:13 UT
Launch Site: ETR / launch complex 17A
Scientific Instruments:
1) ionization chamber
2) magnetometer
3) micrometeoroid detector
4) NOTS infrared imaging system
5) temperature sensor

Results: Although the USAF actually conducted the mission, this was the first U.S. space mission under the aegis of the recently formed National Aeronautics and Space Administration (NASA). The spacecraft was very similar in design to the Able 1 probe. During the mission, the Thor second stage shut down 10 seconds early due to incorrect information from an accelerometer measuring incremental velocity. The launch vehicle thus imparted insufficient velocity for the probe to escape the Earth's gravity. An attempt to insert the spacecraft into high-Earth orbit at 128,700 x 32,200 kilometers by using its retromotor failed because internal temperatures had fallen too much for the batteries to provide adequate power. The probe did, however, reach an altitude of 115,400 kilometers by 11:42 UT, verifying the existence of the Van Allen belts and returning other useful data before reentering 43 hours 17 minutes after launch. Investigators later concluded that an accelerometer had mistakenly cut off the Able stage because of an incorrect setting of a valve. The mission has been retroactively known as "Pioneer 1."

4)
no name / [Luna]
Nation: USSR (2)
Objective(s): lunar impact
Spacecraft: Ye-1 (no. 2)
Spacecraft Mass: c. 360 kg (with upper stage)
Mission Design and Management: OKB-1
Launch Vehicle: 8K72 (no. B1-4)
Launch Date and Time: 11 October 1958 / 23:41:58 UT
Launch Site: NIIP-5 / launch site 1
Scientific Instruments:
1) three-component magnetometer
2) two gas-discharge counters
3) piezoelectric detector
4) scintillation counter
5) ion traps

Results: The second attempt to impact the Moon failed when, again, the probe never left Earth's atmosphere. The launch vehicle exploded at T+104 seconds due to longitudinal resonant vibrations in the strap-on boosters.

5)
Pioneer 2
Nation: U.S. (3)
Objective(s): lunar orbit
Spacecraft: Able 3
Spacecraft Mass: 39.6 kg
Mission Design and Management: USAF BMD / NASA

Launch Vehicle: Thor-Able I (no. 2 / Thor no. 129 / DM-1812-6)
Launch Date and Time: 8 November 1958 / 07:30 UT
Launch Site: ETR / launch complex 17A
Scientific Instruments:
1) ionization chamber
2) magnetometer
3) temperature sensor
4) micrometeoroid sensor
5) proportional counter
6) imaging system

Results: For this third Air Force launch of a lunar orbiter, engineers introduced a number of changes to the Thor-Able launcher. The probe included a new TV scanner and a new type of battery, as well as a new cosmic-ray telescope to study the Cherenkov Effect. Pioneer 2, like its predecessors, never reached its target. A signal from the ground shut down the Thor launch vehicle's stage 2 earlier than planned. Additionally, when the X-248 third-stage engine separated, it failed to fire. As a result, the probe burned up in Earth's atmosphere only 45 minutes after launch. During its brief mission, it reached an altitude of 1,550 kilometers and sent back data that suggested that Earth's equatorial region had higher flux and energy levels than previously thought. The information also indicated that micrometeoroid density was higher near Earth than in space. Investigators concluded that the third-stage engine had failed to fire because of a broken wire.

6)
no name / [Luna]
Nation: USSR (3)
Objective(s): lunar impact
Spacecraft: Ye-1 (no. 3)
Spacecraft Mass: c. 360 kg (with upper stage)
Mission Design and Management: OKB-1
Launch Vehicle: 8K72 (no. B1-5)
Launch Date and Time: 4 December 1958 / 18:18:44 UT
Launch Site: NIIP-5 / launch site 1
Scientific Instruments:
1) three-component magnetometer
2) two gas-discharge counters
3) piezoelectric detector
4) scintillation counter
5) ion traps

Results: This mission was the third failure in a row in Soviet attempts to send a Ye-1 lunar impact probe to the Moon. The thrust level of the core engine of the R-7 booster dropped abruptly at T+245 seconds, leading eventually to premature engine cutoff. The payload never reached escape velocity. Later investigation showed that a pressurized seal cooling in the hydrogen peroxide pump of the main engine had lost integrity in vacuum conditions. The malfunction caused the main turbine to cease working and thus led to engine failure.

7)
Pioneer 3
Nation: U.S. (4)
Objective(s): lunar flyby
Spacecraft: N/A
Spacecraft Mass: 5.87 kg
Mission Design and Management: NASA / ABMA / JPL
Launch Vehicle: Juno II (no. AM-11)
Launch Date and Time: 6 December 1958 / 05:44:52 UT
Launch Site: ETR / launch complex 5
Scientific Instruments:
1) photoelectric sensor trigger
2) two Geiger-Mueller counters

Results: This mission was the first of two U.S. Army launches to the Moon. Pioneer 3 was a spin-stabilized probe (up to 700 rpm) whose primary goal was to fly by the Moon. Two special 0.21-ounce weights were to spin out on 1.5-meter wires and reduce spin to 12 rpm once the mission was under way. The spacecraft carried an optical sensor to test a future imaging system. If the sensor received, from a source such as the Moon, a collimated beam of light that was wide enough to pass through a lens and fall simultaneously on two photocells, then the sensor would send a signal to switch on an imaging system (not carried on this spacecraft). In the event, the main booster engine shut down 4 seconds earlier than planned due to propellant depletion. Once put on its trajectory, Pioneer 3 was about 1,030 kilometers per hour short of escape velocity. It eventually reached 102,322 kilometers and burned up over Africa 38 hours 6 minutes after launch. The spacecraft contributed to the major scientific discovery of dual bands of radiation around Earth.

1959

8)
Cosmic Rocket / [Luna 1]
Nation: USSR (4)
Objective(s): lunar impact
Spacecraft: Ye-1 (no. 4)
Spacecraft Mass: 361.3 kg (with upper stage)
Mission Design and Management: OKB-1
Launch Vehicle: 8K72 (no. B1-6)
Launch Date and Time: 2 January 1959 / 16:41:21 UT
Launch Site: NIIP-5 / launch site 1
Scientific Instruments:
1) three-component magnetometer
2) two gas-discharge counters
3) piezoelectric detector
4) scintillation counter
5) ion traps

Results: Although this Soviet spacecraft was the first humanmade object to reach escape velocity, its trajectory was less than accurate due to a problem in the guidance system, and the probe missed its main target, the Moon. The spacecraft (which, with its launch vehicle, was referred to as "Cosmic Rocket" in the Soviet press) eventually passed by the Moon at a distance of 6,400 kilometers about 34 hours following launch. Before the flyby, at 00:57 UT on 3 January 1959, the attached upper stage released one kilogram of natrium at a distance of 113,000 kilometers from Earth and was photographed by astronomers on Earth.

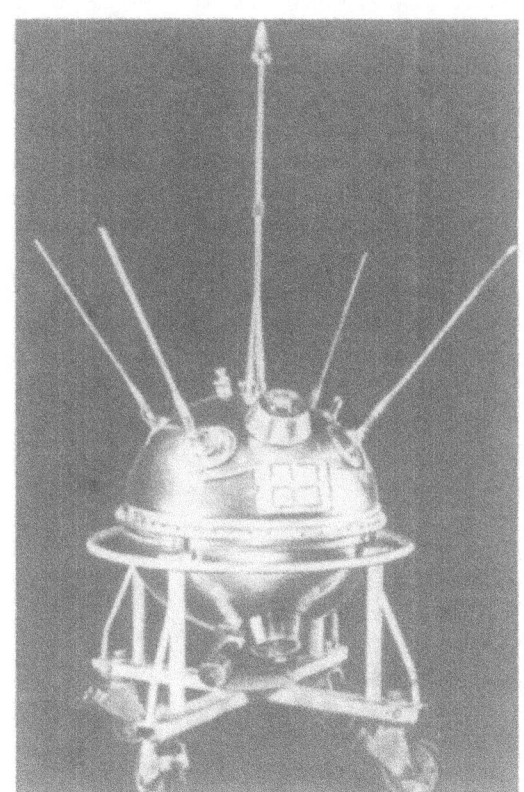

The first robotic explorer to the Moon, Luna 1.

Ground controllers lost contact with Cosmic Rocket (retroactively named Luna 1 in 1963) approximately 62 hours after launch. The probe became the first spacecraft to enter orbit around the Sun.

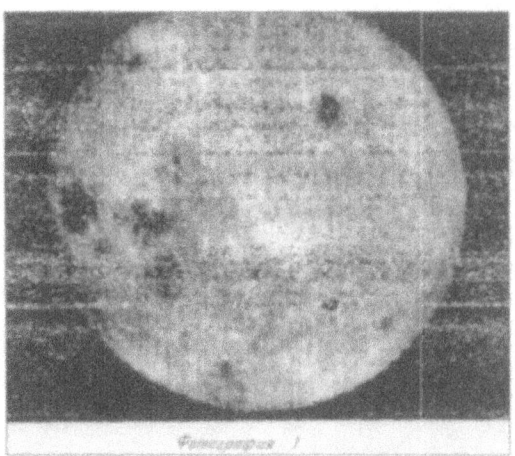

The Luna 3 spacecraft returned the first views ever of the far side of the Moon. The first image was taken at 03:30 UT on 7 October at a distance of 65,200 kilometers, after Luna 3 had passed the Moon and looked back at the sunlit far side. The last image was taken 40 minutes later from 66,700 kilometers. Altogether, twenty-nine photographs were taken, covering 70 percent of the far side. The photographs were very noisy and of low resolution, but many features could be recognized. This was the first image returned by Luna 3; taken by the wide-angle lens, it showed that the far side of the Moon was very different from the near side, most noticeably in its lack of lunar maria (the dark areas). The right three-quarters of the disk are the far side. The dark spot at upper right is Mare Moscoviense; the dark area at lower left is Mare Smythii. The small dark circle at lower right with the white dot in the center is the crater Tsiolkovskiy and its central peak. The Moon is 3,475 kilometers in diameter, and north is up in this image.

9)
Pioneer 4
Nation: U.S. (5)
Objective(s): lunar flyby
Spacecraft: N/A
Spacecraft Mass: 6.1 kg
Mission Design and Management: NASA / ABMA / JPL
Launch Vehicle: Juno II (no. AM-14)
Launch Date and Time: 3 March 1959 / 05:10:45 UT
Launch Site: ETR / launch complex 5
Scientific Instruments:
   1) photoelectric sensor trigger
   2) two Geiger-Mueller counters
Results: Although it did not achieve its primary objective to photograph the Moon during a flyby, Pioneer 4 was the first U.S. spacecraft to reach escape velocity. During the launch, the Sergeants of the second stage did not cut off on time and caused the azimuths and elevation angles of the trajectory to change. The spacecraft thus passed by the Moon at a range of 59,545 kilometers (instead of the planned 32,000 kilometers)—not close enough for the imaging scanner to function. The closest approach was at 10:25 UT on 4 March 1959. The craft's tiny radio transmitted information for 82 hours before contact was lost at a distance of 655,000 kilometers from Earth, the greatest tracking distance for a humanmade object to date. The probe eventually entered heliocentric orbit and became the first American spacecraft to do so. Scientists received excellent data on radiation in space.

10)
no name / [Luna]
Nation: USSR (5)
Objective(s): lunar impact
Spacecraft: Ye-1A (no. 5)
Spacecraft Mass: c. 390 kg (with upper stage)
Mission Design and Management: OKB-1
Launch Vehicle: 8K72 (no. I1-7)
Launch Date and Time: 18 June 1959 / 08:08 UT
Launch Site: NIIP-5 / launch site 1
Scientific Instruments:
   1) three-component magnetometer
   2) two gas-discharge counters
   3) piezoelectric detector
   4) scintillation counter
   5) ion traps
Results: The Soviet Ye-1A probe, like the Ye-1, was designed for lunar impact. Engineers had incorporated some minor modifications to the scientific instruments (a modified antenna housing for the magnetometer, six instead of four gas-discharge counters, and an improved piezoelectric detector) as a result of information received from the first Cosmic Rocket (Luna 1) and the American Pioneer 4. The launch was originally scheduled for 16 June but was postponed for two days as a result of the negligence of a young lieutenant who inadvertently permitted fuelling of the upper stage with the wrong propellant. During the actual launch, one of the gyroscopes of the inertial guidance system failed at T+153 seconds, and the wayward booster was subsequently destroyed by command from the ground.

11)
Second Cosmic Rocket / Luna 2
Nation: USSR (6)
Objective(s): lunar impact
Spacecraft: Ye-1A (no. 7)
Spacecraft Mass: 390.2 kg (with upper stage)
Mission Design and Management: OKB-1
Launch Vehicle: 8K72 (no. I1-7b)
Launch Date and Time: 12 September 1959 / 06:39:42 UT
Launch Site: NIIP-5 / launch site 1
Scientific Instruments:
1) three-component magnetometer
2) six gas-discharge counters
3) piezoelectric detector
4) scintillation counter
5) ion traps

Results: After an aborted launch on 9 September, the Ye-1A probe successfully lifted off and reached escape velocity three days later. Officially named the "Second Soviet Cosmic Rocket," the spacecraft released its one kilogram of natrium on 12 September at a distance of 156,000 kilometers from Earth in a cloud that expanded out to 650 kilometers in diameter and was clearly visible from the ground. Fortunately, this sixth attempt at lunar impact was much more accurate than its predecessors. The spacecraft successfully reached the surface of the Moon at 23:02:23 UT on 14 September 1959, thus becoming the first object of human origin to make contact with another celestial body. The probe's impact point was approximately at 30° north latitude and 0° longitude on the slope of the Autolycus crater, east of Mare Serenitatis. Luna 2 (as it was called after 1963) deposited Soviet emblems on the lunar surface carried in 9 x 15-centimeter metallic spheres. The spacecraft's magnetometer measured no significant lunar magnetic field as close as 55 kilometers to the lunar surface. The radiation detectors also found no hint of a radiation belt.

12)
Automatic Interplanetary Station / Luna 3
Nation: USSR (7)
Objective(s): lunar flyby
Spacecraft: Ye-2A (no. 1)
Spacecraft Mass: 278.5 kg
Mission Design and Management: OKB-1
Launch Vehicle: 8K72 (no. I1-8)
Launch Date and Time: 4 October 1959 / 00:43:40 UT
Launch Site: NIIP-5 / launch site 1
Scientific Instruments:
1) Yenisey-2 photographic-TV imaging system
2) micrometeoroid detector
3) cosmic-ray detector

Results: This spacecraft, of the Ye-2A class, was the first Soviet probe designed to take pictures of the far side of the Moon using the Yenisey-2 imaging system (replacing the Yenisey-1 used on the abandoned Ye-2 probe). The TV system consisted of a 35-mm camera with two lenses of 200-mm (wide-angle) and 500-mm (high-resolution) focal lengths and a capacity to read up to 40 images. Strictly speaking, the probe was not meant to reach escape velocity; instead, the launch vehicle inserted the spacecraft, called the Automatic Interplanetary Station (AMS) in the Soviet press, into a highly elliptical orbit around the Earth at 48,280 x 468,300 kilometers, sufficient to reach lunar distance. During the coast to the Moon, the AMS suffered overheating problems and poor communications, but the vehicle eventually passed over the Moon's southern polar cap at a range of 7,900 kilometers on 6 October before climbing up over the Earth-Moon plane. At a distance of 65,200 kilometers from the Moon, on 7 October, cameras began taking the first of 29 pictures of the far side of the Moon. The exposed film was then developed, fixed, and dried automatically, after which a special light beam of up to 1,000 lines per image scanned the film for transmission to Earth. Images were finally received the next day (after a few aborted attempts). Seventeen of the images were of usable quality and showed parts of the Moon never before seen by human eyes. The spacecraft, named Luna 3 after 1963, photographed about 70 percent of the far side and found fewer mare areas on the far side, prompting scientists to revise their theories of lunar evolution.

13)
Able IVB / "Pioneer"
Nation: U.S. (6)
Objective(s): lunar orbit
Spacecraft: P-3 / Able IVB
Spacecraft Mass: 169 kg

Mission Design and Management: AFBMD / NASA
Launch Vehicle: Atlas-Able (no. 1 / Atlas D no. 20)
Launch Date and Time: 26 November 1959 / 07:26 UT
Launch Site: ETR / launch complex 14
Scientific Instruments:
1) high-energy radiation counter
2) ionization chamber
3) Geiger-Mueller tube
4) low-energy radiation counter
5) two magnetometers
6) photo-scanning device
7) micrometeoroid detector
8) aspect indicator
9) radio receiver to detect natural radio waves
10) transponder to measure electron densities

Results: This mission used the first of four spacecraft designed by Space Technology Laboratories for a lunar assault in 1959 and 1960; two of them had originally been slated for Venus orbit (in June 1959), but mission planners had redirected their missions after the success of the Soviet Luna 3 mission. All the scientific experiments and internal instrumentation were powered by nickel-cadmium batteries charged from 1,100 solar cells on 4 paddles. Each probe also carried an internal hydrazine monopropellant motor for lunar orbit insertion at a range of 8,000 kilometers from the Moon. Ideal lunar orbital parameters were planned as 6,400 x 4,800 kilometers. The missions also inaugurated the first use of the Atlas-with-an-upper-stage combination, affording increased payload weight. During this first launch, the nose fairing began to break away just 45 seconds after liftoff. Aerodynamic forces then caused the third stage and payload to break away and explode. The ground lost contact with the tumbling booster at T+104 seconds. Investigation showed that the 3-meter fiberglass shroud failed because there had been no measures to compensate for pressure differentials as the rocket gained altitude.

1960

14)
Pioneer 5
Nation: U.S. (7)
Objective(s): heliocentric orbit
Spacecraft: P-2 / Able 6
Spacecraft Mass: 43.2 kg
Mission Design and Management: NASA GSFC / USAF BMD
Launch Vehicle: Thor-Able IV (no. 4 / Thor no. 219 / DM-1812-6A)
Launch Date and Time: 11 March 1960 / 13:00:07 UT
Launch Site: ETR / launch complex 17A
Scientific Instruments:
1) magnetometer
2) ionization chamber
3) Geiger-Mueller tube
4) micrometeoroid momentum spectrometer
5) photoelectric cell aspect indicator
6) proportional counter telescope

Results: Launched on a direct solar orbit trajectory, Pioneer 5 successfully reached heliocentric orbit between Earth and Venus to demonstrate deep space technologies and to provide the first map of the interplanetary magnetic field. The spacecraft had originally been intended for a Venus flyby, but the mission was switched to a solar flyby. Pioneer 5 carried Telebit, the first digital telemetry system operationally used on a U.S. spacecraft; it was first tested on Explorer 6. The system used a 5-watt or a 150-watt transmitter, with a 5-watt transmitter acting as driver. Information rates varied from 64 to 8 to 1 bit per second. Controllers maintained contact with Pioneer 5 until 26 June 1960, to a record distance of 36.2 million kilometers from Earth (later surpassed by Mariner 2). The probe, using its 18.1-kilogram suite of scientific instruments, confirmed the existence of previously conjectured interplanetary magnetic fields.

15)
no name / [Luna]
Nation: USSR (8)
Objective(s): lunar farside photography
Spacecraft: Ye-3 (no. 1)
Spacecraft Mass: unknown
Mission Design and Management: OKB-1
Launch Vehicle: 8K72 (no. 1l-9)
Launch Date and Time: 15 April 1960 / 15:06:44 UT
Launch Site: NIIP-5 / launch site 1
Scientific Instruments:
1) Yenisey-2 photographic-TV imaging system
2) micrometeoroid detector
3) cosmic-ray detector

Results: After the spectacular success of Luna 3, this spacecraft was launched to return more detailed photos of the lunar far side. The Ye-3 class vehicle was essentially a Ye-2A probe using a modified radio-telemetry system, but with the old Yenisey-2 imaging system. (A more advanced Ye-3 type with a new imaging system had been abandoned earlier.) During the launch, the probe received insufficient velocity after premature third-stage engine cutoff. The spacecraft reached an altitude of 200,000 kilometers and then fell back to Earth and burned up in Earth's atmosphere, much like some of the early American Pioneer probes.

16)
no name / [Luna]
Nation: USSR (9)
Objective(s): farside lunar photography
Spacecraft: Ye-3 (no. 2)
Spacecraft Mass: unknown
Mission Design and Management: OKB-1
Launch Vehicle: 8K72 (no. Il-9a)
Launch Date and Time: 19 April 1960 / 16:07:43 UT
Launch Site: NIIP-5 / launch site 1
Scientific Instruments:
1) Yenisey-2 photographic-TV imaging system
2) micrometeoroid detector
3) cosmic-ray detector

Results: This was the last of the "first-generation" Soviet probes to the Moon. Like its immediate predecessor, it was designed to photograph the far side of the Moon. Unfortunately, the probe never left Earth's atmosphere. Instead, immediately after launch, at T+10 seconds, the launch vehicle began to fall apart. As each strap-on fell away, parts of the booster landed separately over a large area near the launch site. Thundering explosions broke windows in many nearby buildings.

17)
Able VA / "Pioneer"
Nation: U.S. (8)
Objective(s): lunar orbit
Spacecraft: P-30 / Able VA
Spacecraft Mass: 175.5 kg
Mission Design and Management: AFBMD / NASA
Launch Vehicle: Atlas-Able (no. 2 / Atlas D no. 80)
Launch Date and Time: 25 September 1960 / 15:13 UT
Launch Site: ETR / launch complex 12
Scientific Instruments:
1) high-energy radiation counter
2) ionization chamber
3) Geiger-Mueller tube
4) low-energy radiation counter
5) two magnetometers
6) scintillation spectrometer
7) micrometeoroid detector
8) plasma probe
9) Sun scanner

Results: This probe, Able VA, had a slightly different instrument complement from that of its predecessor Able IVB (launched in November 1959), but it had similar mission goals. Able VA was to enter lunar orbit about 62.5 hours after launch with parameters of 4,000 x 2,250 kilometers in a period of 10 hours. During the launch, although the first stage performed without problems, the Able second stage ignited abnormally and shut down early because of an oxidizer system failure. The third stage never fired, and the probe burned up in Earth's atmosphere 17 minutes after launch. Although the mission was a failure, ground controllers fired Able VA's onboard liquid propellant hydrazine rocket engine—the first time that an onboard motor was fired on a space vehicle. Later, on 15 November 1960, NASA announced that two objects from the Able VA payload had been found in Transvaal, South Africa.

18)
no name / [Mars]
Nation: USSR (10)
Objective(s): Mars flyby
Spacecraft: 1M (no. 1)
Spacecraft Mass: 480 kg
Mission Design and Management: OKB-1
Launch Vehicle: 8K78 (no. L1-4M)
Launch Date and Time: 10 October 1960 / 14:27:49 UT
Launch Site: NIIP-5 / launch site 1
Scientific Instruments:
1) ultraviolet spectrograph
2) radiation detector
3) cosmic-ray detector

Results: This was the first of two Soviet Mars spacecraft intended to fly past Mars. It also was the first attempt by humans to send spacecraft to the vicinity of Mars. Although the spacecraft initially included a TV imaging system and a spectroreflectometer (to detect organic life on Mars), mass constraints forced engineers to remove both instruments a week before launch. The mission profile called for the probe to first enter Earth orbit and then use a new fourth stage (called "Blok L") to gain enough additional velocity to fly to a Mars encounter. During the launch, violent vibrations caused a gyroscope to malfunction. As a result, the booster began to veer from its planned attitude. The guidance system failed at T+309 seconds, and the third-stage engine was shut down after the trajectory deviated to a pitch of greater than 7 degrees. The payload eventually burned up in Earth's atmosphere over eastern Siberia without reaching Earth orbit. The Mars flyby was planned for 13 May 1961.

19)
no name / [Mars]
Nation: USSR (11)
Objective(s): Mars flyby
Spacecraft: 1M (no. 2)
Spacecraft Mass: 480 kg
Mission Design and Management: OKB-1
Launch Vehicle: 8K78 (no. L1-5M)
Launch Date and Time: 14 October 1960 / 13:51:03 UT
Launch Site: NIIP-5 / launch site 1
Scientific Instruments:
   1) ultraviolet spectrograph
   2) radiation detector
   3) cosmic-ray detector

Results: Like its predecessor, this spacecraft never reached Earth orbit. During the launch trajectory, there was a failure in the third-stage engine at T+290 seconds as a result of frozen kerosene in the pipeline feeding its turbopump (which prevented a valve from opening). The third and fourth stages, along with the payload, burned up over Earth's atmosphere over eastern Siberia. The Mars flyby had been planned for 15 May 1961.

20)
Able VB / "Pioneer"
Nation: U.S. (9)
Objective(s): lunar orbit
Spacecraft: P-31 / Able VB
Spacecraft Mass: 176 kg
Mission Design and Management: AFBMD / NASA
Launch Vehicle: Atlas-Able (no. 3 / Atlas D no. 91)
Launch Date and Time: 15 December 1960 / 09:10 UT
Launch Site: ETR / launch complex 12
Scientific Instruments:
   1) micrometeoroid detector
   2) high-energy radiation counter
   3) ionization chamber
   4) Geiger-Mueller tube
   5) low-energy radiation counter
   6) two magnetometers
   7) Sun scanner
   8) plasma probe
   9) scintillation spectrometer
   10) solid state detector

Results: The mission of Able VB, as with its two unsuccessful predecessors, was to enter lunar orbit. Scientific objectives included studying radiation near the Moon, recording the incidence of micrometeoroids, and detecting a lunar magnetic field. Planned lunar orbital parameters were 4,300 x 2,400 kilometers with a period of 9 to 10 hours. The spacecraft had a slightly different scientific instrument complement from that of its predecessors. This was third and last attempt by NASA to launch a probe to orbit the Moon in the 1959–60 period. Unfortunately, the Atlas-Able booster exploded 68 seconds after launch at an altitude of about 12.2 kilometers. Later investigation indicated that the cause was premature Able stage ignition while the first stage was still firing.

1961

21)
Tyazhelyy Sputnik / [Venera]
Nation: USSR (12)
Objective(s): Venus impact
Spacecraft: 1VA (no. 1)
Spacecraft Mass: c. 645 kg
Mission Design and Management: OKB-1
Launch Vehicle: 8K78 (no. L1-7)
Launch Date and Time: 4 February 1961 / 01:18:04 UT
Launch Site: NIIP-5 / launch site 1
Scientific Instruments:
1) three-component magnetometer
2) variometer
3) charged-particle traps

Results: This mission was the first attempt to send a spacecraft to Venus. Original intentions had been to send the 1V spacecraft to take pictures of the Venusian surface, but this proved to be far too ambitious a goal. Engineers instead downgraded the mission and used the 1VA spacecraft for a simple Venus atmospheric entry. The 1VA was essentially a modified 1M spacecraft used for Martian exploration. The spacecraft contained a small globe containing various souvenirs and medals commemorating the mission. This flight was also the first occasion on which the Soviets used an intermediate Earth orbit to launch a spacecraft into interplanetary space. Although the booster successfully placed the probe into Earth orbit, the fourth stage (the Blok L) never fired to send the spacecraft to Venus. A subsequent investigation showed that there had been a failure in the PT-200 DC transformer that ensured power supply to the Blok L guidance system. The system had evidently not been designed to work in a vacuum. The "spacecraft + upper-stage stack" reentered Earth's atmosphere on 26 February 1961. The Soviets announced the total weight of the combination as 6,483 kilograms.

22)
Venera
Nation: USSR (13)
Objective(s): Venus impact
Spacecraft: 1VA (no. 2)
Spacecraft Mass: 643.5 kg
Mission Design and Management: OKB-1
Launch Vehicle: 8K78 (no. L1-6)
Launch Date and Time: 12 February 1961 / 00:34:37 UT
Launch Site: NIIP-5 / launch site 1
Scientific Instruments:
1) three-component magnetometer
2) variometer
3) charged-particle traps

Results: This was the second of two Venus impact probes that the Soviets launched in 1961. This time, the probe successfully exited Earth orbit and headed toward

The Ranger fleet of spacecraft launched in the mid-sixties provided live television transmissions of the Moon. These transmissions resolved surface features as small as 10 inches across and provided over 17,000 images of the lunar surface. These detailed photographs allowed scientists and engineers to study the Moon in greater detail than ever before, thus allowing for the design of a spacecraft that would one day land men of Earth on its surface.

Venus. Despite some initial problems with the solar orientation system, the spacecraft responded properly during a communications session on 17 February 1961 at a distance of 1.9 million kilometers. Unfortunately, controllers were unable to regain contact during a subsequent communications attempt on 22 February. A later investigation indicated that the spacecraft had lost its "permanent" solar orientation due to a faulty optical sensor that malfunctioned because of excess heat after the spacecraft's thermal control system failed. The inert spacecraft eventually passed by Venus on 19 and 20 May 1961 at a distance of about 100,000 kilometers and entered heliocentric orbit.

23)
Ranger 1
Nation: U.S. (10)
Objective(s): highly elliptical Earth orbit
Spacecraft: P-32
Spacecraft Mass: 306.18 kg
Mission Design and Management: NASA JPL
Launch Vehicle: Atlas-Agena B (no. 1 / Atlas D no. 111 / Agena B no. 6001)
Launch Date and Time: 23 August 1961 / 10:04 UT
Launch Site: ETR / launch complex 12
Scientific Instruments:
1) electrostatic analyzer
2) photoconductive particle detectors
3) Rubidium vapor magnetometer
4) triple-coincidence cosmic-ray telescope
5) cosmic-ray integrating ionization chamber
6) x-ray scintillation detectors
7) micrometeoroid dust particle detectors
8) Lyman alpha scanning telescope

Results: Ranger 1 was the first in a series of standardized spacecraft designed to rough-land simple instrumented capsules on the surface of the Moon and take photos of the lunar surface during its descent to the Moon. The spacecraft consisted of a tubular central body connected to a hexagonal base containing basic equipment required for control and communications. Power was provided by solar cells and a silver-zinc battery. Ranger 1's specific mission was to test performance of the new technologies intended for operational Ranger flights and to study the nature of particles and fields in interplanetary space. Its intended orbit was 60,000 x 1.1 million kilometers. Ranger 1 was the first American spacecraft to use a parking orbit around Earth prior to its deep space mission. In this case, the Agena B upper stage cut off almost immediately after its ignition for translunar injection (instead of firing for 90 seconds). The probe remained stranded in low-Earth orbit (501 x 168 kilometers), and telemetry ceased by 27 August, when the main battery went dead. The spacecraft reentered Earth's atmosphere three days later. The cause of the Agena failure was traced to a malfunctioning switch that had prematurely choked the flow the red fuming nitric acid to the rocket engine.

24)
Ranger 2
Nation: U.S. (11)
Objective(s): highly elliptical Earth orbit
Spacecraft: P-33
Spacecraft Mass: 306.18 kg
Mission Design and Management: NASA JPL
Launch Vehicle: Atlas-Agena B (no. 2 / Atlas D no. 117 / Agena B no. 6002)
Launch Date and Time: 18 November 1961 / 08:12 UT
Launch Site: ETR / launch complex 12
Scientific Instruments:
1) electrostatic analyzer for solar plasma
2) photoconductive particle detectors
3) Rubidium vapor magnetometer
4) triple-coincidence cosmic-ray telescope
5) cosmic-ray integrating ionization chamber
6) x-ray scintillation detectors
7) micrometeoroid dust particle detectors
8) Lyman alpha scanning telescope

Results: Like its predecessor, Ranger 2 was designed to operate in a highly elliptical Earth orbit that would take it into deep space beyond the Moon. Mission planners expected that during five months of operation, they could verify both the technical design of the vehicle and conduct key scientific experiments to study the space environment over a prolonged period. Since the Block I Rangers

Ranger 7 took this image of the Moon on 31 July 1964 at 13:09 UT (9:09 A.M. EDT), about 17 minutes before impacting the lunar surface. The area photographed is centered at 13° south latitude and 10° west longitude and covers about 360 kilometers from top to bottom. The large crater at center right is the 108-kilometer-diameter Alphonsus. Above it is Ptolemaeus and below it Arzachel. The terminator is at the bottom right corner. Mare Nubium is at center and left. North is at about 11:00 at the center of the frame. The Ranger 7 impact site is off the frame, to the left of the upper left corner. (Ranger 7, B001) The Ranger series of spacecraft were designed solely to take high-quality pictures of the Moon and transmit them back to Earth in real time. The images were to be used for scientific study, as well as for selecting landing sites for the Apollo Moon missions. Ranger 7 was the first of the Ranger series to be entirely successful. It transmitted 4,308 high-quality images over the last 17 minutes of flight, the final image having a resolution of 0.5 meters per pixel. Ranger 7 was launched on 28 July 1964 and arrived at the Moon on 31 July 1964.

(Ranger 1 and 2) carried no rocket engine, they could not alter their trajectories. On this attempt, Ranger 2, like its predecessor, failed to leave low-Earth orbit. This time, the Agena B stage failed to fire. In its low orbit, Ranger 2 lost its solar orientation and then eventually lost power; it reentered Earth's atmosphere on 19 November 1961. The most probable cause of the failure was inoperation of the roll-control gyroscope on the Agena B guidance system. As a result, the stage had used up all attitude-control propellant for its first orbit insertion burn. At the time of the second burn, without proper attitude, the engine failed to fire.

1962

25)
Ranger 3
Nation: U.S. (12)
Objective(s): lunar impact
Spacecraft: P-34
Spacecraft Mass: 330 kg
Mission Design and Management: NASA JPL
Launch Vehicle: Atlas-Agena B (no. 3 / Atlas D no. 121 / Agena B no. 6003)
Launch Date and Time: 26 January 1962 / 20:30 UT
Launch Site: ETR / launch complex 12
Scientific Instruments:
  1) imaging system
  2) gamma-ray spectrometer
  3) single-axis seismometer
  4) surface-scanning pulse radio experiment

Results: This was the first U.S. attempt to achieve impact on the lunar surface. The Block II Ranger spacecraft carried a TV camera that used an optical telescope that would allow imaging down to about 24 kilometers above the lunar surface during the descent. The main bus also carried a 42.6-kilogram instrument capsule that would separate from the bus at 21.4 kilometers altitude and then independently impact on the Moon. Protected by a balsa-wood outer casing, the capsule was designed to bounce several times on the lunar surface before coming to rest. The primary onboard instrument was a seismometer. Because of a malfunction in the Atlas guidance system (due to faulty transistors), the probe was inserted into a lunar transfer trajectory with an excessive velocity. A subsequent incorrect course change ensured that the spacecraft reached the Moon 14 hours early and missed it by 36,793 kilometers on 28 January. The central computer and sequencer failed and the spacecraft returned no TV images. The probe did, however, provide scientists with the first measurements of interplanetary gamma-ray flux. Ranger 3 eventually entered heliocentric orbit.

26)
Ranger 4
Nation: U.S. (13)
Objective(s): lunar impact
Spacecraft: P-35
Spacecraft Mass: 331.12 kg
Mission Design and Management: NASA JPL
Launch Vehicle: Atlas-Agena B (no. 4 / Atlas D no. 133 / Agena B no. 6004)
Launch Date and Time: 23 April 1962 / 20:50 UT
Launch Site: ETR / launch complex 12
Scientific Instruments:
  1) imaging system
  2) gamma-ray spectrometer
  3) single-axis seismometer
  4) surface-scanning pulse radio experiment

Results: This spacecraft, similar in design to Ranger 3, was the first U.S. spacecraft to reach another celestial body. A power failure in the central computer and sequencer stopped the spacecraft's master clock and prevented the vehicle from performing any of its preplanned operations, such as opening its solar panels. Drifting aimlessly and without any midcourse corrections, Ranger 4 impacted the Moon on its far side at 12:49:53 UT on 26 April 1962. Impact coordinates were 15°30' south latitude and 130°42' west longitude. Although the spacecraft did not achieve its primary objective, the Atlas-Agena-Ranger combination performed without fault for the first time.

27)
Mariner 1
Nation: U.S. (14)
Objective(s): Venus flyby
Spacecraft: P-37 / Mariner R-1
Spacecraft Mass: 202.8 kg
Mission Design and Management: NASA JPL
Launch Vehicle: Atlas-Agena B (no. 5 / Atlas D no. 145 / Agena B no. 6901)
Launch Date and Time: 22 July 1962 / 09:21:23 UT
Launch Site: ETR / launch complex 12
Scientific Instruments:
1) microwave radiometer
2) infrared radiometer
3) fluxgate magnetometer
4) cosmic dust detector
5) solar plasma spectrometer
6) energetic particle detectors

Results: After approval by NASA Headquarters in September 1961, JPL prepared three spacecraft based on the design of the Ranger Block I series (therefore named Mariner R) to fly by Venus in late 1962. Each spacecraft carried a modest suite (9 kilograms) of scientific instrumentation but had no imaging capability. The spacecraft included 54,000 components and was designed to maintain contact with Earth for 2,500 hours—an ambitious goal given that the (still unsuccessful) Ranger was designed for only 65 hours of contact. Mariner 1 would have flown by Venus at a range of 29,000 kilometers on 8 December 1962, but due to an incorrect trajectory during launch, range safety had to destroy the booster and its payload at T+290 seconds.

28)
no name / [Venera]
Nation: USSR (14)
Objective(s): Venus impact
Spacecraft: 2MV-1 (no. 1)
Spacecraft Mass: 1,097 kg
Mission Design and Management: OKB-1
Launch Vehicle: 8K78 (no. T103-12)
Launch Date and Time: 25 August 1962 / 02:18:45 UT
Launch Site: NIIP-5 / launch site 1
Scientific Instruments: unknown

Results: This mission was the first of a second generation of Soviet deep space probes based on a unified platform called 2MV ("2" for the second generation, "MV" for Mars and Venus) designed to study Mars and Venus. The series included four variants with the same bus but with different payload complements: 2MV-1 (for Venus impact), 2MV-2 (for Venus flyby), 2MV-3 (for Mars impact), and 2MV-4 (for Mars flyby). The landers carried pressurized capsules; the Venus landers were cooled with an ammonia-based system, while the Mars landers used a system of air conditioners. Both landers were sterilized with a special substance on recommendation from the Academy of Sciences's Institute of Microbiology. The buses were powered by solar panels with an area of 2.5 square meters capable of providing 2.6 A. For Venus, the Soviets prepared three spacecraft for the August-September 1962 launch window, one flyby spacecraft and two landers. This first spacecraft was successfully launched into Earth orbit, but the Blok L upper stage cut off its interplanetary burn after only 45 seconds (instead of the planned 240 seconds). Later investigation showed that the stage had been set on a tumbling motion prior to main engine ignition due to asymmetrical firing of stabilizing motors. The spacecraft remained in Earth orbit for three days before reentering Earth's atmosphere.

29)
Mariner 2
Nation: U.S. (15)
Objective(s): Venus flyby
Spacecraft: P-38 / Mariner R-2
Spacecraft Mass: 203.6 kg
Mission Design and Management: NASA JPL
Launch Vehicle: Atlas-Agena B (no. 6 / Atlas D no. 179 / Agena B no. 6902)

Launch Date and Time: 27 August 1962 / 06:53:14 UT
Launch Site: ETR / launch complex 12
Scientific Instruments:
1) microwave radiometer
2) infrared radiometer
3) fluxgate magnetometer
4) cosmic dust detector
5) solar plasma spectrometer
6) energetic particle detectors

Results: NASA brought the Mariner R-2 spacecraft out of storage and launched it just thirty-six days after the failure of Mariner 1. Mariner 2, as it was known after launch, was equipped with an identical complement of instrumentation to that of its predecessor (see Mariner 1). The mission proved to be the first fully successful interplanetary mission performed by any nation. After a midcourse correction on 4 September, the spacecraft flew by Venus at a range of 34,762 kilometers on 14 December 1962. During a 42-minute scan of the planet, Mariner 2 gathered significant data on the Venusian atmosphere and surface before continuing on to heliocentric orbit. NASA maintained contact until 07:00 UT on 3 January 1963, when the spacecraft was 87.4 million kilometers from Earth, a new record for a deep space probe. The data returned showed that the surface temperature on Venus was at least 425°C with minimal differentiation between the day and night sides of the planet. Mariner 2 also found that there was a dense cloud layer that extended from 56 to 80 kilometers above the surface. The spacecraft detected no discernable planetary magnetic field; this lack is partly explained by the great distance of the flyby. After this successful mission, NASA elected to stand down the third spacecraft in the series (Mariner R-3), scheduled for the 1964 launch window.

30)
no name / [Venera]
Nation: USSR (15)
Objective(s): Venus impact
Spacecraft: 2MV-1 (no. 2)
Spacecraft Mass: c. 1,100 kg
Mission Design and Management: OKB-1
Launch Vehicle: 8K78 (no. T103-13)
Launch Date and Time: 1 September 1962 / 02:12:30 UT
Launch Site: NIIP-5 / launch site 1
Scientific Instruments: unknown
Results: This was the second of three Venus spacecraft launched by the Soviets in 1962. Like its predecessor launched in August 1962 (also a Venus impact probe), the spacecraft never left parking orbit around Earth because of a malfunction in the Blok L upper stage designed to send the probe out of Earth orbit toward Venus. Evidently, the valve that controlled the delivery of fuel into the combustion chamber of the Blok L engine (the S1.5400) never opened. As a result, the engine never fired. The payload decayed within five days of launch.

31)
no name / [Venera]
Nation: USSR (16)
Objective(s): Venus flyby
Spacecraft: 2MV-2 (no. 1)
Spacecraft Mass: unknown
Mission Design and Management: OKB-1
Launch Vehicle: 8K78 (no. T103-114)
Launch Date and Time: 12 September 1962 / 00:59:13 UT
Launch Site: NIIP-5 / launch site 1
Scientific Instruments:
1) imaging system
   (remainder unknown)

Results: Like its two predecessors (launched on 25 August and 1 September 1962), this Soviet Venus probe never left parking orbit around the Earth. The Blok L upper stage, designed to send the spacecraft toward Venus, fired for only 0.8 seconds before shutting down because of unstable attitude. Later investigation indicated that the upper stage had been put into a tumble by the violent shutdown of the third stage. The tumble had mixed air bubbles within the propellant tanks, preventing a clean firing of the engine. Unlike its predecessors, this probe was designed for a Venus flyby rather than atmospheric entry and impact. The spacecraft reentered Earth's atmosphere two days after launch.

32)
Ranger 5
Nation: U.S. (16)
Objective(s): lunar impact
Spacecraft: P-36
Spacecraft Mass: 342.46 kg

Mission Design and Management: NASA JPL
Launch Vehicle: Atlas-Agena B (no. 7 / Atlas D no. 215 / Agena no. 6005)
Launch Date and Time: 18 October 1962 / 16:59:00 UT
Launch Site: ETR / launch complex 12
Scientific Instruments:
1) imaging system
2) gamma-ray spectrometer
3) single-axis seismometer
4) surface-scanning pulse radio experiment

Results: This was the third attempt to impact the lunar surface with a Block II Ranger spacecraft. On this mission, just 15 minutes after normal operation, a malfunction led to the transfer of power from solar to battery power. Normal operation never resumed; battery power was depleted after 8 hours, and all spacecraft systems died. The first midcourse correction was never implemented, and Ranger 5 passed the Moon at a range of 724 kilometers on 21 October and entered heliocentric orbit. It was tracked to a distance of 1,271,381 kilometers. Before loss of signal, the spacecraft sent back about 4 hours of data from the gamma-ray experiment.

33)
no name / [Mars]
Nation: USSR (17)
Objective(s): Mars flyby
Spacecraft: 2MV-4 (no. 1)
Spacecraft Mass: c. 900 kg
Mission Design and Management: OKB-1
Launch Vehicle: 8K78 (no. T103-15)
Launch Date and Time: 24 October 1962 / 17:55:04 UT
Launch Site: NIIP-5 / launch site 1
Scientific Instruments:
1) imaging system
2) magnetometer

Results: This was the first of three "second-generation" interplanetary probes (two flyby probes and one impact probe), designed to reach Mars, prepared by the Soviets for the late-1962 launch window. Because of the repeated failures of the Blok L upper stage during deep space missions, engineers elected to outfit the stage for the Mars missions with supplementary control and measurement equipment. As a result, most of the scientific instruments were removed from the Mars spacecraft. The three missions were primarily technological test flights rather than scientific missions. In this case, the Blok L interplanetary stage failed again. Just 17 seconds after trans-Mars injection ignition, the main engine (the S1.5400A1) turbopump exploded, destroying the payload. The problem was traced to leaking lubricant. As many as twenty-four fragments were later tracked, the largest of which reentered on 29 October. The original probe was designed to fly by Mars on 17 June 1963.

34)
Mars 1
Nation: USSR (18)
Objective(s): Mars flyby
Spacecraft: 2MV-4 (no. 4)
Spacecraft Mass: 893.5 kilograms
Mission Design and Management: OKB-1
Launch Vehicle: 8K78 (no. T103-16)
Launch Date and Time: 1 November 1962 / 16:14:16 UT
Launch Site: NIIP-5 / launch site 1
Scientific Instruments:
1) imaging system
2) magnetometer

Results: The second of three Soviet spacecraft intended for the 1962 Mars launch window, Mars 1 was the first spacecraft sent by any nation to fly past Mars. Its primary mission was to photograph the surface. This time the upper stage successfully fired the probe toward Mars, but immediately after engine cutoff, controllers discovered that pressure in one of the nitrogen gas bottles for the spacecraft's attitude-control system had dropped to zero (due to incomplete closure of a valve). On 6 and 7 November, controllers used a backup gyroscope system to keep the solar panels constantly exposed to the Sun during the coast phase, although further midcourse corrections became impossible. Controllers maintained contact with the vehicle until 21 March 1963, when the probe was 106 million kilometers from Earth. Mars 1 eventually silently flew by Mars at a distance of 197,000 kilometers on 19 June 1963. Prior to loss of contact, scientists were able to collect data on interplanetary space (on cosmic-ray intensity, Earth's magnetic fields, ionized gases from the Sun, and meteoroid impact densities) up to a distance of 1.24 AU.

35)
no name / [Mars]
Nation: USSR (19)
Objective(s): Mars impact
Spacecraft: 2MV-3 (no. 1)
Spacecraft Mass: unknown
Mission Design and Management: OKB-1
Launch Vehicle: 8K78 (no. T103-17)
Launch Date and Time: 4 November 1962 / 15:35:15 UT
Launch Site: NIIP-5 / launch site 1
Scientific Instruments: unknown
Results: This was the third and last of the Soviet "second-generation" Mars attempts in 1962 and also the only lander in the series. During the trans-Mars injection firing of the Blok L stage, the main engine (the S1.5400A1) prematurely shut down after 33 seconds due to a malfunction in the programmed timer for the stage. The problem was later traced to excessive vibrations of the second stage during liftoff. These vibrations evidently also jarred loose a pyrotechnic igniter from its support, preventing the Blok L upper stage from firing. The spacecraft remained stranded in orbit and reentered Earth's atmosphere on 5 November. The spacecraft had been intended to fly by Mars on 21 June 1963.

1963

36)
no name / [Luna]
Nation: USSR (20)
Objective(s): lunar soft-landing
Spacecraft: Ye-6 (no. 2)
Spacecraft Mass: 1,420 kg
Mission Design and Management: OKB-1
Launch Vehicle: 8K78 (no. T103-09)
Launch Date and Time: 4 January 1963 / 08:49 UT
Launch Site: NIIP-5 / launch site 1
Scientific Instruments:
 1) imaging system
 2) radiation detector
Results: This spacecraft was the first "second-generation" Soviet lunar probe (known as Ye-6). These were designed to accomplish a survivable landing on the surface of the Moon. The Ye-6 probes were equipped with simple lander capsules (called the ALS) whose primary objective was to send back photographs from the lunar surface. Each egg-shaped ALS was installed on a roughly cylindrical-shaped main bus. Like the Mars and Venera deep space probes, the Ye-6 Luna spacecraft were also launched by the four-stage 8K78 (Molniya) booster but modified for lunar missions. Like many of its deep space predecessors, this first Luna probe failed to escape Earth orbit because of a failure in the Blok L translunar injection stage. There was apparently a failure in the inverter in the power system of the I-100 guidance system (which controlled both the Blok L and the spacecraft), which failed to issue a command to fire the Blok L engine. The spacecraft remained in Earth orbit, unacknowledged by the Soviets.

37)
no name / [Luna]
Nation: USSR (21)
Objective(s): lunar soft-landing
Spacecraft: Ye-6 (no. 3)
Spacecraft Mass: 1,420 kg
Mission Design and Management: OKB-1
Launch Vehicle: 8K78 (no. G103-10)
Launch Date and Time: 3 February 1963 / 09:29:14 UT
Launch Site: NIIP-5 / launch site 1
Scientific Instruments:
 1) imaging system
 2) radiation detector
Results: This was the second Soviet attempt to accomplish a soft-landing on the Moon. This time, the spacecraft failed to reach Earth orbit. Following separation of the second stage, the booster lost attitude control and deposited its third and fourth stages in the Pacific Ocean near Midway Island. Later investigation indicated that the I-100 guidance system provided incorrect information to the booster's trajectory control system.

38)
Luna 4
Nation: USSR (22)
Objective(s): lunar soft-landing
Spacecraft: Ye-6 (no. 4)
Spacecraft Mass: 1,422 kilograms
Mission Design and Management: OKB-1
Launch Vehicle: 8K78 (no. G103-11)
Launch Date and Time: 2 April 1963 / 08:16:37 UT
Launch Site: NIIP-5 / launch site 1
Scientific Instruments:
1) imaging system
2) radiation detector

Results: The third Soviet attempt to perform a lunar soft-landing was the first in which the spacecraft actually left Earth orbit. During the coast to the Moon, the spacecraft's Yupiter astronavigation system suffered a major failure (probably in its thermal control system) and left the probe in an incorrect attitude. As a result, Luna 4 was unable to perform its planned midcourse correction. Although communications were maintained with the spacecraft, it passed by the Moon at a range of 8,500 kilometers on 6 April and eventually entered heliocentric orbit (after being in an intermediate barycentric orbit).

39)
Kosmos 21 / [Zond]
Nation: USSR (23)
Objective(s): lunar flyby
Spacecraft: 3MV-1A (no. 1)
Spacecraft Mass: c. 800 kg
Mission Design and Management: OKB-1
Launch Vehicle: 8K78 (no. G103-18)
Launch Date and Time: 11 November 1963 / 06:23:35 UT
Launch Site: NIIP-5 / launch site 1
Scientific Instruments:
1) radiation detector
2) charged-particle detector
3) magnetometer
4) piezoelectric detector
5) atomic hydrogen detector
6) radio telescope
7) ultraviolet and Roentgen solar radiation experiment
8) technology experiment
9) plasma engines

Results: This was the first of the Soviet Union's "third-generation" deep space planetary probes of the 3MV series. Like the second generation, Soviet engineers projected four types of the 3MV: the 3MV-1 (for Venus impact), 3MV-2 (for Venus flyby), 3MV-3 (for Mars impact), and 3MV-4 (for Mars flyby). The primary difference over the second generation was vastly improved (and in many cases doubled) orientation system elements. While these four versions were meant to study Mars and Venus, the Soviets conceived of two additional variants of the series, similar but not identical to the 3MV-1 and 3MV-4 versions. These "test variants" were designed to verify key technological systems during simpler missions on flyby missions to the Moon and the near planets. On this particular launch, the first to fly a "test variant," the third and fourth stages separated abnormally; after the craft reached Earth orbit, ground control lost telemetry from the Blok L upper stage designed to send the vehicle past the Moon. The stage's main engine turbopump probably exploded upon ignition, destroying the payload. With this mission, the Soviets began the practice of giving Kosmos designations to lunar and planetary probes that remained stranded in Earth orbit.

1964

40)
Ranger 6
Nation: U.S. (17)
Objective(s): lunar impact
Spacecraft: P-53 / Ranger-A
Spacecraft Mass: 364.69 kg
Mission Design and Management: NASA JPL
Launch Vehicle: Atlas-Agena B (no. 8 / Atlas D no. 199 / Agena B no. 6008)
Launch Date and Time: 30 January 1964 / 15:49:09 UT
Launch Site: ETR / launch complex 12
Scientific Instruments:
   1) imaging system (six TV cameras)

Results: This fourth American attempt at lunar impact was the closest success. The spacecraft, the first Block III type vehicle with a suite of six TV cameras, was sterilized to avoid contaminating the lunar surface. The series would also serve as a test bed for future interplanetary spacecraft by deploying systems (such as solar panels) that could be used for more ambitious missions. The Block III spacecraft carried a 173-kilogram TV unit (replacing the impact capsule carried on the Block II Ranger spacecraft). The six cameras included two full-scan and four partial-scan cameras. Ranger 6 flew to the Moon successfully and impacted precisely on schedule at 09:24:32 UT on 2 February. Unfortunately, the power supply for the TV camera package had short-circuited three days previously during Atlas booster separation and left the system inoperable. The cameras were to have transmitted high-resolution photos of the lunar approach from 1,448 kilometers to 6.4 kilometers range in support of Project Apollo. Impact coordinates were 9°24' north latitude and 21°30' east longitude.

41)
no name / [Zond]
Nation: USSR (24)
Objective(s): Venus flyby
Spacecraft: 3MV-1A (no. 4A)
Spacecraft Mass: c. 800 kg
Mission Design and Management: OKB-1
Launch Vehicle: 8K78 (no. T15000-19)
Launch Date and Time: 19 February 1964 / 05:47:40 UT
Launch Site: NIIP-5 / launch site 1
Scientific Instruments:
   1) radiation detector
   2) charged-particle detector
   3) magnetometer
   4) piezoelectric detector
   5) atomic hydrogen detector
   6) radio telescope
   7) ultraviolet and Roentgen solar radiation experiment
   8) technology experiment
   9) plasma engines

Results: This was another Soviet "third-generation" deep space probe that failed to accomplish its mission of a Venus flyby. This spacecraft failed to reach Earth orbit due to a malfunction in the launch vehicle's third stage. Later investigation indicated that a liquid oxygen leak through an unpressurized valve seal froze propellant in the main pipeline. As a result, the pipeline cracked, leading to an explosion in the third stage.

42)
no name / [Luna]
Nation: USSR (25)
Objective(s): lunar soft-landing
Spacecraft: Ye-6 (no. 6)
Spacecraft Mass: c. 1,420 kg
Mission Design and Management: OKB-1
Launch Vehicle: 8K78M (no. T15000-20)
Launch Date and Time: 21 March 1964 / 08:15:35 UT
Launch Site: NIIP-5 / launch site 1
Scientific Instruments:
1) imaging system
2) radiation detector

Results: This fourth Soviet attempt to achieve a soft-landing on the Moon failed to reach an intermediate orbit around Earth. During the boost phase, the launcher's third-stage engine's main liquid oxygen valve failed to open when the valve rod broke off. As a result, the third-stage engine never reached full thrust and eventually cut off prematurely at T+489 seconds. The spacecraft never reached Earth orbit.

43)
Kosmos 27 / [Zond]
Nation: USSR (26)
Objective(s): Venus impact
Spacecraft: 3MV-1 (no. 5)
Spacecraft Mass: 948 kg
Mission Design and Management: OKB-1
Launch Vehicle: 8K78 (no. T15000-22)
Launch Date and Time: 27 March 1964 / 03:24:42 UT
Launch Site: NIIP-5 / launch site 1
Scientific Instruments:
Bus:
1) radiation detector
2) charged-particle detector
3) magnetometer
4) piezoelectric detector
5) atomic hydrogen detector

Lander:
1) barometer
2) thermometer
3) radiation detector
4) micro-organism detection experiment
5) atmospheric composition experiment
6) acidity measurement experiment
7) electro-conductivity experiment
8) luminosity experiment

Results: The probe, designed to accomplish atmospheric entry into Venus, successfully reached Earth orbit but failed to leave for Venus when the Blok L upper stage malfunctioned. The upper stage evidently lost stable attitude due to a failure in the circuit of the power supply for the attitude-control system. The spacecraft burned up in Earth's atmosphere the following day. Had this mission been successful, it would probably have been given a Zond designation.

44)
Zond 1
Nation: USSR (27)
Objective(s): Venus impact
Spacecraft: 3MV-1 (no. 4)
Spacecraft Mass: 948 kg
Mission Design and Management: OKB-1
Launch Vehicle: 8K78 (no. T15000-23)
Launch Date and Time: 2 April 1964 / 02:42:40 UT
Launch Site: NIIP-5 / launch site 1
Scientific Instruments:
Bus:
1) radiation detector
2) charged-particle detector
3) magnetometer
4) piezoelectric detector
5) atomic hydrogen detector
Lander:
1) barometer
2) thermometer
3) radiation detector
4) micro-organism detection experiment
5) atmospheric composition experiment
6) acidity measurement experiment
7) electro-conductivity experiment
8) luminosity experiment

Results: Although this Venus impact probe was successfully sent toward Venus, ground controllers discovered a series of major malfunctions in the spacecraft during its coast to the planet. These included depressurization of the main spacecraft bus when the glass cover of a solar-stellar attitude-control sensor cracked. Additionally, the internal radio transmitters of the spacecraft were automatically switched on at the wrong time—during depressurization, when the gas discharge created high-voltage currents that shorted out the system. Contact was maintained with the still-pressurized 290-kilogram lander module until 25 May 1964, by which time controllers had managed to conduct two major course corrections (at 560,000 kilometers and 13 to 14 million kilometers from Earth, respectively), the first time such actions had been performed on a Soviet interplanetary spacecraft. The inert spacecraft eventually flew by Venus on 19 July 1964 at a range of 110,000 kilometers. The Soviets later published some data on cosmic-ray flux measured by Zond 1.

45)
no name / [Luna]
Nation: USSR (28)
Objective(s): lunar soft-landing
Spacecraft: Ye-6 (no. 5)
Spacecraft Mass: c. 1,420 kg
Mission Design and Management: OKB-1
Launch Vehicle: 8K78M (no. T15000-21)
Launch Date and Time: 20 April 1964 / 08:08:28 UT
Launch Site: NIIP-5 / launch site 1
Scientific Instruments:
 1) imaging system
 2) radiation detector
Results: This was the fifth Soviet attempt at a lunar soft-landing. The mission was aborted early when during the ascent to Earth orbit, the launch vehicle's third-stage engine prematurely shut down. A subsequent investigation indicated that the engine cut off due to loss of power when a circuit between a battery in the fourth stage (which powered the third-stage engine) and the I-100 guidance unit was broken.

46)
Ranger 7
Nation: U.S. (18)
Objective(s): lunar impact
Spacecraft: P-54 / Ranger-B
Spacecraft Mass: 365.6 kg
Mission Design and Management: NASA JPL
Launch Vehicle: Atlas-Agena B (no. 9 / Atlas D no. 250 / Agena B no. 6009)
Launch Date and Time: 28 July 1964 / 16:50:07 UT
Launch Site: ETR / launch complex 12
Scientific Instruments:
 1) imaging system (six TV cameras)
Results: Ranger 7, the second of the Block III Ranger series, was the first unequivocal success in U.S. efforts to explore the Moon—after thirteen consecutive failures. In some ways, it marked a major milestone in American deep space exploration because the ratio in favor of successes increased dramatically after this point. After a nominal midcourse correction on 29 July, Ranger 7 approached the Moon precisely on target two days later. Just 15 minutes prior to impact, the suite of TV cameras began sending back spectacular photos of the approaching surface to JPL's Goldstone dish in California. The last of 4,316 images was transmitted only 2.3 seconds prior to impact at 13:25:49 UT on 31 July 1964. The impact point was at 10°38' south latitude and 20°36' west longitude on the northern rim of the Sea of Clouds. Scientists on the ground were more than satisfied with Results; image resolution was, in many cases, one thousand times better than photos taken from Earth. Scientists concluded that an Apollo crewed landing would be possible in the mare regions of the lunar surface, given their relative smoothness.

47)
Mariner 3
Nation: U.S. (19)
Objective(s): Mars flyby
Spacecraft: Mariner-64C / Mariner-C
Spacecraft Mass: 260.8 kg
Mission Design and Management: NASA JPL
Launch Vehicle: Atlas-Agena D (no. 11 / Atlas D no. 289 / Agena D no. AD68/6931)
Launch Date and Time: 5 November 1964 / 19:22:05 UT
Launch Site: ETR / launch complex 13
Scientific Instruments:
 1) imaging system
 2) cosmic dust detector
 3) cosmic-ray telescope
 4) ionization chamber
 5) magnetometer
 6) trapped radiation detector
 7) solar plasma probe
 8) occultation experiment

Results: NASA approved two probes for the Mariner-Mars 1964 project in November 1962. The primary goal of the two spacecraft was to photograph the Martian surface using a single TV camera fixed on a scan platform that could return up to twenty-one pictures after an eight-month journey. During the launch of Mariner 3, the first of the two probes, the booster payload shroud failed to separate from the payload. Additionally, battery power mysteriously dropped to zero (at T+8 hours 43 minutes), and the spacecraft's solar panels apparently never unfurled to replenish the power supply. As a result, ground control lost contact with the spacecraft, which eventually entered heliocentric orbit. A later investigation indicated that the shroud's inner fiberglass layer had separated from the shroud's outer skin, thus preventing jettisoning.

48)
Mariner 4
Nation: U.S. (20)
Objective(s): Mars flyby
Spacecraft: Mariner-64D / Mariner-D
Spacecraft Mass: 260.8 kg
Mission Design and Management: NASA JPL
Launch Vehicle: Atlas-Agena D (no. 12 / Atlas D no. 288 / Agena D no. AD69 / 6932)
Launch Date and Time: 28 November 1964 / 14:22:01 UT
Launch Site: ETR / launch complex 12
Scientific Instruments:
    1) imaging system
    2) cosmic dust detector
    3) cosmic-ray telescope
    4) ionization chamber
    5) magnetometer
    6) trapped radiation detector
    7) solar plasma probe
    8) occultation experiment

Results: The Mariner 4 mission, the second of two Mars flyby attempts in 1964 by NASA, was one of the great early successes of the Agency, returning the very first photos of another planet from deep space. Using a new all-metal shroud, the spacecraft lifted off without any problems and was successfully boosted toward Mars by the Agena D upper stage. A single midcourse correction on 5 December ensured that the spacecraft would fly between 8,000 and 9,660 kilometers from the Martian surface. Approximately 40 minutes prior to closest

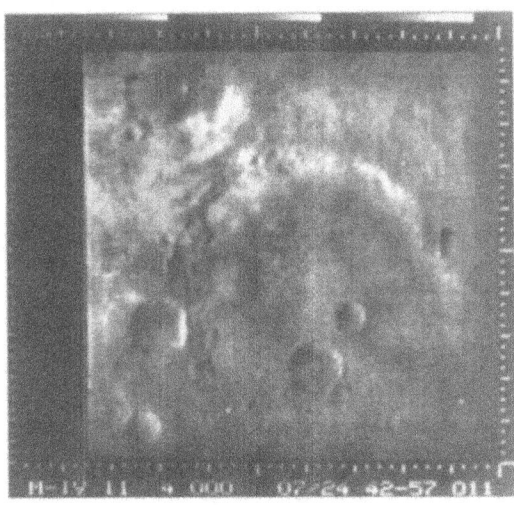

Eleventh picture of Mars from Mariner 4 (in "raw" state) taken through the green filter from 12,500 kilometers away, showing a crater 121 kilometers in diameter in the Atlantis region. Mariner 4 was the first spacecraft to get a close look at Mars. Flying as close as 9,846 kilometers, Mariner 4 revealed Mars to have a cratered, rust-colored surface, with signs on some parts of the planet that liquid water had once etched its way into the soil. Mariner 4 was launched on 28 November 1964 and arrived at Mars on 14 July 1965.

approach (which was at 01:00:57 UT on 15 July 1965 at a range of 9,846 kilometers), the TV camera began taking the first of twenty-one images (plus twenty-two lines of a twenty-second) through red and green filters. About 1.25 hours after the encounter, Mariner 4 dipped behind the right-hand side of Mars (as viewed from Earth) in order to refract its radio signals through the Martian atmosphere. Data indicated that surface pressure was quite low—future Mars landers would have to be equipped with retro-rocket engines in addition to parachutes. The probe detected daytime surface temperatures of about –100°C. A very weak radiation belt, about 0.1 percent of that of Earth's, was also detected. The day after the closest encounter, Mariner 4 began transmitting its photos back to Earth. The images clearly showed Mars to be an ancient Moon-like body with widespread cratering. Given the thin atmosphere, scientists believed it unlikely that Mars harbored any life. NASA maintained contact with the spacecraft until 1 October 1965, when the probe was 309 million kilometers from Earth. Two years later, in October 1967, the spacecraft was reactivated for attitude control tests in support of the Mariner 5 mission to Venus, which used a similar spacecraft bus. Final contact was lost on 21 December 1967.

49)
Zond 2
Nation: USSR (29)
Objective(s): Mars flyby
Spacecraft: 3MV-4 (no. 2)
Spacecraft Mass: 996 kg
Mission Design and Management: OKB-1
Launch Vehicle: 8K78
Launch Date and Time: 30 November 1964 / 13:12 UT
Launch Site: NIIP-5 / launch site 1
Scientific Instruments:
1) radiation detector
2) charged-particle detector
3) magnetometer
4) piezoelectric detector
5) radio telescope
6) nuclear component of cosmic-ray experiment
7) ultraviolet and Roentgen solar radiation experiment
8) imaging system

Results: Zond 2 was the Soviet Union's first third-generation ("3MV") spacecraft sent toward Mars. This particular model, the 3MV-4, was designed to fly by the planet and take photographs. After the spacecraft successfully entered a trans-Mars trajectory, ground controllers discovered that the probe's solar panels had not completely unfurled, which deprived the vehicle of full power. Later investigation indicated that a tug cord, designed to pull the panels free at the moment of separation from the Blok L upper stage, had broken off. Controllers were able to fully open the panel only on 15 December 1964, but by then the time for the first midcourse correction to fly by Mars had already passed. Additionally, between communications sessions, there had been a failure in the onboard programmed timer immediately after transinterplanetary injection that led to inappropriate thermal conditions for the spacecraft. On 18 December, before loss of contact, Zond 2 successfully fired six plasma electric rocket engines (twice) as a technology demonstrator for future deep space missions. The spacecraft was to have flown by Mars on 6 August 1965. It eventually entered heliocentric orbit.

1965

50)
Ranger 8
Nation: U.S. (21)
Objective(s): lunar impact
Spacecraft: Ranger-C
Spacecraft Mass: 366.87 kg
Mission Design and Management: NASA JPL
Launch Vehicle: Atlas-Agena B (no. 13 / Atlas D no. 196 / Agena B no. 6006)
Launch Date and Time: 17 February 1965 / 17:05:00 UT
Launch Site: ETR / launch complex 12
Scientific Instruments: Imaging system (six TV cameras)
Results: As successful as its predecessor, Ranger 8 returned 7,137 high-resolution photographs of the lunar surface prior to its scheduled impact at 09:57:37 UT on 20 February. Unlike Ranger 7, however, Ranger 8 turned on its cameras about 8 minutes earlier to return pictures with resolution comparable to Earth-based telescopes (for calibration and comparison purposes). Controllers attempted to align the cameras along the main velocity vector (to reduce imagine smear) but abandoned this maneuver to allow greater area coverage. There had also been a mysterious loss of telemetry during a midcourse correction on 18 February that gave rise for concern, although the mission was completed successfully. Ranger 8 impacted at 2°43' north latitude and 24°38' east longitude, just 24 kilometers from its intended target point in the equatorial region of the Sea of Tranquillity—an area that Apollo mission planners were particularly interested in studying.

51)
"Atlas-Centaur 5"
Nation: U.S. (22)
Objective(s): highly elliptical orbit
Spacecraft: SD-1
Spacecraft Mass: 951 kg
Mission Design and Management: NASA JPL
Launch Vehicle: Atlas-Centaur (AC-5 / Atlas C no. 156D / Centaur C)
Launch Date and Time: 2 March 1965 / 13:25 UT
Launch Site: ETR / launch complex 36A
Scientific Instruments: none
Results: This mission was designed to rehearse a complete Centaur upper-stage burn in support of the Surveyor lunar lander program. On a nominal mission, the Centaur would boost its payload on a direct-ascent trajectory to the Moon. On this test flight, SD-1, a nonfunctional dynamic model, would be boosted on a simulated lunar transfer trajectory to a hypothetical Moon with an orbit of 167 x 926,625 kilometers. During the actual launch, less than 1 second after liftoff, a faulty valve caused both Atlas main engines to shut down. As a result, the booster fell back onto the pad and exploded.

52)
Kosmos 60 / [Luna]
Nation: USSR (30)
Objective(s): lunar soft-landing
Spacecraft: Ye-6 (no. 9)
Spacecraft Mass: c. 1,470 kg
Mission Design and Management: OKB-1
Launch Vehicle: 8K78 (no. R103-25)
Launch Date and Time: 10 April 1965 / N/A
Launch Site: NIIP-5
Scientific Instruments:
   1) imaging system
   2) radiation detector

Results: Yet another Soviet attempt to soft-land a Ye-6 probe on the lunar surface ended in failure when the Blok L upper stage failed to fire for the translunar injection burn. Instead, the spacecraft remained stranded in Earth orbit. A later investigation indicated that there had been a short circuit in an inverter within the I-100 guidance system of the spacecraft (which also controlled the Blok L stage) preventing engine ignition. The spacecraft's orbit decayed five days later.

53)
Ranger 9
Nation: U.S. (23)
Objective(s): lunar impact
Spacecraft: Ranger-D
Spacecraft Mass: 366.87 kg
Mission Design and Management: NASA JPL
Launch Vehicle: Atlas-Agena B (no. 14 / Atlas D no. 204 / Agena B no. 6007)
Launch Date and Time: 21 March 1965 / 21:37:02 UT
Launch Site: ETR / launch complex 12
Scientific Instruments:
   1) imaging system (six TV cameras)

Results: Ranger 9 was the final Ranger mission of the Block III series and closed out the program as a whole. Since both Ranger 7 and Ranger 8 had provided sufficient photographs of the mare regions (potential landing sites for the early Apollo missions), Ranger 9 was targeted to the more geologically interesting Alphonsus crater in the lunar highlands, at that time a possible site for recent volcanic activity. Following a midcourse correction on 23 March, the spacecraft headed directly to its impact point. Only 20 minutes prior to impact, Ranger 9 began taking the first of 5,814 pictures from an altitude of 2,100 kilometers. Unlike its predecessors, the cameras this time were aimed directly in the direction of travel and provided some spectacular shots as the spacecraft approached the lunar surface. These pictures were converted for live viewing on commercial TV. Best resolution was up to 25 centimeters just prior to impact. The spacecraft crashed into the Moon at 14:08:20 UT on 24 March at 12.83° south latitude and 357.63° east longitude, about 6.5 kilometers from its scheduled target.

54)
no name / [Luna]
Nation: USSR (31)
Objective(s): lunar soft-landing
Spacecraft: Ye-6 (no. 8)
Spacecraft Mass: c. 1,470 kg
Mission Design and Management: OKB-1
Launch Vehicle: 8K78 (no. R103-26)
Launch Date and Time: 10 April 1965 / N/A
Launch Site: NIIP-5 / launch site 1
Scientific Instruments:
   1) imaging system
   2) radiation detector

Results: This was the seventh consecutive failure to accomplish a lunar soft-landing by the Soviets. On this mission, engineers redesigned the problematic I-100 guidance system that had caused most of the previous failures. Previously, the I-100 unit had controlled both the Blok L upper stage and the spacecraft itself. On this mission (and subsequent Lunas), the fourth stage and the Ye-6 spacecraft had separate systems. Unfortunately, this probe never reached Earth orbit. During the launch, depressurization of a nitrogen pipe for the liquid oxygen tank on the third stage had prevented third-stage engine ignition. The spacecraft broke up over the Pacific without reaching orbit.

55)
Luna 5
Nation: USSR (32)
Objective(s): lunar soft-landing
Spacecraft: Ye-6 (no. 10)
Spacecraft Mass: 1,476 kg
Mission Design and Management: OKB-1
Launch Vehicle: 8K78M (no. U103-30)
Launch Date and Time: 9 May 1965 / 07:49:37 UT
Launch Site: NIIP-5 / launch site 1

Scientific Instruments:
1) imaging system
2) radiation detector

Results: In May 1965, Luna 5 became the first Soviet probe to head for the Moon in two years. Following the midcourse correction on 10 May, the spacecraft began spinning around its main axis due to a problem in a flotation gyroscope in the I-100 guidance system unit. A subsequent attempt to fire the main engine failed because of ground control error, and the engine never fired. After loss of control as a result of the gyroscope problem, Luna 5 crashed. Landing coordinates were 31° south latitude and 8° west longitude. It was the second Soviet spacecraft to land on the Moon (following Luna 2 in 1959).

56)
Luna 6
Nation: USSR (33)
Objective(s): lunar soft-landing
Spacecraft: Ye-6 (no. 7)
Spacecraft Mass: 1,442 kg
Mission Design and Management: OKB-1
Launch Vehicle: 8K78M (no. U103-31)
Launch Date and Time: 8 June 1965 / 07:40 UT
Launch Site: NIIP-5 / launch site 1
Scientific Instruments:
1) imaging system
2) radiation detector

Results: On this ninth Soviet attempt at a lunar soft-landing, the mission proceeded as planned until the major midcourse correction late on 9 June. Although the main retro-rocket engine (the S5.5A) ignited on time, it failed to cut off and continued to fire until propellant supply was exhausted. An investigation later indicated that the problem had been due to human error; a command had been mistakenly sent to the timer that ordered the main engine to shut down. Although the spacecraft was sent on a completely wrong trajectory, ground controllers put the spacecraft through a series of steps to practice an actual landing, all of which were satisfactorily accomplished. Luna 6 passed by the Moon late on 11 June at a range of 161,000 kilometers and eventually entered heliocentric orbit. Contact was maintained to a distance of 600,000 kilometers from Earth.

57)
Zond 3
Nation: USSR (34)
Objective(s): lunar flyby
Spacecraft: 3MV-4 (no. 3)
Spacecraft Mass: 950 kg
Mission Design and Management: OKB-1
Launch Vehicle: 8K78
Launch Date and Time: 18 July 1965 / N/A
Launch Site: NIIP-5 / launch site 1
Scientific Instruments:
1) imaging system
2) ultraviolet spectrograph
3) ultraviolet and infrared spectrophotometer
4) meteoroid detectors
5) radiation sensors (cosmic rays, solar wind)
6) magnetometer
7) ion thrusters
8) radio telescope

Results: This "third-generation" deep space probe had originally been slated for a Mars flyby in late 1964 but could not be prepared on time. Instead, Soviet designers diverted the mission for a simple lunar flyby in 1965 to test its basic systems and photograph the far side of the Moon. After a successful translunar injection burn, Zond 3 approached the Moon after only a 33-hour flight. Its imaging mission began on 20 July at a range of 11,570 kilometers from the near side of the Moon. The camera system used a similar system to that of Luna 3, with onboard exposure, development, fixing, and drying prior to scanning for transmission to Earth. In total, the spacecraft took twenty-five visual and three ultraviolet images during its flyby. The closest approach was to 9,220 kilometers. These pictures were successfully transmitted back to Earth on 29 July, nine days after Zond 3's lunar encounter, when it was 2.2 million kilometers from Earth. Further communications sessions occurred on 23 October (involving photo transmissions) when Zond 3 was 31.5 million kilometers from Earth. The last contact was sometime in early March 1966, when the spacecraft was 153.5 million kilometers away. During the mission, it had photographed the unseen 30 percent of the far side of the Moon. Zond 3 also demonstrated successful course correction using both solar and stellar orientation, a first for a Soviet spacecraft.

58)
Surveyor Model 1
Nation: U.S. (24)
Objective(s): highly elliptical orbit
Spacecraft: SD-2
Spacecraft Mass: 950 kg
Mission Design and Management: NASA JPL
Launch Vehicle: Atlas-Centaur (AC-6 / Atlas D no. 151D / Centaur D)
Launch Date and Time: 11 August 1965 / 14:31:04 UT
Launch Site: ETR / launch complex 36B
Scientific Instruments: none
Results: This was the second attempt to launch a dummy Surveyor lunar lander spacecraft into a barycentric orbit toward a simulated Moon. Unlike the results of the previous attempt (in March 1965), all systems worked without fault; the Surveyor dynamic model was inserted on a simulated lunar trajectory so precise that it would have landed on the Moon without a trajectory correction on an actual mission. The spacecraft reentered Earth's atmosphere after thirty-one days.

59)
Luna 7
Nation: USSR (35)
Objective(s): lunar soft-landing
Spacecraft: Ye-6 (no. 11)
Spacecraft Mass: 1,506 kg
Mission Design and Management: OKB-1
Launch Vehicle: 8K78 (no. U103-27)
Launch Date and Time: 4 October 1965 / 07:56:40 UT
Launch Site: NIIP-5 / launch site 1
Scientific Instruments:
   1) imaging system
   2) radiation detector
Results: Unlike its predecessors, Luna 7 successfully carried out its midcourse correction on 5 October on the way to the Moon, in anticipation of a soft-landing two days later. Unfortunately, immediately prior to planned retro-fire during the approach to the lunar surface, the spacecraft suddenly lost attitude control and failed to regain it. Automatic programmed systems then prevented the main engine from firing. As controllers observed helplessly, Luna 7 plummeted to the lunar surface at a very high speed, crashing at 22:08:24 UT on 7 October west of the Kepler crater, relatively near the actual intended target. Impact coordinates were 9° north latitude and 49° west longitude. Later investigation indicated that the optical sensor of the astronavigation system had been set at the wrong angle and had lost sight of Earth during the critical attitude-control maneuver. It was the tenth consecutive failure in the Ye-6 program.

60)
Venera 2
Nation: USSR (36)
Objective(s): Venus flyby
Spacecraft: 3MV-4 (no. 4)
Spacecraft Mass: 963 kg
Mission Design and Management: OKB-1
Launch Vehicle: 8K78M
Launch Date and Time: 12 November 1965 / N/A
Launch Site: NIIP-5 / launch site 31
Scientific Instruments:
   1) three-component magnetometer
   2) imaging system
   3) solar x-radiation detector
   4) cosmic-ray gas-discharge counters
   5) piezoelectric detectors
   6) ion traps
   7) photon Geiger counter
   8) cosmic radio emission receivers
Results: Although the 3MV-3 and 3MV-4 type spacecraft were originally intended for Mars exploration, the Soviets re-equipped three of the series, left over from the 1964 Mars launch windows, for Venus exploration in 1965. This particular vehicle was scheduled to fly past the sunlit side of Venus at no more than a 40,000-kilometer range and take photographs. During the outbound flight, communications with the spacecraft were poor. Immediately before closest approach in late February 1966, ground control commanded to switch on all the onboard scientific instrumentation. The closest approach to the planet was at 02:52 UT on 27 February 1966 at about a 24,000-kilometer range. After its flyby, when the spacecraft was supposed to relay back the collected information, ground control was unable to regain contact. Controllers finally gave up all attempts at communication on 4 March. Venera 2 eventually entered heliocentric orbit. Later investigation indicated that improper functioning of

40 thermal radiator elements caused a sharp increase in gas temperatures in the spacecraft. As a result, elements of the receiving and decoding units failed, the solar panels overheated, and contact was lost. Ironically, the scientific instruments may have collected valuable data, but none of it was ever transmitted back to Earth.

61)
Venera 3
Nation: USSR (37)
Objective(s): Venus impact
Spacecraft: 3MV-3 (no. 1)
Spacecraft Mass: 958 kg
Mission Design and Management: OKB-1
Launch Vehicle: 8K78M
Launch Date and Time: 16 November 1965 / N/A
Launch Site: NIIP-5 / launch site 31
Scientific Instruments:
  Bus:
  1) radiation detector
  (rest unknown)
Results: This was the second of three 3MV spacecraft the Soviets attempted to launch toward Venus in late 1965. Venera 3 successfully left Earth orbit and released a small 0.9-meter-diameter, 337-kilogram (some sources say 310-kilogram) landing capsule to explore the Venusian atmosphere and transmit data on pressure, temperature, and composition of the Venusian atmosphere back to Earth during the descent by parachute. During the outbound trajectory, ground controllers successfully performed a midcourse correction on 26 December 1965 and completed 93 communications sessions. However, contact was lost on 16 February 1966, shortly before the Venusian encounter, although the spacecraft automatically released its sterilized lander probe, which landed inertly on the Venusian surface at 06:56 UT on 1 March 1966. It was the first time a humanmade object had made physical contact with another planetary body besides the Moon. Later investigation confirmed that Venera 3 suffered many of the same failures as Venera 2, such as overheating of internal components and the solar panels.

62)
Kosmos 96 / [Venera]
Nation: USSR (38)
Objective(s): Venus flyby

Spacecraft: 3MV-4 (no. 6)
Spacecraft Mass: c. 950 kg
Mission Design and Management: OKB-1
Launch Vehicle: 8K78M
Launch Date and Time: 23 November 1965 / N/A
Launch Site: NIIP-5 / launch site 31
Scientific Instruments:
  1) three-component magnetometer
  2) imaging system
  3) solar x-radiation detector
  4) cosmic-ray gas-discharge counters
  5) piezoelectric detectors
  6) ion traps
  7) photon Geiger counter
  8) cosmic radio emission receivers
Results: This was the third and last spacecraft prepared for a Venus encounter by the Soviets in 1965. All three spacecraft had originally been intended for Mars exploration in 1964 and 1965. However, during coast to orbit, a combustion chamber in the booster's third-stage engine exploded due to a crack in the fuel pipeline. Although the payload reached Earth orbit, the Blok L upper stage was tumbling and was unable to fire for trans-Venus trajectory injection. The probe remained stranded in Earth orbit, and the Soviets named it Kosmos 96 to disguise its true mission. The probe's orbit decayed on 9 December 1965.

63)
Luna 8
Nation: USSR (39)
Objective(s): lunar soft-landing
Spacecraft: Ye-6 (no. 12)
Spacecraft Mass: 1,552 kg
Mission Design and Management: OKB-1
Launch Vehicle: 8K78 (no. U103-28)
Launch Date and Time: 3 December 1965 / 10:46:14 UT
Launch Site: NIIP-5 / launch site 31
Scientific Instruments:
  1) imaging system
  2) radiation detector
Results: This, the tenth Soviet attempt to achieve a lunar soft-landing, nearly succeeded. After a successful midcourse correction on 4 December, the spacecraft headed toward the Moon without any apparent problems. Just prior to the planned retro-fire burn, a command was sent to inflate cushioning airbags around the ALS lander probe.

Unfortunately, a plastic mounting bracket apparently pierced one of the two bags. The resulting expulsion of air put the spacecraft into a spin of 12 degrees per second. The vehicle momentarily regained attitude, long enough for a 9-second retro-engine firing, but then lost it again. Without a full retro-fire burn to reduce approach velocity sufficient for a survivable landing, Luna 8 plummeted to the lunar surface and crashed at 21:51:30 UT on 6 December just west of the Kepler crater. Impact coordinates were 9°8' north latitude and 63°18' west longitude.

64)
Pioneer 6
Nation: U.S. (25)
Objective(s): heliocentric orbit
Spacecraft: Pioneer-A
Spacecraft Mass: 62.14 kg
Mission Design and Management: NASA ARC
Launch Vehicle: Thor-Delta E (no. 35 / Thor no. 460/DSV-3E)
Launch Date and Time: 16 December 1965 / 07:31:21 UT
Launch Site: ETR / launch complex 17A
Scientific Instruments:
1) single-axis fluxgate magnetometer
2) Faraday-cup plasma probe
3) plasma analyzer
4) cosmic-ray telescope
5) cosmic-ray-anisotropy detector
6) radio wave propagation experiment
7) celestial mechanics experiment

Results: Pioneer 6 was the first of four NASA spacecraft designed to study interplanetary phenomena in space. The spacecraft successfully provided simultaneous scientific measurements at widely dispersed locations in heliocentric orbit. It returned the first data on the tenuous solar atmosphere and later recorded the passage of Comet Kohoutek's tail in 1974. Along with Pioneers 7, 8, and 9, the spacecraft formed a ring of solar weather stations spaced along Earth's orbit. Measurements by the four Pioneers were used to predict solar storms for approximately 1,000 primary users, including the Federal Aviation Administration; commercial airlines; power companies; communication companies; military organizations; and entities involved in surveying, navigation, and electronic prospecting. By December 1990, Pioneer 6 had circled the Sun twenty-nine times (traveling 24.8 billion kilometers) and had been operational for twenty years—a record for a deep space probe. Its original slated lifetime had been only six months. On 15 December 1996, the spacecraft's primary transmitter failed, but during a track on 11 July 1996, ground controllers switched on the backup transmitter. Of the spacecraft's six scientific instruments, two (the plasma analyzer and the cosmic-ray detector) still continue to function. NASA maintains contact with the spacecraft once or twice each year. For example, 1 hour's worth of scientific data was collected on 29 July and 15 December 1995 (although the primary transmitter failed soon after that), and again on 6 October 1997, more than thirty years after launch. The probe's solar arrays continue to deteriorate, although the transmitters can be turned on at perihelion when the solar flux is strong enough to provide sufficient power. On 8 December 2000, to commemorate its thirty-fifth anniversary of operation, ground controllers established successful contact with the spacecraft for about 2 hours.

1966

65)
Luna 9
Nation: USSR (40)
Objective(s): lunar soft-landing
Spacecraft: Ye-6M (no. 202)
Spacecraft Mass: 1,538 kg
Mission Design and Management: GSMZ Lavochkin
Launch Vehicle: 8K78M (no. U103-32)
Launch Date and Time: 31 January 1966 / 11:41:37 UT
Launch Site: NIIP-5 / launch site 31
Scientific Instruments:
 1) imaging system
 2) SBM-10 radiation detector

Results: With this mission, the Soviets accomplished another spectacular first in the space race, the first survivable landing of a human-made object on another celestial body. Luna 9 was the twelfth attempt at a soft-landing by the Soviets; it was also the first deep space probe built by the Lavochkin design bureau, which ultimately would design and build almost all Soviet (and Russian) lunar and interplanetary spacecraft. All operations prior to landing occurred without fault, and the 58-centimeter spheroid ALS capsule landed on the Moon at 18:45:30 UT on 3 February 1966 west of the Reiner and Marius craters in the Ocean of Storms (at 7°8' north latitude and 64°22' west longitude). Approximately 5 minutes after touchdown, Luna 9 began transmitting data to Earth, but it was 7 hours (after the Sun climbed to 7° elevation) before the probe began sending the first of nine images (including five panoramas) of the surface of the Moon. These were the first images sent from the surface of another planetary body. The radiation detector, the only scientific instrument on board, measured a dosage of 30 millirads per day. Perhaps the most important discovery of the mission was determining that a foreign object would not simply sink into the lunar dust, that is, that the ground could support a heavy lander. Last contact with the spacecraft was at 22:55 UT on 6 February 1966.

66)
Kosmos 111 / [Luna]
Nation: USSR (41)
Objective(s): lunar orbit
Spacecraft: Ye-6S (no. 204)
Spacecraft Mass: c. 1,580 kg
Mission Design and Management: GSMZ Lavochkin
Launch Vehicle: 8K78M (no. N103-41)
Launch Date and Time: 1 March 1966 / 11:03:49 UT
Launch Site: NIIP-5 / launch site 31
Scientific Instruments:
 1) magnetometer
 2) gamma-ray spectrometer
 3) five gas-discharge counters

4) two ion traps and a charged-particle trap
5) piezoelectric micrometer detector
6) infrared detector
7) low-energy x-ray photon counters

Results: In early 1966, the Soviets began hastily putting together an interim lunar orbiter program, the Ye-6S, partly to upstage the American Lunar Orbiter project and partly to commemorate the 23rd Congress of the Communist Party held in March 1966. Engineers quickly designed a set of two rudimentary probes using the old Ye-6 (lander) buses for these missions. The first of them was prepared in less than a month but failed to leave Earth orbit. During Earth orbit operations, the Blok L upper stage lost roll control and failed to fire to send the probe towards the Moon. The official Soviet media named the stranded satellite Kosmos 111; it reentered Earth's atmosphere two days after launch.

67)
Luna 10
Nation: USSR (42)
Objective(s): lunar orbit
Spacecraft: Ye-6S (no. 206)
Spacecraft Mass: 1,582 kg
Mission Design and Management: GSMZ Lavochkin
Launch Vehicle: 8K78M (no. N103-42)
Launch Date and Time: 31 March 1966 / 10:47 UT
Launch Site: NIIP-5 / launch site 31
Scientific Instruments:
1) magnetometer
2) gamma-ray spectrometer
3) five gas-discharge counters
4) two ion traps and a charged-particle trap
5) piezoelectric micrometer detector
6) infrared detector
7) low-energy x-ray photon counters

Results: After a midcourse correction on 1 April, Luna 10, the second of two hastily prepared Soviet Ye-6S probes (that is, the backup), successfully entered lunar orbit two days later at 18:44 UT, thus becoming the first humanmade object to go into orbit around another planetary body. A 245-kilogram instrument compartment separated from the main bus, which was in a 350 x 1,000-kilometer orbit inclined at 71.9° to the lunar equator. The spacecraft carried a set of solid-state oscillators that had been programmed to reproduce the notes of the Internationale so that it could be broadcast live to the 23rd Communist Party Congress. During a rehearsal on the night of 3 April, the playback went well, but the following morning, controllers discovered a missing note and played the previous night's tape to the assembled gathering at the Congress–claiming it was a live broadcast from the Moon. Luna 10 conducted extensive research in lunar orbit, gathering important data on the weakness of the Moon's magnetic field, its radiation belts, and the nature of lunar rocks (which were found to be comparable to terrestrial basalt rocks), cosmic radiation, and micrometeoroid density. Perhaps its most important finding was the first evidence of mass concentrations (called "mascons")—areas of high density below the mare basins that distort lunar orbital trajectories. Their discovery has usually been credited to the American Lunar Orbiter series. Last contact was on 30 May 1966.

68)
Surveyor Model 2
Nation: U.S. (26)
Objective(s): highly elliptical orbit
Spacecraft: SD-3
Spacecraft Mass: 784 kg
Mission Design and Management: NASA JPL
Launch Vehicle: Atlas-Centaur (AC-8 / Atlas no. 184D / Centaur D)
Launch Date and Time: 8 April 1966 / 01:00:02 UT
Launch Site: ETR / launch complex 36B
Scientific Instruments: none
Results: This was a test to launch a dummy Surveyor lunar lander spacecraft into a barycentric orbit toward a simulated Moon. Unlike the two previous Surveyor mass model tests, this flight was supposed to demonstrate a restart capability for the Centaur upper stage. The Centaur-Surveyor combination successfully achieved parking orbit around Earth, but at the desired time, the Centaur engines fired for only a few seconds. A thrust imbalance left the payload tumbling. The problem was later traced to a hydrogen peroxide leak in the ullage motors of the Centaur stage. With no hope of reaching its ultimate

orbit, the spacecraft reentered Earth's atmosphere on 5 May 1966.

69)
Surveyor 1
Nation: U.S. (27)
Objective(s): lunar soft-landing
Spacecraft: Surveyor-A
Spacecraft Mass: 995.2 kg
Mission Design and Management: NASA JPL
Launch Vehicle: Atlas-Centaur (AC-10 / Atlas D no. 290 / Centaur D)
Launch Date and Time: 30 May 1966 / 14:41:01 UT
Launch Site: ETR, launch complex 36A
Scientific Instruments:
1) imaging system

Results: NASA initially (c. 1963) conceived of the Surveyor program as a landing and orbiting robotic lunar project, but it scaled down plans to a more specific program of ten lunar soft-landers (seven were eventually launched) geared toward basic engineering goals rather than scientific exploration. The primary "scientific instrument" was an imaging system. Unlike the Soviet Luna landers, Surveyor was a true soft-lander, comprising a 3-meter-tall vehicle based on a 27-kilogram, thin-walled aluminum triangular structure with one of three legs at each corner and a large solid-propellant retro-rocket engine (that comprised over 60 percent of the spacecraft's overall mass) in the center. The spacecraft was equipped with a Doppler velocity-sensing system that fed information into the spacecraft computer to implement a controllable descent to the surface. Each of the three landing pads also carried aircraft-type shock absorbers and strain gauges to provide data on landing characteristics, important for future Apollo missions. Surveyor 1, the first in the series, was an unprecedented success. NASA accomplished the first true soft-landing on the Moon on its very first try when the probe landed in the southwest region of the Ocean of Storms at 06:17:36 UT on 2 June 1966, just 63.6 hours after launch from Cape Canaveral. Touchdown coordinates were 2°27' south latitude and 43°13' west longitude, just 14 kilometers from the planned target. At landing, the spacecraft weighed 294.3 kilograms. The initial panoramic views from the lunar surface indicated that Surveyor 1 was resting in a 100-kilometer-diameter crater that contained boulders of more than 1 meter in length scattered all around. The photos showed crestlines of low mountains in the distant horizon. The lander transmitted 11,350 images over two separate communications sessions by 6 July. Although the primary mission was completed by 13 July, NASA maintained contact until 7 January 1967. Without doubt, Surveyor 1 was one of the great successes of NASA's early lunar and interplanetary program.

Image of Surveyor 1's shadow against the lunar surface in the late lunar afternoon, with the horizon at the upper right. Surveyor 1 was the first U.S. mission to make a successful soft-landing on the Moon. In addition to transmitting over 11,000 pictures, it sent information on the bearing strength of the lunar soil, the radar reflectivity, and temperature.

70)
Explorer 33
Nation: U.S. (28)
Objective(s): lunar orbit
Spacecraft: IMP-D
Spacecraft Mass: 93.4 kg
Mission Design and Management: NASA GSFC
Launch Vehicle: Thor-Delta E-1 (no. 39 / Thor no. 467 / DSV-3E)
Launch Date and Time: 1 July 1966 / 16:02:25 UT
Launch Site: ETR / launch complex 17A
Scientific Instruments :
 1) fluxgate magnetometers
 2) thermal ion probe
 3) ion chamber
 4) tubes plus p-on-n junction
 5) Faraday-cup probe

Results: Explorer 33 was designed to become the first U.S. spacecraft to enter lunar orbit (planned parameters were 1,300 x 6,440 kilometers at 175° inclination), but the Thor Delta E-1 second stage accelerated too rapidly for compensation by the probe's retro-rocket to achieve lunar orbit. Instead, the spacecraft (56.7 kg by this time) went into an eccentric Earth orbit of 15,897 x 435,330 kilometers. The main solid-propellant retro-rocket engine later stabilized the orbit to a less eccentric 30,550 x 449,174-kilometer orbit at 28.9° inclination. In its new orbit, the probe returned key data on Earth's magnetic tail, the interplanetary magnetic field, and radiation.

71)
Lunar Orbiter 1
Nation: U.S. (29)
Objective(s): lunar orbit
Spacecraft: LO-A
Spacecraft Mass: 385.6 kg
Mission Design and Management: NASA LaRC
Launch Vehicle: Atlas-Agena D (no. 17 / Atlas D no. 5801 / Agena D no. AD121 / 6630)
Launch Date and Time: 10 August 1966 / 19:26:00 UT
Launch Site: ETR / launch complex 13
Scientific Instruments:
 1) imaging system
 2) micrometeoroid detectors
 3) radiation dosimeters

Results: The Lunar Orbiter program originated as a response to the need to obtain 1-meter-resolution photographs of potential Apollo landing sites. NASA planned launches of a series of three-axis stabilized spacecraft with four solar panels and a main engine (derived from an Apollo attitude control thruster) for lunar orbit insertion. The primary instrument on board was a 68-kilogram Eastman-Kodak imaging system (using wide- and narrow-angle lenses) that could develop exposed film, scan the images, and send them back to Earth. The narrow-angle pictures provided resolution of up to 60 to 80 meters, while the wide-angle photos showed resolutions up to 0.5 kilometers. Lunar Orbiter 1 entered a 191 x 1,854-kilometer orbit around the Moon on 24 August, becoming the first U.S. spacecraft to do so. The spacecraft's primary mission was to photograph nine potential Apollo landing sites, seven secondary areas, and the Surveyor 1 landing site. During its mission, the probe took 207 frames of the lunar surface covering an area of 5.18 million square kilometers. The high-resolution photos were blurred from smearing, but the medium-resolution images were the best lunar surface images returned to date. One of the images returned, taken on 23 August, was the first picture of Earth from the Moon. Lunar Orbiter 1 returned its last picture on 30 August and was commanded to crash on to the lunar surface on 29 October to prevent its transmissions from interfering with future Lunar Orbiters. Impact coordinates were 6°42' north latitude and 162° east longitude (at 13:30 UT).

72)
Pioneer 7
Nation: U.S. (30)
Objective(s): heliocentric orbit
Spacecraft: Pioneer-B
Spacecraft Mass: 62.75 kg
Mission Design and Management: NASA ARC
Launch Vehicle: Thor-Delta E-1 (no. 40 / Thor no. 462 / DSV-3E)
Launch Date and Time: 17 August 1966 / 15:20:17 UT
Launch Site: ETR / launch complex 17A
Scientific Instruments:
 1) single-axis fluxgate magnetometer
 2) Faraday-cup plasma probe
 3) plasma analyzer
 4) cosmic-ray telescope
 5) cosmic-ray-anisotropy detector

6) radio wave propagation experiment
7) celestial mechanics experiment

Results: Identical to Pioneer 6, Pioneer 7 was put into heliocentric orbit at 0.814 x 0.985 AU to study the solar magnetic field, the solar wind, and cosmic rays at widely separated points in solar orbit. On 7 September 1968, the spacecraft was correctly aligned with the Sun and Earth to begin studying Earth's magnetic tail. In 1977, eleven years after its launch, Pioneer 7 registered the magnetic tail 19.3 million kilometers out, three times further into space than recorded previously. On 20 March 1986, the spacecraft flew within 12.3 million kilometers of Halley's Comet and monitored the interaction between the cometary hydrogen tail and the solar wind. As with Pioneer 6 and Pioneer 8, NASA continues to maintain intermittent contact with Pioneer 7, more than thirty years after its mission began. On 31 March 1995, for example, the plasma analyzer was turned on during 2 hours of contact with the ground.

73)
Luna 11
Nation: USSR (43)
Objective(s): lunar orbit
Spacecraft: Ye-6LF (no. 101)
Spacecraft Mass: 1,640 kg
Mission Design and Management: GSMZ Lavochkin
Launch Vehicle: 8K78M (no. N103-43)
Launch Date and Time: 24 August 1966 / 08:03 UT
Launch Site: NIIP-5
Scientific Instruments:
1) imaging system
2) gamma-ray detector
3) magnetometer
4) radiation detectors
5) infrared radiometer
6) meteoroid detectors
7) R-1 gear transmission experiment

Results: This subset of the "second-generation" Luna spacecraft, the Ye-6LF, was designed to take the first photographs of the surface of the Moon from lunar orbit. A secondary objective was to obtain data on mass concentrations ("mascons") on the Moon first detected by Luna 10. Using the basic Ye-6 bus, a suite of scientific instruments (plus an imaging system similar to the one used on Zond 3) replaced the small lander capsule used on the soft-landing flights. The resolution of the photos was reportedly 15 to 20 meters. A technological experiment included testing the efficiency of gear transmission in vacuum as a test for a future lunar rover. Luna 11, launched only two weeks after the U.S. Lunar Orbiter, successfully entered lunar orbit at 21:49 UT on 27 August. Parameters were 160 x 1,193 kilometers. During the mission, the TV camera failed to return usable images because the spacecraft lost proper orientation to face the lunar surface when a foreign object was lodged in the nozzle of one of the attitude-control thrusters. The other instruments functioned without fault before the mission formally ended on 1 October 1966 after the power supply had been depleted.

74)
Surveyor 2
Nation: U.S. (31)
Objective(s): lunar soft-landing
Spacecraft: Surveyor-B
Spacecraft Mass: 995.2 kg
Mission Design and Management: NASA JPL
Launch Vehicle: Atlas-Centaur (AC-7 / Atlas D no. 194 / Centaur D)
Launch Date and Time: 20 September 1966 / 12:32:00 UT
Launch Site: ETR / launch complex 36A
Scientific Instruments:
1) imaging system

Results: Surveyor 2, similar in design to its predecessor, was aimed for a lunar soft-landing in Sinus Medii. During the coast to the Moon, at 05:00 UT on 21 September, one of three thrusters failed to ignite for a 9.8-second midcourse correction and thus put the spacecraft into an unwanted spin. Despite as many as thirty-nine repeated attempts to fire the recalcitrant thruster, the engine failed to ignite, and Surveyor 2 headed to the Moon without proper control. Just 30 seconds after retro-fire ignition at 09:34 UT on 22 September, communications fell out, and the lander crashed on to the surface of the Moon at 5°30' north latitude and 12° west longitude, just southeast of Copernicus crater.

75)
Luna 12
Nation: USSR (44)
Objective(s): lunar orbit
Spacecraft: Ye-6LF (no. 102)
Spacecraft Mass: 1,620 kg
Mission Design and Management: GSMZ Lavochkin
Launch Vehicle: 8K78M (no. N103-44)
Launch Date and Time: 22 October 1966 / 08:42 UT
Launch Site: NIIP-5 / launch site 31
Scientific Instruments:
1) imaging system
2) gamma-ray detector
3) magnetometer
4) radiation detectors
5) infrared radiometer
6) meteoroid detectors
7) R-1 gear transmission experiment

Results: Luna 12 was launched to complete the mission that Luna 11 had failed to accomplish—take high-resolution photos of the Moon's surface from lunar orbit. Luna 12 successfully reached the Moon on 25 October 1966 and entered a 133 x 1,200-kilometer orbit. The Soviet press released the first photos taken of the surface on 29 October—pictures that showed the Sea of Rains and the Aristarchus crater. Resolution was as high as 15 to 20 meters. Film was developed, fixed, dried automatically, and scanned for transmission to Earth. No further photos were ever released. After completing its main imaging mission, Luna 12 was put into a spin-stabilized roll to carry out its scientific mission, which was fulfilled quite successfully. Contact was finally lost on 19 January 1967 after 302 communications sessions.

76)
Lunar Orbiter 2
Nation: U.S. (32)
Objective(s): lunar orbit
Spacecraft: LO-B
Spacecraft Mass: 385.6 kg
Mission Design and Management: NASA LaRC
Launch Vehicle: Atlas-Agena D (no. 18 / Atlas D no. 5802 / Agena D no. AD122 / 6631)
Launch Date and Time: 6 November 1966 / 23:21:00 UT
Launch Site: ETR / launch complex 13
Scientific Instruments:
1) imaging system
2) micrometeoroid detectors
3) radiation dosimeters

Results: Lunar Orbiter 2's mission was to photograph thirteen primary and seventeen secondary landings sites for the Apollo program in the northern region of the Moon's near side equatorial area. On 10 November 1966, the spacecraft entered a 196 x 1,871-kilometer orbit around the Moon. By 6 December, when the probe transmitted back its last photograph, 211 pictures had been taken of both the near side and large areas of the far side. These photos covered nearly four million square kilometers of the lunar surface. The high-gain transmitter failed on the same day, but did not significantly affect the coverage afforded by the photos. Lunar Orbiter 2 returned perhaps the most memorable photo of any in the series, a spectacular shot looking across the Copernicus crater from an altitude of only 45 kilometers, which vividly emphasized the three-dimensional nature of the lunar surface. On 8 December, after the main photographic mission was over, Lunar Orbiter 2 fired its main engine to change its orbital plane in order to provide tracking data of the Moon's gravitational field over a wider swath. Finally, on 11 October 1967, when attitude control gas was almost depleted, a retro-burn deliberately crashed the spacecraft onto the lunar surface at 4° south latitude and 98° east longitude on the far side to prevent communications interference on future missions.

77)
Luna 13
Nation: USSR (45)
Objective(s): lunar soft-landing
Spacecraft: Ye-6M (no. 205)
Spacecraft Mass: 1,620 kg
Mission Design and Management: GSMZ Lavochkin
Launch Vehicle: 8K78M (no. N103-45)
Launch Date and Time: 21 December 1966 / 10:17 UT
Launch Site: NIIP-5 / launch site 1
Scientific Instruments:
1) TV cameras
2) infrared radiometer
3) penetrometer

4) radiation densitometer
5) radiation detector

Results: Luna 13 became the second Soviet spacecraft to successfully soft-land on the surface of the Moon. The probe landed in the Ocean of Storms at 18:01 UT on 24 December 1966, between the Krafft and Seleucus craters at 18°52' north latitude and 62°3' west longitude. Unlike its predecessor, the heavier Luna 13 lander (113 kilograms) carried a suite of scientific instruments in addition to the usual imaging system. A three-axis accelerometer within the pressurized frame of the lander recorded the landing forces during impact to determine the soil structure down to a depth of 20 to 30 centimeters. A pair of spring-loaded booms was also deployed. Both were equipped with titanium-tipped rods that were driven into the ground with a powerful force by small explosive charges to measure soil density (found at roughly 0.8 grams per cubic centimeter). Four radiometers recorded infrared radiation from the surface indicating a noon temperature of $117 \pm 3°C$ while a radiation detector indicated that radiation levels would be less than hazardous for humans. The lander returned a total of five panoramas of the lunar surface, showing a more smooth terrain than seen by Luna 9. One of the two cameras (intended to return stereo images) failed, but this did not diminish the quality of the photographs. After a fully successful mission, contact was lost at 06:13 UT on 28 December when the onboard batteries were exhausted.

1967

78)
Lunar Orbiter 3
Nation: U.S. (33)
Objective(s): lunar orbit
Spacecraft: LO-C
Spacecraft Mass: 385.6 kg
Mission Design and Management: NASA LaRC
Launch Vehicle: Atlas-Agena D (no. 20 / Atlas D no. 5803 / Agena D no. AD128 / 6632)
Launch Date and Time: 5 February 1967 / 01:17:01 UT
Launch Site: ETR / launch complex 13
Scientific Instruments:
 1) imaging system
 2) micrometeoroid detectors
 3) radiation dosimeters
Results: Lunar Orbiter 3 was the final Lunar Orbiter mission to study potential Apollo landing sites; further missions would be dedicated to scientific and global surveys. The spacecraft arrived in lunar orbit on 7 February 1967. Initial orbital parameters were 200 x 1,850 kilometers at 21° inclination. During its eight-month mission, the spacecraft took 211 frames of pictures, although only 182 were actually returned to Earth because of a problem on 24 February with the motor that rewound the film. Despite the minor glitch, Lunar Orbiter fulfilled its original mission objectives, returning images of 15.5 million square kilometers of the near side and 650,000 square kilometers of the far side. On 30 August 1967, ground controllers commanded the vehicle to circularize its orbit to 160 kilometers in order to simulate an Apollo trajectory. Later, on 9 October 1967, the probe was intentionally crashed onto the lunar surface at 14°36' north latitude and 91°42' west longitude. The photographs from the first three Lunar Orbiters allowed NASA scientists to pick eight preliminary landing sites for Apollo by early April 1967, including site 2 in the Sea of Tranquillity, where Apollo 11 would land, and site 5 in the Ocean of Storms, where Apollo 12 (and also Surveyor 3) would disembark.

79)
Surveyor 3
Nation: U.S. (34)
Objective(s): lunar soft-landing
Spacecraft: Surveyor-C
Spacecraft Mass: 997.9 kg
Mission Design and Management: NASA JPL
Launch Vehicle: Atlas-Centaur (AC-12 / Atlas D no. 292 / Centaur D)
Launch Date and Time: 17 April 1967 / 07:05:01 UT
Launch Site: ETR / launch complex 36B
Scientific Instruments:
 1) imaging system
 2) surface sampler
Results: Surveyor 3 was the third engineering flight of the series; for the first time, it car-

Charles Conrad, Jr., Apollo 12 Commander, examines the unpiloted Surveyor 3 spacecraft during the second extravehicular activity (EVA-2). The Lunar Module (LM) *Intrepid* is in the right background. This picture was taken by astronaut Alan L. Bean, Lunar Module pilot. The *Intrepid* landed on the Moon's Ocean of Storms only 600 feet from Surveyor 3. The television camera and several other components were taken from Surveyor 3 and brought back to Earth for scientific analysis. Surveyor 3 soft-landed on the Moon on 19 April 1967.

ried a soil-sampling instrument that could reach up to 1.5 meters from the lander and dig up to 0.5 meters deep. Unlike the previous Surveyors, Surveyor 3 began its mission from parking orbit around Earth with a burn from the Centaur upper stage, now capable of multiple firings. Although the landing radar cut out prematurely, basic inertial control ensured that Surveyor 3 landed on the lunar surface with minimal vertical velocity at 00:04:17 UT on 20 April 1967 in the southeastern region of Oceanus Procellarum, at 2°56' north latitude and 23°20' west longitude. A fairly strong sideways motion made the lander hop twice before coming to a standstill. Less than an hour after landing, the spacecraft began transmitting the first of 6,315 TV pictures of the surrounding areas. The most exciting experiment of the mission was the deployment of the remote scooper arm, which, via commands from Earth, dug four trenches and performed four bearing tests and thirteen impact tests. Based on these experiments, scientists concluded that lunar soil had a consistency similar to wet sand, with a bearing strength of 0.7 kilograms per square centimeter—solid enough for an Apollo Lunar Module. Last contact was made on 4 May 1967, two days after the lunar night began. More than three years later, Apollo 12 astronauts Charles Conrad, Jr., and Alan L. Bean landed the Intrepid LM near the inactive Surveyor 3 lander on 18 November 1969. The astronauts recovered parts from Surveyor 3, including the soil scoop and camera system, to allow scientists to evaluate the effects of nearly two and one-half years of exposure on the Moon's surface.

80)
Lunar Orbiter 4
Nation: U.S. (35)
Objective(s): lunar orbit
Spacecraft: LO-D
Spacecraft Mass: 385.6 kg
Mission Design and Management: NASA LaRC
Launch Vehicle: Atlas-Agena D (no. 22 / Atlas D no. 5804 / Agena D no. AD131 / 6633)
Launch Date and Time: 4 May 1967 / 22:25:00 UT
Launch Site: ETR / launch complex 13

Scientific Instruments:
1) imaging system
2) micrometeoroid detectors
3) radiation dosimeters

Results: Lunar Orbiter 4 was the first in the series dedicated to scientific surveys of the Moon. After a burn at 21:54 UT on 8 May 1967, the spacecraft entered a 2,705 x 6,034-kilometer orbit inclined at 85.48 degrees, becoming the first vehicle to enter polar orbit around the Moon. Controllers successfully overcame a problem with the Thermal Camera Door, and subsequently, during its two-month mission, the orbiter took pictures of 99 percent of the near side and 75 percent of the far side of the Moon in a total of 193 frames. The images had a resolution of up to 60 meters. In early June, controllers lowered the spacecraft's orbit to match that of Lunar Orbiter 5 so that scientists could collect gravitational data in support of the latter mission. Before losing contact on 17 July, Lunar Orbiter 4 took the first photos of the lunar south pole and discovered a 240-kilometer-long crustal fault on the far side. Since contact was lost before controlled impact, the spacecraft naturally crashed onto the Moon on 6 October 1967 due to gravitational anomalies.

81)
Kosmos 159 / [Luna]
Nation: USSR (46)
Objective(s): highly elliptical orbit around Earth
Spacecraft: Ye-6LS (no. 111)
Spacecraft Mass: unknown
Mission Design and Management: GSMZ Lavochkin
Launch Vehicle: 8K78M (no. Ya716-56)
Launch Date and Time: 16 May 1967 / 21:43:57 UT
Launch Site: NIIP-5 / launch site 1
Scientific Instruments: unknown
Results: This spacecraft was a one-off high-apogee Earth satellite developed to acquire data on trajectory measurement techniques on future lunar orbital missions. By perfecting such techniques, engineers could accurately measure trajectories of future lunar orbiters affected by anomalies in the Moon's gravitational field. Mission designers had planned to send the probe into a highly elliptical orbit with an apogee of 250,000 kilometers, but the

Blok L upper stage evidently cut off too early. Instead, the spacecraft, named Kosmos 159, entered a lower orbit of 260 x 60,710 kilometers at 51.7° inclination. Despite the incorrect orbit, controllers no doubt used the spacecraft for its original mission. No data is available on when the ground lost contact with the spacecraft. Kosmos 159 reentered Earth's atmosphere on 11 November 1967.

82)
Venera 4
Nation: USSR (47)
Objective(s): Venus impact
Spacecraft: 1V (no. 310)
Spacecraft Mass: 1,106 kg
Mission Design and Management: GSMZ Lavochkin
Launch Vehicle: 8K78M
Launch Date and Time: 12 June 1967 / 02:39:45 UT
Launch Site: NIIP-5 / launch site 1
Scientific Instruments:
   Lander:
   1) radio altimeter
   2) aneroid barometer
   3) eleven gas-analyzer cartridges
   4) two resistance thermometers
   5) ionization densitometer
   Bus:
   1) magnetometer
   2) cosmic-ray counters
   3) charged-particle traps
   4) ultraviolet photometer

Results: Venera 4 was the first Venus probe built by the Lavochkin design bureau, although Lavochkin engineers retained the basic design layout of the earlier Korolev probes. The spacecraft consisted of a main bus about 3.5 meters high and a 383-kilogram lander probe designed to transmit data as it descended through the Venusian atmosphere. This capsule was designed to endure loads as high as 350 g and land on both land and liquid. For atmospheric entry, it was equipped with a thick ablative heatshield. After a midcourse correction on 29 July 1967, Venera 4 approached Venus on 18 October and released the lander at 04:34 UT, immediately prior to entry of the bus. Parachuting into the planet's atmosphere, the lander turned on its scientific instruments 5 minutes later when the rate of descent lowered to 10 meters per second (at 55 kilometers altitude). The probe continued to transmit for 93 minutes as it slowly fell through the atmosphere. Initially, Soviet scientists believed that the probe transmitted until contact with the surface. In reality, transmissions ceased at an altitude of 27 kilometers when the high atmospheric pressure and temperatures crushed the probe. The data implied that surface temperatures and pressure were 500°C and 75 atmospheres respectively. Venera 4's gas analyzers also found that the planet's atmosphere was composed of 90 to 95 percent carbon dioxide with no nitrogen. The spacecraft bus measured the planet's weak magnetic field and found no ring of radiation belts. It detected a very weak atmosphere of atomic hydrogen about 9,900 kilometers above the planet. Venera 4 was the first spacecraft to transmit data from a planet's atmosphere.

83)
Mariner 5
Nation: U.S. (36)
Objective(s): Venus flyby
Spacecraft: Mariner-67E / Mariner-E
Spacecraft Mass: 244.9 kg
Mission Design and Management: NASA JPL
Launch Vehicle: Atlas-Agena D (no. 23 / Atlas D no. 5401 / Agena D no. AD157 / 6933)
Launch Date and Time: 14 June 1967 / 06:01:00 UT
Launch Site: ETR / launch complex 12
Scientific Instruments:
   1) ultraviolet photometer
   2) S-band occultation experiment
   3) dual-frequency occultation experiment
   4) solar plasma probe
   5) magnetometer
   6) trapped-radiation detector
   7) celestial mechanics experiment

Results: In December 1965, NASA approved a project to modify the Mariner 4 backup spacecraft to conduct a closer flyby of Venus than the only other NASA probe to fly past Venus, Mariner 2. Unlike Mariner 4, however, Mariner 5 did not carry an imaging instrument. Initially, NASA had planned to send Mariner 5 on a flyby at a miss distance of 8,165 kilometers, but the Agency altered its plan in favor of a more modest 75,000-kilometer flyby in order to prevent the nonsterilized vehicle from crashing into the planet.

After a midcourse correction on 19 June, Mariner 5 began transmitting data about Venus on 19 October during its encounter. Closest approach was at 17:34:56 UT at a range of 4,094 kilometers. Mariner 5 found no radiation belts trapped by Venus' magnetic field. The ultraviolet photometer detected a hydrogen corona (as did the Soviet Venera 4), but no oxygen emission. Mariner 5's instruments indicated that the planet's surface temperature and pressure were 527°C and 75 to 100 atmospheres respectively—which countered the Soviet claim that its Venera 4 spacecraft had managed to transmit from the planet's surface. On 4 December 1967, NASA lost contact with the spacecraft, although controllers briefly regained contact on 14 October 1968. The spacecraft did not transmit any further telemetry, and NASA eventually stopped attempts to communicate with the vehicle, now in heliocentric orbit.

84)
Kosmos 167 / [Venera]
Nation: USSR (48)
Objective(s): Venus impact
Spacecraft: 1V (no. 311)
Spacecraft Mass: c. 1,100 kg
Mission Design and Management: GSMZ Lavochkin
Launch Vehicle: 8K78M
Launch Date and Time: 17 June 1967 / 02:36:38 UT
Launch Site: NIIP-5 / launch site 1
Scientific Instruments:
  Lander:
  1) radio altimeter
  2) aneroid barometer
  3) eleven gas-analyzer cartridges
  4) two resistance thermometers
  5) ionization densitometer
  Bus:
  1) magnetometer
  2) cosmic-ray counters
  3) charged-particle traps
  4) ultraviolet photometer
Results: This identical twin craft to Venera 4 failed to leave Earth orbit when its Blok L transinterplanetary stage failed to fire, apparently because the engine's turbopump had not been cooled prior to ignition. The spacecraft remained stranded in Earth orbit and reentered Earth's atmosphere on 25 June 1967.

85)
Surveyor 4
Nation: U.S. (37)
Objective(s): lunar soft-landing
Spacecraft: Surveyor-D
Spacecraft Mass: 1,037.4 kg
Mission Design and Management: NASA JPL
Launch Vehicle: Atlas Centaur (AC-11 / Atlas D no. 291 / Centaur D)
Launch Date and Time: 14 July 1967 / 11:53:29 UT
Launch Site: ETR / launch complex 36A
Scientific Instruments:
  1) imaging system
  2) surface sampler
  3) soil magnet
Results: Like Surveyor 3, Surveyor 4 was equipped with a surface claw (with a magnet in the claw) to detect and measure ferrous elements in the lunar surface. The mission was completely successful until all communications were abruptly lost 2 seconds prior to retro-rocket cutoff at 02:03 UT on 17 July 1967, with only 2.5 minutes left to landing on the Moon. The landing target was Sinus Medii (Central Bay) at 0.4° north latitude and 1.33° west longitude. NASA concluded that the lander might have exploded when contact was lost.

86)
Explorer 35 / International Monitoring Platform 6
Nation: U.S. (38)
Objective(s): lunar orbit
Spacecraft: IMP-E
Spacecraft Mass: 104.3 kg
Mission Design and Management: NASA GSFC
Launch Vehicle: Thor-Delta E-1 (no. 50 / Thor no. 488 / DSV-3E)
Launch Date and Time: 19 July 1967 / 14:19:02 UT
Launch Site: ETR / launch complex 17B
Scientific Instruments:
  1) magnetometers
  2) thermal ion detector
  3) ion chambers and Geiger tubes
  4) Geiger tubes and p-on-n junction
  5) micrometeoroid detector
  6) Faraday cup
Results: Explorer 35 was designed to study interplanetary space phenomena—particularly the solar wind, the interplanetary magnetic field, dust distribution near the Moon, the lunar gravitational field, the weak lunar

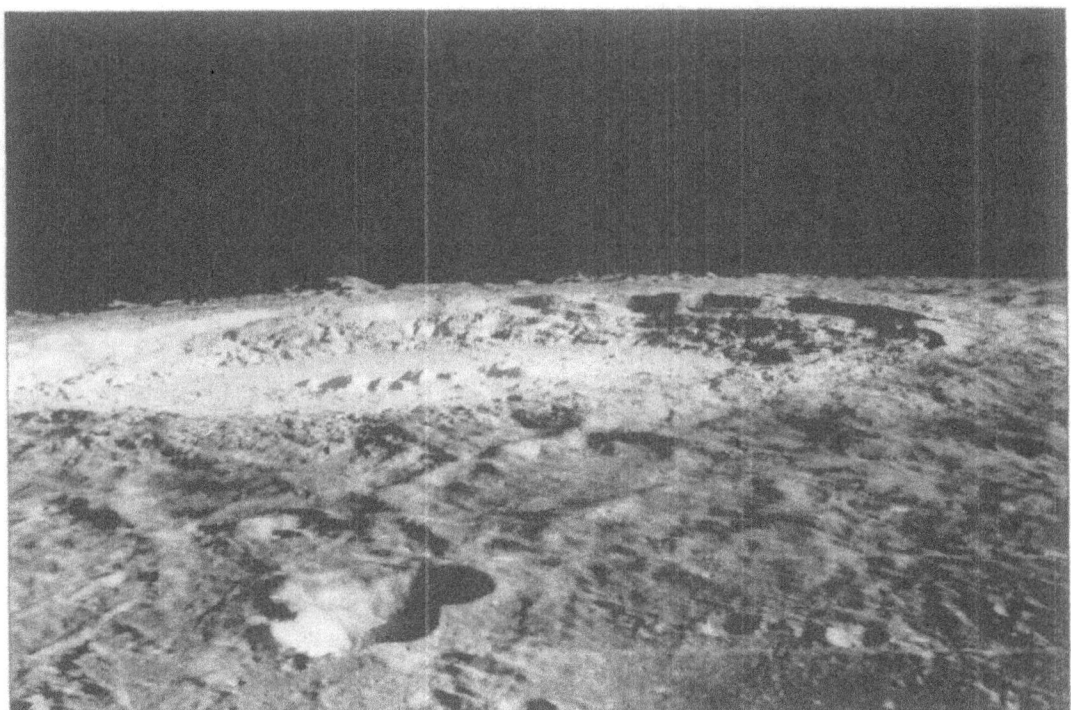

This image from Lunar Orbiter 5 shows crater Copernicus, 93 kilometers wide and located within the Mare Imbrium Basin at the northern near side of the Moon (10° north latitude and 20° west longitude). The picture shows the crater floor, floor mounds, rim, and rayed ejecta. Rays from the ejecta are superposed on all other surrounding terrains, which places the crater in its namesake age group: the Copernican system, established as the youngest assemblage of rocks on the Moon.

ionosphere, and the radiation environment. The spacecraft left Earth on a direct ascent trajectory and entered lunar orbit on 21 July 1967. Initial orbital parameters were 800 x 7,692 kilometers at 147° inclination. The spacecraft, similar to Explorer 33, also in lunar orbit, found that the Moon has no magnetosphere, that solar wind particles impact directly against the surface, and that the Moon creates a "cavity" in the solar wind stream. After six years of successful operation, the satellite was turned off on 24 June 1973. Explorer 35 was launched by the fiftieth Thor-Delta booster, of which only three had failed, giving the booster a success rating of 94 percent.

87)
Lunar Orbiter 5
Nation: U.S. (39)
Objective(s): lunar orbit
Spacecraft: LO-E
Spacecraft Mass: 385.6 kg
Mission Design and Management: NASA LaRC
Launch Vehicle: Atlas-Agena D (no. 24 / Atlas D no. 5805 / Agena D no. AD159 / 6634)
Launch Date and Time: 1 August 1967 / 22:33:00 UT
Launch Site: ETR / launch complex 13
Scientific Instruments:
 1) imaging system
 2) micrometeoroid detectors
 3) radiation dosimeters
Results: Lunar Orbiter 5 was the last in a series of highly successful missions to map the Moon for potential landing sites and conduct general observational surveys. Two days after a midcourse correction on 3 August, it entered lunar orbit at 16:48 UT. Initial orbital parameters were 196 x 6,040 kilometers at 85.0° inclination. The spacecraft photographed thirty-six different areas on the near side and mapped most of the far side via a set of 212 frames during its first month in orbit. These included five potential Apollo landing sites, as well as possible targets for Surveyor missions. Controllers also extensively used the spacecraft to map the Moon's gravitational field in order to predict orbital perturbations

on future lunar orbital missions. The probe also obtained spectacular high-quality photos of Earth showing Africa and the Middle East. Lunar Orbiter 5 was commanded to land on the lunar surface and did so at 0° north latitude and 70° west longitude on 31 January 1968. In total, the five Lunar Orbiters photographed 99 percent of the lunar surface.

88)
Surveyor 5
Nation: U.S. (40)
Objective(s): lunar soft-landing
Spacecraft: Surveyor-E
Spacecraft Mass: 1,006 kg
Mission Design and Management: NASA JPL
Launch Vehicle: Atlas-Centaur (AC-13 / Atlas 3C no. 5901C / Centaur D-1A)
Launch Date and Time: 8 September 1967 / 07:57:01 UT
Launch Site: ETR, launch complex 36B
Scientific Instruments:
  1) imaging system
  2) alpha-scattering instrument
  3) surface sampler
  4) footpad magnet
Results: Brilliantly overcoming a near-fatal helium leak in a pressure regulator, engineers from JPL and Hughes Aircraft Company (the prime contractor for the spacecraft) managed to safely deposit Surveyor 5 on the surface of the Moon in the south-eastern region of Mare Tranquillitatis at 1°25' north latitude and 23°11' east longitude at 00:46:42 UT on 11 September 1967. The malfunction put the lander about 29 kilometers away from its target in an angular incline within the slope of the rimless crater. Surveyor 5 was, however, the most successful of the series. The lander returned 18,006 photos before lunar night descended on 24 September. Controllers successfully commanded the vehicle to take further photographs during the second lunar day between 15 and 24 October 1967 and the fourth lunar day in December. In total, 20,018 pictures were transmitted. In another experiment, on 13 September, controllers fired the main engine for 0.55 seconds to examine the effects of disturbing the lunar surface. NASA announced that no new craters were created, nor was there any significant dust cloud. The alpha-scattering instrument had earlier been released onto the surface and found the soil to be composed of more than half oxygen with amounts of silicon and aluminum. Contact was lost with the lander on 16 December 1967.

89)
no name / [Zond]
Nation: USSR (49)
Objective(s): circumlunar flight
Spacecraft: 7K-L1 (no. 4L)
Spacecraft Mass: c. 5,375 kg
Mission Design and Management: TsKBEM
Launch Vehicle: 8K82K + Blok D (Proton-K no. 229-01 / Blok D no. 12L)
Launch Date and Time: 27 September 1967 / 22:11:54 UT
Launch Site: NIIP-5 / launch site 81L
Scientific Instruments: unknown
Results: This spacecraft, a 7K-L1 type, was the first of a series of spacecraft that the Soviets tried to send on circumlunar missions as part of a larger project to send cosmonauts around the Moon. The program, which was officially approved in October 1965, was set off by two technological flights in Earth orbit in March and April 1967. The 7K-L1 spacecraft was a stripped-down version of the larger 7K-OK Soyuz spacecraft intended for Earth-orbital operations. During this launch, one of the six first-stage engines failed to fire because of blockage of a propellant line, and the launch vehicle was destroyed at T+97.4 seconds.

90)
Surveyor 6
Nation: U.S. (41)
Objective(s): lunar soft-landing
Spacecraft: Surveyor-F
Spacecraft Mass: 1,008.3 kg
Mission Design and Management: NASA JPL
Launch Vehicle: Atlas-Centaur (AC-14 / Atlas 3C no. 5902C / Centaur D-1A)
Launch Date and Time: 7 November 1967 / 07:39:01 UT
Launch Site: ETR / launch complex 36B
Scientific Instruments:
  1) imaging system
  2) alpha-scattering instrument
  3) surface sampler
  4) footcomplex magnet
Results: Surveyor 6 landed safely on the Moon at 01:01:04 UT on 10 November 1967 in the Sinus Medii (Central Bay) at 2.45° south latitude and 43.21° west longitude. The spacecraft

returned 29,952 images of the lunar surface during less than two weeks of operation before the onset of lunar night on 24 November. Although controllers regained contact briefly on 14 December 1967, primary landing operations had ceased by this time. On 17 November 1967, before termination of operations, Surveyor 6 was commanded to fire its three main liquid-propellant thrusters for 2.5 seconds. As a result, the lander became the first spacecraft to be launched from the lunar surface. Surveyor 6 lifted up to about 3 meters before landing 2.5 meters west of its original landing point. Cameras then studied the original landing footprints in order to determine the soil's mechanical properties and, now that the source point had been displaced, also accomplish some stereo imaging.

91)
no name / [Zond]
Nation: USSR (50)
Objective(s): circumlunar flight
Spacecraft: 7K-L1 (no. 5L)
Spacecraft Mass: c. 5,375 kg
Mission Design and Management: TsKBEM
Launch Vehicle: 8K82K + Blok D (Proton-K no. 230-01 / Blok D no. 13L)
Launch Date and Time: 22 November 1967 / 19:07:59 UT
Launch Site: NIIP-5 / launch site 81P
Scientific Instruments: unknown
Results: This was the second Soviet attempt at a robotic circumlunar mission. On this launch, one of the four second-stage engines of the Proton rocket failed to ignite at T+125.5 seconds due to a break in the engine nozzle. The wayward booster was then destroyed on command from the ground at T+129.9 seconds.

92)
Pioneer 8
Nation: U.S. (42)
Objective(s): heliocentric orbit
Spacecraft: Pioneer-C
Spacecraft Mass: 65.36 kg
Mission Design and Management: NASA ARC
Launch Vehicle: Thor-Delta E-1 (no. 55 / Thor no. 489 / DSV-3E)
Launch Date and Time: 13 December 1967 / 14:08 UT
Launch Site: ETR / launch complex 17B
Scientific Instruments:
    1) single-axis fluxgate magnetometer
    2) plasma analyzer
    3) cosmic-ray telescope
    4) radio-wave propagation experiment
    5) cosmic-ray gradient detector
    6) electric field detector
    7) cosmic dust detector
    8) celestial mechanics experiment
Results: Pioneer 8, like its two predecessors, was sent to heliocentric orbit to study interplanetary space, particularly to carry collected information on magnetic fields, plasma, and cosmic rays. Although the spacecraft carried a different complement of scientific instruments from those of Pioneers 6 and 7, its findings were correlated with those of the other two probes. The spacecraft was launched into a path ahead of Earth to provide the vehicle with added velocity in solar orbit in order to move out beyond Earth's orbit at 1.0 x 1.1. AU. It arrived at Earth's magnetospheric bounds at 19:00 UT on 15 December 1967. Later, on 18 January 1968, Pioneer 8, the Sun, and Earth were perfectly aligned to allow investigation of Earth's magnetic tail in detail, first performed by Pioneer 7 in 1968. Controllers have intermittently maintained contact with the spacecraft for nearly thirty years, although only one instrument, the electric field detector, remained operational past 1982. During tracking on 23 July 1995, NASA was unable to switch on Pioneer 8's transmitter, probably because the spacecraft was too far away from the Sun to charge the solar panels. On 22 August 1996, contact was reacquired via a backup transmitter. The electric field detector remains functional as of June 2001, nearly thirty-six years after launch.

1968

93)
Surveyor 7
Nation: U.S. (43)
Objective(s): lunar soft-landing
Spacecraft: Surveyor-G
Spacecraft Mass: 1,040.1 kg
Mission Design and Management: NASA JPL
Launch Vehicle: Atlas-Centaur (AC-15 / Atlas 3C no. 5903C / Centaur D-1A)
Launch Date and Time: 7 January 1968 / 06:30:00 UT
Launch Site: ETR / launch complex 36A
Scientific Instruments:
1) imaging system
2) alpha-scattering instrument
3) surface sampler
4) footpad magnet

Results: Since Surveyors 1, 3, 5, and 6 successfully fulfilled requirements in support of Apollo, NASA opted to use the last remaining Surveyor for a purely scientific mission outside of exploring a potential landing site for the early Apollo flights. After an uneventful coast to the Moon, Surveyor 7 successfully set down at 01:05:36 UT on 10 January 1968 on the ejecta blanket emanating from the bright Tycho crater in the south of the near side. Landing coordinates were 40.86° south latitude and 11.47° west longitude, about 29 kilometers north of Tycho's rim and 2.4 kilometers from the craft's target. Initial photos from the surface showed surprisingly few craters, much like the mare sites, although the general area was rougher. About 21 hours after landing, ground controllers fired a pyrotechnic charge to drop the alpha-scattering instrument on the lunar surface. When the instrument failed to move, controllers used the robot arm to force it down. The scoop on the arm was used numerous times for picking up soil, digging trenches, and conducting at least sixteen surface-bearing tests. Apart from taking 21,274 photographs (many of them in stereo), Surveyor 7 also served as a target for Earth-based lasers (of 1-watt power) to accurately measure the distance between Earth and the Moon. Although it was successfully reactivated after the lunar night, Surveyor 7 finally shut down on 21 February 1968. In total, the five successful Surveyors returned more than 87,000 photos of the lunar surface and demonstrated the feasibility of soft-landing a spacecraft on the lunar surface.

94)
no name / [Luna]
Nation: USSR (51)
Objective(s): lunar orbit
Spacecraft: Ye-6LS (no. 112)
Spacecraft Mass: unknown
Mission Design and Management: GSMZ Lavochkin
Launch Vehicle: 8K78M (no. Ya716-57)

Launch Date and Time: 7 February 1968 / 10:43:54 UT
Launch Site: NIIP-5 / launch site 1
Scientific Instruments: unknown
Results: During launch to Earth orbit, the third-stage engine cut off prematurely because of an excessive propellant consumption rate via the gas generator. The spacecraft never reached Earth orbit. The goal of the mission was evidently to test communications systems in support of the N1-L3 human lunar landing program.

95)
Zond 4
Nation: USSR (52)
Objective(s): deep space mission
Spacecraft: 7K-L1 (no. 6L)
Spacecraft Mass: c. 5,375 kg
Mission Design and Management: TsKBEM
Launch Vehicle: 8K82K + Blok D (Proton-K no. 232-01)
Launch Date and Time: 2 March 1968 / 18:29:23 UT
Launch Site: NIIP-5 / launch site 81L
Scientific Instruments: unknown
Results: The Soviets decided to send this next 7K-L1 spacecraft, not on a circumlunar flight, but to about 330,000 kilometers into deep space in the opposite direction of the Moon in order to test the main spacecraft systems without the perturbing effects of the Moon (much like the Surveyor model test flights in 1965 and 1966). The spacecraft was successfully boosted on its trajectory and reached an apogee of 354,000 kilometers. During the flight, although a key attitude-control sensor worked only intermittently, controllers managed to aim the spacecraft for a guided reentry back into Earth's atmosphere. Unfortunately, the same sensor failed at reentry, preventing the vehicle from maintaining stable orientation. Instead, Zond 4 began to carry out a direct ballistic reentry for landing in the Indian Ocean. An emergency destruct system, however, destroyed the returning capsule over the Gulf of Guinea to prevent foreign observers from recovering the wayward spacecraft.

96)
Luna 14
Nation: USSR (53)
Objective(s): lunar orbit
Spacecraft: Ye-6LS (no. 113)
Spacecraft Mass: unknown
Mission Design and Management: GSMZ Lavochkin
Launch Vehicle: 8K78M (no. Ya716-58)
Launch Date and Time: 7 April 1968 / 10:09:32 UT
Launch Site: NIIP-5 / launch site 1
Scientific Instruments: unknown
Results: Luna 14 successfully entered lunar orbit at 19:25 UT on 10 April 1968. Initial orbital parameters were 160 x 870 kilometers at 42° inclination. The primary goal of the flight was to test communications systems in support of the N1-L3 piloted lunar landing project. Ground tracking of the spacecraft's orbit also allowed controllers to accurately map lunar gravitational anomalies in order to predict trajectories of future lunar missions such as those of the LOK and LK lunar landing vehicles. Luna 14 also carried scientific instruments to study cosmic rays and charged particles from the Sun, although few details have been revealed.

97)
no name / [Zond]
Nation: USSR (54)
Objective(s): circumlunar flight
Spacecraft: 7K-L1 (no. 7L)
Spacecraft Mass: c. 5,375 kg
Mission Design and Management: TsKBEM
Launch Vehicle: 8K82K + Blok D (Proton K no. 232-01 / Blok D no. 15L)
Launch Date and Time: 22 April 1968 / 23:01:27 UT
Launch Site: NIIP-5 / launch site 81P
Scientific Instruments: unknown
Results: During this third attempt at a circumlunar mission, the Proton rocket's second-stage engine spuriously shut down at T+194.64 seconds due to an erroneous signal from the payload. The emergency rescue system was activated, and the 7K-L1 capsule was later recovered about 520 kilometers from the launch pad.

98)
Zond 5
Nation: USSR (55)
Objective(s): circumlunar flight
Spacecraft: 7K-L1 (no. 9L)
Spacecraft Mass: c. 5,375 kg

Mission Design and Management: TsKBEM
Launch Vehicle: 8K82K + Blok D upper stage (Proton-K no. 234-01 / Blok D no. 17)
Launch Date and Time: 14 September 1968 / 21:42:11 UT
Launch Site: NIIP-5 / launch site 81L
Scientific Instruments:
1) biological payload
2) radiation detectors
3) imaging system

Results: Zond 5 was the first Soviet spacecraft to complete a successful circumlunar mission—after three failures. During the flight to the Moon, the main stellar attitude control sensor failed due to contamination of the sensor's optical surface. Controllers used less accurate backup sensors to perform two midcourse corrections. The spacecraft successfully circled around the far side of the Moon at a range of 1,950 kilometers on 18 September, taking high-resolution photos of the Moon and Earth. On the return leg of the flight, a second attitude-control sensor failed and the spacecraft's three-axis stabilization platform switched off the guided reentry system. As a result, Zond 5 performed a direct ballistic reentry (instead of a guided one) and splashed down safely in the backup target area in the Indian Ocean at 32°38' south latitude and 65°33' east longitude, about 105 kilometers from the nearest Soviet tracking ship. Landing time was 16:08 UT on 21 September. Zond 5 carried an extensive biological payload including two steppe tortoises to measure the effects of circumlunar flight. The tortoises survived the trip and were returned to Moscow.

99)
Pioneer 9
Nation: U.S. (44)
Objective(s): solar orbit
Spacecraft: Pioneer-D
Spacecraft Mass: 65.36 kg
Mission Design and Management: NASA ARC
Launch Vehicle: Thor-Delta E-1 (no. 60 / Thor no. 479 / DSV-3E)
Launch Date and Time: 8 November 1968 / 09:46:29 UT
Launch Site: ETR / launch complex 17B
Scientific Instruments:
1) triaxial fluxgate magnetometer
2) plasma analyzer
3) cosmic-ray-anisotropy detector
4) cosmic-ray gradient detector
5) radio wave propagation experiment
6) electric field detector
7) cosmic dust detector
8) celestial mechanics experiment

Results: Pioneer 9 was the fourth in a series of probes designed to study interplanetary space from heliocentric orbit. In its 297.5-day orbit at 0.75 x 1.0 AU, the cylindrical, spin-stabilized spacecraft obtained valuable data on the properties of the solar wind, cosmic rays, and interplanetary magnetic fields. The Delta launch vehicle also carried the Test and Training Satellite (TETR-B), which was put into Earth orbit to test ground-based communications systems in support of the Apollo program. NASA maintained contact with Pioneer 9 until 19 May 1983. Subsequent attempts to use Search for Extraterrestrial Intelligence (SETI) equipment to establish contact with the probe on 3 March 1987 failed, and the Agency officially declared the spacecraft inactive.

100)
Zond 6
Nation: USSR (56)
Objective(s): circumlunar flight
Spacecraft: 7K-L1 (no. 12L)
Spacecraft Mass: c. 5,375 kg
Mission Design and Management: TsKBEM
Launch Vehicle: 8K82K + Blok D (Proton-K no. 235-01 / Blok D no. 19)
Launch Date and Time: 10 November 1968 / 19:11:31 UT
Launch Site: NIIP-5 / launch site 81L
Scientific Instruments:
1) biological payload
2) radiation detectors
3) imaging system
4) photo-emulsion camera
5) micrometeoroid detector

Results: Zond 6 was the second spacecraft that the Soviets sent around the Moon. Soon after translunar injection, ground controllers discovered that the vehicle's high-gain antenna had failed to deploy. Given that the main attitude-control sensor was installed on the antenna boom, controllers had to make plans to use a backup sensor for further attitude control. The spacecraft circled the far side of the Moon at a range of 2,420 kilometers, once again taking black-and-white photographs of the Moon. During the return flight, temperatures in a hydrogen peroxide tank for the attitude-control thrusters dropped far below acceptable levels. Engineers attempted to heat the tank by direct sunlight, but as they later discovered, such a procedure affected the weak pressurization seal of the main hatch and led to slow decompression of the main capsule. Despite the failures, Zond 6 successfully carried a fully automated guided reentry into the primary landing zone in Kazakhstan. A radio altimeter, not designed for work in depressurized spacecraft, issued an incorrect command to jettison the main parachutes. As a result, the spacecraft plummeted to the ground and was destroyed. Although the main biological payload was lost, rescuers salvaged film from the cameras.

1969

101)
Venera 5
Nation: USSR (57)
Objective(s): Venus landing
Spacecraft: 2V (no. 330)
Spacecraft Mass: 1,130 kg
Mission Design and Management: GSMZ Lavochkin
Launch Vehicle: 8K78M
Launch Date and Time: 5 January 1969 / 06:28:08 UT
Launch Site: NIIP-5 / launch site 1
Scientific Instruments:
 Lander:
 1) radio altimeter
 2) aneroid barometer
 3) eleven gas analyzer cartridges
 4) two resistance thermometers
 5) ionization densitometer
 6) photoelectric sensors
 Bus:
 1) magnetometer
 2) cosmic-ray counters
 3) charged-particle traps
 4) ultraviolet photometer

Results: Veneras 5 and 6 were two identical spacecraft designed to penetrate Venus's atmosphere and transmit a variety of scientific to Earth during descent. Both spacecraft were targeted to reach Venus only a day apart, thus allowing some cross-calibration of data. Although both spacecraft used a similar bus-lander system as the 1V-type spacecraft (flown as Venera 4), the two new landers (each weighing 405 kilograms) were designed to endure g-loads as high as 450 (as opposed to 300 for their predecessors). The landers also used smaller parachutes for descent, allowing the probes to descend faster through the atmosphere to increase chances of operating close to the surface. After performing seventy-three communications sessions with ground control and completing one midcourse correction on 14 March 1966, Venera 5 approached the dark side of Venus on 16 May 1969 and detached its lander, whose speed reduced from 1,100.17 meters per second to 210 meters per second after it hit the Venusian atmosphere at 06:01 UT. One minute later, controllers reestablished contact with the lander and began receiving transmitted data on pressure, temperature, and composition of the Venusian atmosphere for 53 minutes. Contact was lost at an altitude of about 24 to 26 kilometers when the pressure exceeded 26.1 atmospheres. Impact coordinates were 3° south latitude and 18° longitude. Information extrapolated from Venera 5's data suggested that ground temperature and pressure at the Venusian surface were 140 atmospheres and 530°C, respectively.

102)
Venera 6
Nation: USSR (58)
Objective(s): Venus landing
Spacecraft: 2V (no. 331)
Spacecraft Mass: 1,130 kg
Mission Design and Management: GSMZ Lavochkin
Launch Vehicle: 8K78M
Launch Date and Time: 10 January 1969 / 05:51:52 UT
Launch Site: NIIP-5 / launch site 1
Scientific Instruments:
    Lander:
    1) radio altimeter
    2) aneroid barometer
    3) eleven gas-analyzer cartridges
    4) two resistance thermometers
    5) ionization densitometer
    6) photoelectric sensors
    Bus:
    1) magnetometer
    2) cosmic-ray counters
    3) charged-particle traps
    4) ultraviolet photometer

Results: Identical to Venera 5, Venera 6 reached Venus after performing sixty-three communications sessions with Earth and one midcourse correction at a range of 15.7 million kilometers from Earth on 16 March 1969. Its 405-kilogram lander separated from the main bus 25,000 kilometers from the planet and entered the Venusian atmosphere at a velocity of 11.17 kilometers per second at 06:05 UT on 17 May 1969. The Venera 6 capsule transmitted data for 51 minutes before contact was lost, probably at an altitude of about 10 to 12 kilometers. Pressure was similar at the time to that measured by Venera 5 at a much higher altitude, indicating that Venera 6 may have come down over a mountain or high plateau. Landing coordinates were -5° latitude and 23° longitude. Results from the Venera 5 and 6 missions, published by the Soviets in March 1970, seemed to confirm and sharpen earlier findings from Venera 4. The two new spacecraft found that Venus's atmosphere was composed of roughly 93 to 97 percent carbon dioxide (the remainder was split among nitrogen, oxygen, and inert gases). Data from Venera 6 suggested that the ground pressure was about 60 atmospheres and ground temperature was about 400°C. This compared with Venera 4's readings, which indicated pressure at 75 atmospheres and temperature at 500°C.

103)
no name / [Zond]
Nation: USSR (59)
Objective(s): circumlunar flight
Spacecraft: 7K-L1 (no. 13L)
Spacecraft Mass: c. 5,375 kg
Mission Design and Management: TsKBEM
Launch Vehicle: 8K82K + Blok D (Proton-K no. 237-01)
Launch Date and Time: 20 January 1969 / 04:14:36 UT
Launch Site: NIIP-5 / launch site 81L
Scientific Instruments: unknown
Results: This was the sixth attempt at a robotic circumlunar flight in support of the L1 piloted lunar program and the first after the resounding success of the American Apollo 8 in December 1968. The Proton launch vehicle lifted off on time, and first-stage operation was nominal. However, during second-stage firing, one of the four engines of the stage mysteriously switched off at T+313.66 seconds. The other engines continued firing, but subsequently, the primary third-stage engine also switched off during its firing sequence at T+500.03 seconds due to a breakdown in the main pipeline feeding fuel to the fuel gas generator. After a near-ballistic flight, the L1 payload landed near the border between the USSR and Mongolia.

104)
no name / [Luna]
Nation: USSR (60)
Objective(s): lunar roving operations
Spacecraft: Ye-8 (no. 201)
Spacecraft Mass: c. 5,700 kg
Mission Design and Management: GSMZ Lavochkin
Launch Vehicle: 8K82K + Blok D (Proton no. 239-01)
Launch Date and Time: 19 February 1969 / 06:48:15 UT
Launch Site: NIIP-5 / launch site 81P
Scientific Instruments:
    1) imaging system (two low-resolution TVs and four high-resolution photometers)

2) x-ray spectrometer
3) penetrometer
4) laser reflector
5) radiation detectors
6) x-ray telescope
7) odometer/speedometer

Results: The Ye-8 represented the "third generation" of Soviet robotic lunar probes. The basic Ye-8 comprised a lander stage (the "KT") topped off by an eight-wheeled, remote-controlled lunar rover (the "8YeL") for exploring the Moon's surface. Essentially a pressurized magnesium alloy container on wheels, the 8YeL was designed to operate over a period of three lunar days (roughly three Earth months) and collect scientific data from various points on the lunar surface. This first attempt to put the rover on the Moon was a complete failure. At T+51 seconds, the payload stack disintegrated and the booster eventually exploded. Later investigation indicated that maximum dynamic pressure during the ascent trajectory tore a new payload shroud off at its weakest tension points. Despite an intensive effort, searchers were unable to find the polonium-20 radioactive isotope heat source in the rover. Unconfirmed rumors still abound that soldiers at the launch site used the isotope to heat their barracks during the bitter winter of 1968.

105)
no name / [N1 launch test]
Nation: USSR (61)
Objective(s): lunar orbit
Spacecraft: 7K-L1S (no. 2)
Spacecraft Mass: 6,900 kg
Mission Design and Management: TsKBEM
Launch Vehicle: N1 (no. 15003)
Launch Date and Time: 21 February 1969 / 09:18:07 UT
Launch Site: NIIP-5 / launch site 110P
Scientific Instruments: unknown
Results: This was the first attempted launch of the giant N1 booster as part of early test operations in the Soviet piloted lunar landing program. N1 development began in 1962 after two years of initial R&D on heavy booster designs. Although the first launch had been originally planned for 1965, a major redesign of the booster in 1964 and financial and organizational difficulties delayed the launch by four years. On this first launch, the N1 carried a basic 7K-L1 spacecraft (openly known as Zond) modified for operations in lunar orbit (rather than for circumlunar flight). Known as the 7K-L1S, the spacecraft was equipped with an Engine Orientation Complex (DOK) for attitude control in lunar orbit. During the launch, two first-stage engines initially shut down, but the remainder of the engines operated until T+70 seconds when the control system shut them down. The booster crashed about 50 kilometers from the launch site, and the payload successfully used its launch escape system to descend without problem 32 to 35 kilometers from the pad. Investigators believed that booster failed when a pipe for measuring fuel pressure broke at T+23.3 seconds that set in motion a sequence of events that led to a huge fire at T+54.5 seconds in the tail of the first stage. The fire short-circuited the control system and shut down all the engines at approximately T+70 seconds.

106)
Mariner 6
Nation: U.S. (45)
Objective(s): Mars flyby
Spacecraft: Mariner-69F / Mariner-F
Spacecraft Mass: 381 kg
Mission Design and Management: NASA JPL
Launch Vehicle: Atlas-Centaur (AC-20 / Atlas 3C no. 5403C / Centaur D-1A)
Launch Date and Time: 25 February 1969 / 01:29:02 UT
Launch Site: ETR / launch complex 36B
Scientific Instruments:
1) imaging system (two TV cameras)
2) infrared spectrometer
3) ultraviolet spectrometer
4) infrared radiometer
5) celestial mechanics experiment
6) S-band occultation experiment

Results: Mariners 6 and 7, identical spacecraft intended to fly by Mars, were the first Mariner spacecraft launched by the Atlas-Centaur, permitting a heavier instrument suite. Both spacecraft were intended to study the surface and atmosphere of Mars during close flybys. All onboard instrumentation was designed to collect data on Mars; there were no experiments for study of interplanetary space. The 3.35-meter-tall spacecraft was constructed around an eight-sided magnesium framework with four rectangular solar panels for 449 watts power. The heart of the spacecraft was the 11.8-kilogram Control Computer and Sequencer (CC&S), which was designed to operate Mariner independently without intervention from ground control. After a midcourse correction on 1 March 1969 and preliminary imaging sessions (fifty photos) on 28 July, Mariner 6 flew by Mars at 05:19:07 UT on 31 July at a distance of 3,429 kilometers. Just 15 minutes prior to closest approach (just south of the Martian equator), the two TV cameras on a scan platform began taking photos of the planet automatically every 42 seconds. During a period of 17 minutes, Mariner 6 took twenty-four near-encounter photos that were stored and later transmitted to Earth. The photos showed heavily cratered and chaotic areas not unlike parts of the Moon. Images of the south polar region showed intriguing detail of an irregular border. The scientific instruments indicated that the polar cap gave off infrared radiation consistent with solid carbon dioxide. Mariner 6 found surface pressure to be equal to about 30.5 kilometers above Earth's surface. Atmospheric composition was about 98 percent carbon dioxide. Surface temperatures ranged from −73°C at night to −125°C at the south polar cap.

107)
no name / [Mars]
Nation: USSR (62)
Objective(s): Mars orbit
Spacecraft: M-69 (no. 521)
Spacecraft Mass: c. 3,800 kg
Mission Design and Management: GSMZ Lavochkin
Launch Vehicle: 8K82K + Blok D (Proton no. 240-01)
Launch Date and Time: 27 March 1969 / 10:40:45 UT
Launch Site: NIIP-5 / launch site 81L
Scientific Instruments:
 1) radiometer
 2) instrument to measure water vapor levels
 3) ultraviolet spectrometer
 4) radiation detector
 5) gamma spectrometer
 6) hydrogen/helium mass spectrometer
 7) spectrometer
 8) low-energy ion spectrometer
 9) imaging system (three cameras)
Results: The M-69 series of Mars spacecraft was the first of a new generation of Mars probes designed by the Lavochkin design bureau for launch on the heavy Proton booster. Although the 1969 missions were originally meant for both Mars orbit and landing, weight constraints late in mission design forced engineers to delete the lander and focus only on a Mars orbit mission. The probes were designed around a single large spherical tank to which three pressurized compartments were attached. After two en route midcourse corrections, the spacecraft were intended to enter orbit around Mars at roughly 1,700 x 34,000 kilometers at 40° inclination. After an initial photography mission, the probes would lower their pericenter to about 500 to 700 kilometers for a second imaging mission. Total mission lifetime would be about three months. During the launch of the first M-69, the Proton's third stage stopped firing at T+438.66 seconds, after its turbopump had caught on fire because of a faulty rotor bearing. The probe, scheduled to reach Mars orbit on 11 September 1969, never even reached Earth orbit.

108)
Mariner 7
Nation: U.S. (46)
Objective(s): Mars flyby
Spacecraft: Mariner-69G
Spacecraft Mass: 381 kg
Mission Design and Management: NASA JPL
Launch Vehicle: Atlas-Centaur (AC-19 / Atlas 3C no. 5105C / Centaur D-1A)
Launch Date and Time: 27 March 1969 / 22:22:01 UT
Launch Site: ETR / launch complex 36A
Scientific Instruments:
 1) imaging system (two TV cameras)
 2) infrared spectrometer
 3) ultraviolet spectrometer
 4) infrared radiometer
 5) celestial mechanics experiment
 6) S-band occultation experiment
Results: Identical to Mariner 6, Mariner 7 had a similar mission of flying by Mars. After Mariner 6 had returned intriguing photos of Mars's south polar cap, controllers reprogrammed Mariner 7's control system to increase the number of scans of the south pole

for the second spacecraft from twenty-five to thirty-three. Following a perfect midcourse correction on the way to Mars on 8 April 1969, on 30 July, just 7 hours before Mariner 6 was scheduled to fly by Mars, the deep space tracking station at Johannesburg, South Africa, lost contact with the spacecraft's high-gain antenna. One of two stations in Madrid, Spain, was diverted from its original mission of tracking Pioneer 8 and joined the search for Mariner 7. Fortunately, the Pioneer station at Goldstone picked up faint signals from the spacecraft. Controllers sent commands to Mariner 7 to switch to the low-gain antenna, which worked well afterwards. Despite problems with positional calibration, Mariner 7 recorded ninety-three far-encounter and thirty-three near-encounter images of the planet, showing heavily cratered terrain very similar to images recorded by Mariner 6. The closest approach to Mars was at 05:00:49 UT on 5 August 1969, at a distance of 3,430 kilometers. Oddly, despite the high resolution of 300 meters, Mariner 7 found the center of Hellas to be devoid of craters. The spacecraft found a pressure of 3.5 millibars and a temperature of –90°F at 59° south latitude and 28° east longitude in the Hellespontus region, suggesting that this area was elevated about 6 kilometers above the average terrain. One photo from Mariner 7 showed the moon Phobos. Although surface features were not visible, the picture clearly showed the moon to be irregularly shaped.

109)
no name / [Mars]
Nation: USSR (63)
Objective(s): Mars orbit
Spacecraft: M-69 (no. 522)
Spacecraft Mass: c. 3,800 kg
Mission Design and Management: GSMZ Lavochkin
Launch Vehicle: 8K82K + Blok D (Proton no. 233-01)
Launch Date and Time: 2 April 1969 / 10:33:00 UT
Launch Site: NIIP-5 / launch site 81P
Scientific Instruments:
1) radiometer
2) instrument to measure water vapor levels
3) ultraviolet spectrometer
4) radiation detector
5) gamma spectrometer
6) hydrogen/helium mass spectrometer
7) spectrometer
8) low-energy ion spectrometer
9) imaging system (three cameras)

Results: The second M-69 spacecraft was identical to its predecessor (launched six days before) and was intended to enter orbit around Mars on 15 September 1969. Like its twin, it never reached intermediate-Earth orbit. At launch, at T+0.02 seconds, one of the six first-stage engines of the Proton exploded. Although the booster lifted off using the remaining five engines, it began veering off course and eventually assumed horizontal attitude, at which point all the remaining first-stage engines shut down. At T+41 seconds, the booster impacted 3 kilometers from the launch site in a massive fireball.

110)
no name / [Luna]
Nation: USSR (64)
Objective(s): lunar sample return
Spacecraft: Ye-8-5 (no. 402)
Spacecraft Mass: c. 5,700 kg
Mission Design and Management: GSMZ Lavochkin
Launch Vehicle: 8K82K + Blok D (Proton no. 238-01)
Launch Date and Time: 14 June 1969 / 04:00:47 UT
Launch Site: NIIP-5 / launch site 81P
Scientific Instruments:
1) stereo imaging system
2) remote arm for sample collection
3) radiation detector

Results: The Ye-8-5 was a variant of the basic Ye-8 lunar rover spacecraft developed by the Lavochkin design bureau. This particular version, whose development began in 1968, was designed to recover a small portion of soil from the lunar surface and return it to Earth. It had the same basic lander stage ("KT") as that of the rover variant (built around a structure comprising four spherical propellant tanks linked together in a square), which was installed with a robot arm to scoop up lunar soil. The rover was replaced by a new "ascent stage" that was built around three spherical propellant tanks that consisted of a main rocket engine to lift off from the Moon, a pressurized compartment for electronics, and a small, 39-kilogram spherical capsule that would detach from the stage and reenter Earth's atmosphere with its valuable payload of lunar dust. On the first launch attempt of the Ye-8-5 robot scooper, the first three stages of the Proton worked without fault, but the Blok D fourth stage, which was to fire to attain orbital velocity, failed to ignite due to a disruption in the circuit of its guidance system. The spacecraft reentered Earth's atmosphere over the Pacific without reaching orbit.

111)
no name / [N1 test flight]
Nation: USSR (65)
Objective(s): lunar orbit
Spacecraft: 7K-L1S
Spacecraft Mass: c. 6,900 kg
Mission Design and Management: TsKBEM
Launch Vehicle: N1 (no. 15005)
Launch Date and Time: 3 July 1969 / 20:18:32 UT
Launch Site: NIIP-5 / launch site 110P
Scientific Instruments: unknown
Results: This was the second attempt to launch the giant N1 rocket. As with its predecessor, its payload consisted of a basic 7K-L1 ("Zond") spacecraft equipped with additional instrumentation and an attitude-control block to enable operations in lunar orbit. Moments after launch, the first stage of the booster exploded in a massive inferno that engulfed the entire launch pad and damaged nearby buildings and structures for several kilometers around the area. Amazingly, the payload's launch escape system operated without fault, and the Zond descent apparatus (or descent module) was recovered safely 2 kilometers from the pad. An investigation commission traced the cause of the failure to the entry of a foreign object into the oxidizer pump of one of the first-stage engines at T-0.25 seconds. The ensuing explosion started a fire that began to engulf the first stage. The control system shut down all engines except one by T+10.15 seconds. The booster lifted about 200 meters off the pad and then came crashing down in a massive explosion.

112)
Luna 15
Nation: USSR (66)
Objective(s): lunar sample return
Spacecraft: Ye-8-5 (no. 401)
Spacecraft Mass: 5,700 kg
Mission Design and Management: GSMZ Lavochkin
Launch Vehicle: 8K82K + Blok D (Proton no. 242-01)
Launch Date and Time: 13 July 1969 / 02:54:42 UT
Launch Site: NIIP-5 / launch site 81P
Scientific Instruments:
 1) stereo imaging system
 2) remote arm for sample collection
 3) radiation detector
Results: Luna 15, launched only three days before the historic Apollo 11 mission to the Moon, was the second Soviet attempt to recover and bring lunar soil back to Earth. In a race to reach the Moon and return to Earth, the parallel missions of Luna 15 and Apollo 11 were, in some ways, the culmination of the Moon race that defined the space programs of both the United States and the Soviet Union in the 1960s. After a midcourse correction the day after launch, Luna 15 entered lunar orbit at 10:00 UT on 17 July 1969. The spacecraft remained in lunar orbit for two days while controllers checked all onboard systems and performed two orbital maneuvers. After astronauts Armstrong and Aldrin had already set foot on the Moon, Luna 15 fired its main retrorocket engine to initiate descent to the surface at 15:47 UT on 21 July 1969. Unfortunately, transmissions ceased only 4 minutes after deorbit at a calculated altitude of 3 kilometers. The spacecraft had probably crashed onto the side of a mountain. Impact coordinates were 17° north latitude and 60° east longitude in Mare Crisium.

113)
Zond 7
Nation: USSR (67)
Objective(s): circumlunar flight
Spacecraft: 7K-L1 (no. 11)
Spacecraft Mass: c. 5,375 kg
Mission Design and Management: TsKBEM
Launch Vehicle: 8K82K + Blok D (Proton no. 243-01)
Launch Date and Time: 7 August 1969 / 23:48:06 UT
Launch Site: NIIP-5 / launch site 81L

Scientific Instruments:
1) biological payload
2) radiation detectors
3) imaging system

Results: Following a spate of partial successes and catastrophic failures, Zond 7 was the first fully successful Soviet circumlunar mission. The spacecraft had been the last 7K-L1 vehicle manufactured for robotic flight. In the original schedule, the next flight would have been piloted. Like its predecessors, Zond 7 carried a set of biological specimens, including four male steppe tortoises that were part of a group of thirty selected for an experiment. After a midcourse correction on 8 August, the spacecraft successfully circled the far side of the Moon two days later at a range of 1,200 kilometers. Zond 7 performed color imaging sessions on 8 August (of Earth) and 11 August (two sessions of both Earth and the Moon). The only major malfunction during the mission was the failure to deploy the main parabolic antenna (due to a problem in the securing cables), but this did not prevent fulfillment of all the primary goals of the mission. Zond 7 successfully carried out a guided reentry over Earth's atmosphere and landed without problem south of Kustanay in Kazakhstan after a 6-day 18-hour 25-minute flight.

114)
Pioneer
Nation: U.S. (47)
Objective(s): solar orbit
Spacecraft: Pioneer-E
Spacecraft Mass: 65.4 kg
Mission Design and Management: NASA ARC
Launch Vehicle: Thor-Delta L (no. 73 / Thor no. 540)
Launch Date and Time: 27 August 1969 / 15:59 UT
Launch Site: ETR / launch complex 17A
Scientific Instruments:
1) three-axis magnetometer
2) cosmic-ray telescope
3) radio propagation detector
4) electric field detector
5) quadrispherical plasma analyzer
6) cosmic-ray-anisotropy detector
7) cosmic dust detector
8) celestial mechanics experiment

Results: At T+31 seconds in the launch of this Pioneer probe, the hydraulics system of the first stage of the booster developed a problem that eventually culminated in complete loss of pressure at T+213 seconds, only 4 seconds prior to main-engine cutoff of the first stage. Although second-stage performance was nominal, there was no way to compensate for the large pointing error introduced by the malfunctions in the first stage. With the booster veering off course, ground control sent a command to destroy the vehicle at T+484 seconds. Pioneer-E was the last in a series of probes intended for studying interplanetary space from heliocentric orbit. An additional payload on the Thor-Delta L was a Test and Training Satellite (TETR) to test the Apollo ground tracking network.

115)
Kosmos 300 / [Luna]
Nation: USSR (68)
Objective(s): lunar sample return
Spacecraft: Ye-8-5 (no. 403)
Spacecraft Mass: c. 5,700 kg
Mission Design and Management: GSMZ Lavochkin
Launch Vehicle: 8K82K + Blok D (Proton no. 244-01)
Launch Date and Time: 23 September 1969 / 14:07:36 UT
Launch Site: NIIP-5 / launch site 81P
Scientific Instruments:
1) stereo imaging system
2) remote arm for sample collection
3) radiation detector

Results: This was the third attempt to send a sample return spacecraft to the Moon (after failures in June and July 1969). On this attempt, the spacecraft successfully reached Earth orbit but failed to inject itself on a translunar trajectory. Later investigation indicated that the Blok D upper stage had failed to fire a second time for translunar injection because of a problem with a fuel injection valve that had become stuck during the first firing of the Blok D (for Earth orbital insertion). As a result, all the liquid oxygen in the Blok D was depleted. The Soviet press named the vehicle Kosmos 300 without alluding to its lunar goal. The payload's orbit decayed about four days after launch.

116)
Kosmos 305 / [Luna]
Nation: USSR (69)

Objective(s): lunar sample return
Spacecraft: Ye-8-5 (no. 404)
Spacecraft Mass: c. 5,700 kg
Mission Design and Management: GSMZ Lavochkin
Launch Vehicle: 8K82K + Blok D (Proton no. 241-01)
Launch Date and Time: 22 October 1969 / 14:09:59 UT
Launch Site: NIIP-5 / launch site 81P
Scientific Instruments:
1) stereo imaging system
2) remote arm for sample collection
3) radiation detector

Results: Exactly one lunar month after the failure of Kosmos 300, the Soviets launched another Ye-8-5 lunar sample return spacecraft. Once again, the spacecraft failed to leave Earth orbit. When the Blok D upper stage was meant to fire for translunar injection, telemetry readings went off scale and communications were lost. There had apparently been a programming failure in one of the radio-command blocks designed to command the Blok D to fire. The Soviet press merely referred to the probe as Kosmos 305. The spacecraft's orbit decayed over Australia before the craft completed a single orbit of Earth.

1970

117)
no name / [Luna]
Nation: USSR (70)
Objective(s): lunar sample return
Spacecraft: Ye-8-5 (no. 405)
Spacecraft Mass: c. 5,700 kg
Mission Design and Management: GSMZ Lavochkin
Launch Vehicle: 8K82K + Blok D (Proton no. 247-01)
Launch Date and Time: 6 February 1970 / 04:16:06 UT
Launch Site: NIIP-5 / launch site 81
Scientific Instruments:
1) stereo imaging system
2) remote arm for sample collection
3) radiation detector

Results: This attempt continued the spate of failures on the robotic lunar sample return program. On this fifth attempt to recover soil from the Moon, the Proton booster failed to deposit its payload in Earth orbit. An erroneous command shut down the second stage at T+127 seconds, and the booster was destroyed. Subsequently, the design organization responsible for the Proton, the TsKBM, implemented a thorough review of the Proton's performance and completed a simple suborbital diagnostic flight in August 1970 to verify corrective measures.

118)
Venera 7
Nation: USSR (71)
Objective(s): Venus landing
Spacecraft: 3V (no. 630)
Spacecraft Mass: 1,180 kg
Mission Design and Management: GSMZ Lavochkin
Launch Vehicle: 8K78M
Launch Date and Time: 17 August 1970 / 05:38:22 UT
Launch Site: NIIP-5 / launch site 31
Scientific Instruments:
   Bus:
1) solar wind detector
2) cosmic-ray detector
   Lander:
1) resistance thermometer
2) aneroid barometer

Results: Venera 7 was one of a pair of spacecraft prepared by the Soviets in 1970 to make a survivable landing on the surface of Venus. The spacecraft were quite similar in design to Veneras 4, 5, and 6, with a main bus and a spherical lander (now with a mass of 500 kilograms). After the last mission, engineers redesigned the landing capsule to withstand pressures of up to 180 atmospheres and temperatures of up to 540°C. Venera 7 successfully left Earth orbit and implemented two midcourse corrections on 2 October and 17 November, respectively, before beginning its

Venus encounter operations on 12 December 1970 when the lander probe's batteries were charged up (using solar panels on the bus) and the internal temperature lowered. At 04:58:44 UT on 15 December, the lander separated from the bus and entered the Venusian atmosphere at an altitude of 135 kilometers and a velocity of 11.5 kilometers per second. When aerodynamic drag had reduced velocity down to 200 meters per second at an altitude of 60 kilometers, the parachute system deployed. Within 35 minutes, at 05:34:10 UT, the capsule was on the Venusian landscape. Although transmissions appeared to have ended at the moment of landing, Soviet ground tracking stations recorded what at first proved to be unintelligible noise. After computer processing of the data, Soviet scientists discovered a valuable 22 minutes 58 seconds of information from the capsule—the first transmissions of spacecraft from the surface of another planet. Quite likely, the initial loss of signal occurred when the capsule tipped over on its side. Venera 7's data indicated a surface temperature of 475 ± 20°C and a pressure of 90 ± 15 atmospheres. The information was a good fit with previous Soviet and American estimates. Impact point was 5° south latitude and 351° longitude.

119)
Kosmos 359 / [Venera]
Nation: USSR (72)
Objective(s): Venus landing
Spacecraft: 3V (no. 631)
Spacecraft Mass: c. 1,200 kg
Mission Design and Management: GSMZ Lavochkin
Launch Vehicle: 8K78M
Launch Date and Time: 22 August 1970 / 05:06:09 UT
Launch Site: NIIP-5 / launch site 31
Scientific Instruments:
   Bus:
   1)   solar wind detector
   2)   cosmic-ray detector
   Lander:
   1)   resistance thermometer
   2)   aneroid barometer
Results: This was the second of a pair of probes designed to land on Venus and transmit information back to Earth. In this case, after the spacecraft had reached Earth orbit, the main engine of the Blok L upper stage was late in igniting and cut off early (after only 25 seconds) due to incorrect operation of a sequencer and a failure in the DC transformer in the power supply system. The payload remained stranded in orbit, eventually reentering Earth's atmosphere on 6 November 1970. The spacecraft was named Kosmos 359 by the Soviet press to disguise the failure.

120)
Luna 16
Nation: USSR (73)
Objective(s): lunar sample return
Spacecraft: Ye-8-5 (no. 406)
Spacecraft Mass: 5,727 kg
Mission Design and Management: GSMZ Lavochkin
Launch Vehicle: 8K82K + Blok D (Proton-K no. 248-01)
Launch Date and Time: 12 September 1970 / 13:25:53 UT
Launch Site: NIIP-5 / launch site 81L
Scientific Instruments:
   1)   stereo imaging system
   2)   remote arm for sample collection
   3)   radiation detector
Results: Luna 16 was a landmark success for the Soviets in their deep space exploration program; the mission accomplished the first fully automatic recovery of soil samples from the surface of the Moon. The success came after five failures. After a successful coast to the Moon (which included one midcourse correction), Luna 16 entered circular lunar orbit (at 110 kilometers with a 70° inclination) on 17 September. Two further orbital adjustments on 18 and 19 September altered both altitude and inclination in preparation for descent to the Moon. At perilune at 05:12 UT on 20 September, Luna 16 fired its main engine to begin its descent to the surface. Six minutes later, the spacecraft safely soft-landed in its target area at 0°41' south latitude and 56°18' east longitude, in the northeast area of the Sea of Fertility, approximately 100 kilometers east of Webb crater. The mass of the spacecraft at landing was 1,880 kilograms. Less than an hour after landing, at 06:03 UT, an automatic drill penetrated the lunar surface to collect a soil sample. After drilling for 7 minutes, the drill reached a stop at 35 millimeters depth and then withdrew its sample

and lifted it in an arc to the top of the spacecraft, depositing the precious cargo in a small spherical capsule mounted on the main spacecraft bus. Finally, at 07:43 UT on 21 September, the spacecraft's upper stage lifted off from the Moon. Three days later, after a direct ascent traverse with no midcourse corrections, the capsule, with its 105 grams of lunar soil, reentered Earth's atmosphere at a velocity of 11 kilometers per second. The capsule parachuted down 80 kilometers southeast of the town of Dzhezkazgan in Kazakhstan at 05:25 UT on 24 September 1970. Analysis of the dark basalt material indicated a close resemblance to soil recovered by the American Apollo 12 mission.

121)
Zond 8
Nation: USSR (74)
Objective(s): circumlunar flight
Spacecraft: 7K-L1 (no. 14)
Spacecraft Mass: c. 5,375 kg
Mission Design and Management: TsKBEM
Launch Vehicle: 8K82K + Blok D (Proton-K no. 250-01)
Launch Date and Time: 20 October 1970 / 19:55:39 UT
Launch Site: NIIP-5 / launch site 81L
Scientific Instruments:
   1) solar wind collector packages
   2) imaging system

Results: Zond 8 was the last in the series of circumlunar spacecraft designed to rehearse a piloted circumlunar flight. The project was initiated in 1965 to compete with the Americans in the race to the Moon but lost its importance once three astronauts circled the Moon on the Apollo 8 mission in December 1968. After a midcourse correction on 22 October at a distance of 250,000 kilometers from Earth, Zond 8 reached the Moon without any apparent problems, circling its target on 24 October at a range of 1,200 kilometers. The spacecraft took black-and-white photographs of the lunar surface during two separate sessions. After two midcourse corrections on the return leg, Zond 8 flew a return over Earth's northern hemisphere instead of the standard southern approach profile, allowing Soviet ground control stations to maintain near-continuous contact with the ship. The guidance system evidently malfunctioned on the return leg, and the spacecraft performed a simple ballistic (instead of a guided) reentry into Earth's atmosphere. The vehicle's descent module splashed down safely in the Indian Ocean at 13:55 UT on 27 October about 730 kilometers southeast of the Chagos Islands, 24 kilometers from its original target point.

122)
Luna 17 / Lunokhod 1
Nation: USSR (75)
Objective(s): lunar roving operations
Spacecraft: Ye-8 (no. 203)
Spacecraft Mass: 5,700 kg
Mission Design and Management: GSMZ Lavochkin
Launch Vehicle: 8K82K + Blok D (Proton-K no. 251-01)
Launch Date and Time: 10 November 1970 / 14:44:01 UT
Launch Site: NIIP-5 / launch site 81L
Scientific Instruments:
   1) imaging system (two low-resolution TVs and four high-resolution photometers)
   2) x-ray spectrometer
   3) penetrometer
   4) laser reflector
   5) radiation detectors
   6) x-ray telescope
   7) odometer/speedometer

Results: Luna 17 continued the spate of successes in Soviet lunar exploration begun by Luna 16 and Zond 8. Luna 17 carried Lunokhod 1, the first in a series of robot lunar roving vehicles whose conception had begun in the early 1960s, originally as part of the piloted lunar landing operations. This was the second attempt to land such a vehicle on the Moon after a failure in February 1969. The descent stage was equipped with two landing ramps for the "ascent stage," that is, the rover, to disembark onto the Moon's surface. The 756-kilogram rover stood about 1.35 meters high and was 2.15 meters across. Each of its eight wheels could be controlled independently for two forward and two reverse speeds. Its top speed was about 100 meters per hour, with commands issued by a five-man team of "drivers" on Earth who had to deal with the 5-second delay. The set of scientific instruments was powered by solar cells (installed on the inside of the hinged top lid of the rover) and

The Soviet Moon lander, Lunokhod 1.

chemical batteries. After two midcourse corrections en route to the Moon, Luna 17 entered lunar orbit and then landed on the lunar surface at 03:46:50 UT on 17 November 1970 at 38°17' north latitude and 35° west longitude, about 2,500 kilometers from the Luna 16 site in the Sea of Rains. The Lunokhod 1 rover rolled over the ramps and onto the lunar surface at 06:28 UT. The rover had an expected lifetime of three lunar days but operated for eleven. During its 322 Earth days of operation, the rover traveled 10.54 kilometers and returned more than 20,000 TV images and 206 high-resolution panoramas. In addition, Lunokhod 1 performed twenty-five soil analyses with its RIFMA x-ray fluorescence spectrometer and used its penetrometer at 500 different locations. Controllers finished the last communications session with Lunokhod 1 at 13:05 UT on 14 September 1971. Attempts to reestablish contact were finally discontinued on 4 October.

1971

123)
Mariner 8
Nation: U.S. (48)
Objective(s): Mars orbit
Spacecraft: Mariner-71H / Mariner-H
Spacecraft Mass: 997.9 kg
Mission Design and Management: NASA JPL
Launch Vehicle: Atlas-Centaur (AC-24 / Atlas 3C no. 5405C / Centaur D-1A)
Launch Date and Time: 9 May 1971 / 01:11:01 UT
Launch Site: ETR / launch complex 36A
Scientific Instruments:
1) imaging system
2) ultraviolet spectrometer
3) infrared spectrometer
4) infrared radiometer
5) S-band occultation experiment
6) celestial mechanics experiment

Results: Mariner-71H (also called Mariner-H) was the first of a pair of American spacecraft intended to explore the physical and dynamic characteristics of Mars from Martian orbit. The overall goals of the series were to search for an environment that could support life; to collect data on the origin and evolution of the planet; to gather information on planetary physics, geology, planetology, and cosmology; and to provide data that could aid future spacecraft such as the Viking Landers. Launch of Mariner-71H was nominal until just after separation of the Centaur upper stage, when a malfunction occurred in the stage's flight-control system, leading to loss of pitch control at an altitude of 148 kilometers at T+4.7 minutes. As a result, the stack began to tumble and the Centaur engines shut down. The stage and its payload reentered Earth's atmosphere approximately 1,500 kilometers downrange from the launch site.

124)
Kosmos 419 / [Mars]
Nation: USSR (76)
Objective(s): Mars orbit
Spacecraft: M-71S (no. 170)
Spacecraft Mass: 4,549 kg
Mission Design and Management: GSMZ Lavochkin
Launch Vehicle: 8K82K + Blok D (Proton-K no. 253-01)
Launch Date and Time: 10 May 1971 / 16:58:42 UT
Launch Site: NIIP-5 / launch site 81L
Scientific Instruments:
1) fluxgate magnetometer
2) infrared radiometer
3) infrared photometer
4) spectrometer
5) photometer
6) radiometer
7) ultraviolet photometer
8) cosmic-ray detector
9) charged-particle spectrometer

10) imaging system
11) Stereo antenna

Results: Kosmos 419 was the first of the "fifth-generation" Soviet Mars probes (after those launched in 1960, 1962, 1963–64, and 1969). The original plan was to launch two orbiter-lander combinations known as M-71 during the 1971 Mars launch window, but in order to preempt the American Mariner H/I vehicles, Soviet planners added a third mission, the M-71S, a simple orbiter that could become the first spacecraft to go into orbit around Mars. The orbiter could also collect data important for aiming the two landers at precise locations in the Martian system. The spacecraft entered Earth orbit successfully, but the Blok D upper stage failed to fire the second time to send the spacecraft to Mars. Later investigation showed that there was human error in programming the firing time for the Blok D; an eight-digit code to fire the engine had been issued by an operator in reverse order. The stranded spacecraft, which was named Kosmos 419 by the Soviet press, reentered Earth's atmosphere within two days of launch. The Soviets had promised the French that two of their Stereo instruments would be sent to Mars. Since one was lost on Kosmos 419, Soviet officials were forced to lie about its ultimate fate to cover up the failure.

125)
Mars 2
Nation: USSR (77)
Objective(s): Mars orbit and landing
Spacecraft: M-71 (no. 171)
Spacecraft Mass: 4,650 kg
Mission Design and Management: GSMZ Lavochkin
Launch Vehicle: 8K82K + Blok D (Proton-K no. 255-01)
Launch Date and Time: 19 May 1971 / 16:22:44 UT
Launch Site: NIIP-5 / launch site 81P
Scientific Instruments:
  Orbiter:
  1) three-component magnetometer
  2) infrared radiometer
  3) radiotelescope
  4) infrared photometer/CO_2 absorption strips
  5) ultraviolet photometer
  6) imaging system (two cameras)
  7) photometer in visible part of electromagnetic spectrum
  8) cosmic-ray particle detector
  9) energy spectrometer
  10) spectrometer to determine water vapor
  11) Stereo antenna

  Lander:
  1) gamma-ray spectrometer
  2) x-ray spectrometer
  3) thermometer
  4) wind velocity recorder
  5) barometer
  6) imaging system (two cameras)
  7) penetrometer (on mobile PROP-M)
  8) gamma-ray densitometer (on PROP-M)

Results: Mars 2 was the first of two orbiter-lander combination spacecraft sent to Mars by the Soviets during the 1971 launch window. The orbiters were roughly cylindrical structures fixed to a large propellant tank base. The landers were egg-shaped modules with petals that would open on the Martian surface. The 1,000-kilogram landers (of which 350 kilograms was the actual capsule) were fastened to the top of the bus and protected by a braking shell for entry into the Martian atmosphere. After jettisoning the shell, the landers would deploy parachutes to descend to the Martian surface. On the Mars 2 trip to the Red Planet, controllers performed two successful midcourse corrections on 17 June and 20 November 1971, respectively. On 27 November 1971, Mars 2 implemented its final midcourse correction, after which the lander probe separated to initiate atmospheric entry. At this point, the onboard computer was designed to implement final corrections to the trajectory, spin the lander around its longitudinal axis, and fire a solid-propellant engine to initiate reentry in a specific direction. During the flight, after the final midcourse correction, the trajectory of the spacecraft was so accurate that there was no need for further corrective measures. Because of pre-programmed algorithms that assumed a deviated trajectory, the lander was put into an incorrect attitude after separation to compensate for the "error." When the reentry engine fired, the angle of entry proved to be far too steep. The parachute system never deployed, and the lander even-

The Soviet Mars 3 spacecraft.

tually crashed onto the Martian surface at 4° north latitude and 47° west longitude. It was the first humanmade object to make contact with Mars. Meanwhile, the Mars 3 orbiter successfully entered orbit around Mars at 20:19 UT on 27 November 1971. Parameters were 1,380 x 25,000 kilometers at 48.9° inclination. (See entry under Mars 3 for the planned Mars 2 orbiter program.)

126)
Mars 3
Nation: USSR (78)
Objective(s): Mars orbit and landing
Spacecraft: M-71 (no. 172)
Spacecraft Mass: 4,650 kg
Mission Design and Management: GSMZ Lavochkin
Launch Vehicle: 8K82K + Blok D (Proton-K no. 249-01)
Launch Date and Time: 28 May 1971 / 15:26:30 UT
Launch Site: NIIP-5 / launch site 81L
Scientific Instruments:

Orbiter:
1) three-component magnetometer
2) infrared radiometer
3) radiotelescope
4) infrared photometer/CO_2 absorption strips
5) ultraviolet photometer
6) imaging system (two cameras)
7) photometer in visible part of electromagnetic spectrum
8) cosmic-ray particle detector
9) energy spectrometer
10) spectrometer to determine water vapor

Lander:
1) gamma-ray spectrometer
2) x-ray spectrometer
3) thermometer
4) wind velocity recorder
5) barometer
6) imaging system (two cameras)
7) penetrometer (on mobile PROP-M)
8) gamma-ray densitometer (on PROP-M)

Results: Like its predecessor, Mars 3 was successfully sent on a trajectory to the Red Planet. The spacecraft completed three midcourse corrections on 8 June, 14 November, and 2 December 1971. At 09:14 UT on 2 December 1971, the lander separated from the orbiter and, 4.5 hours later, began entry into the Martian atmosphere. Finally, at 13:47 UT, the probe successfully set down intact on the Martian surface, becoming the first human-made object to perform a survivable landing on the planet. Landing coordinates were 45° south latitude and 158° west longitude. The bus, meanwhile, entered orbit around Mars with parameters of 1,500 x 190,700 kilometers at 48.9° inclination, significantly different from the originally planned orbit. At 13:50:35 UT, immediately after landing, the lander probe began transmitting a TV image of the Martian surface, although transmissions abruptly ceased after 20 seconds. Because of a violent dust storm that raged across the planet, controllers surmised that coronal discharge may have shorted all electric instrumentation on the lander. The received image showed only a gray background with no detail, probably because the two imaging "heads" had still not deployed in 20 seconds to their full height to see the surface. After the initial contact, the ground lost all contact with the lander probe. The Mars 3 orbiter, like the Mars 2 orbiter, had problems with its imaging mission. Because the orbiters had to perform their imaging mission soon after entering orbit, they could not wait until the dust storms subsided on the surface. As a result, the orbiter photographs showed few details of the surface. Additionally, controllers had set the cameras at the wrong exposure setting, making the photos far too light to show much detail. Despite the failure of the imaging mission, both orbiters carried out a full cycle of scientific experiments returning valuable data on the planet until contact with both was lost almost simultaneously in July 1972.

127)
Mariner 9
Nation: U.S. (49)
Objective(s): Mars orbit
Spacecraft: Mariner-71I / Mariner-I
Spacecraft Mass: 997.9 kg
Mission Design and Management: NASA JPL
Launch Vehicle: Atlas-Centaur (AC-23 / Atlas 3C no. 5404C / Centaur D-1A)
Launch Date and Time: 30 May 1971 / 22:23:04 UT
Launch Site: ETR / launch complex 36B
Scientific Instruments:
1) imaging system
2) ultraviolet spectrometer
3) infrared spectrometer
4) infrared radiometer
5) S-band occultation experiment
6) celestial mechanics experiment

Results: Mariner 9 was the second in the pair of identical spacecraft launched in 1971 to orbit Mars. The first spacecraft, Mariner 8, failed to reach Earth orbit. Based on a wide octagonal structure, these vehicles used a bipropellant propulsion system with a fixed thrust of 136 kilograms for orbital insertion around Mars. All scientific instrumentation on the spacecraft was mounted on a movable scan platform "underneath" the main bodies. The span of the spacecraft over its extended solar panels was 6.9 meters. Following an en route midcourse correction on 5 June 1971, Mariner 9 ignited its main engine for 915.6 seconds on 14 November 1971 at 00:18 UT, becoming the first humanmade object to enter orbit around a planet. Initial orbital parameters were 1,398 x 17,916 kilometers at 64.3° inclination. The primary goal of the mission was to map about 70 percent of the surface during the first three months of operation. The dedicated imaging mission began in late November, but because of the major dust storm at the planet during this time, photos taken prior to about mid-January 1972 did not show great detail. Once the dust storm had subsided, Mariner 9 began to return spectacular photos of the deeply pitted Martian landscape, showing for the first time such features as the great system of parallel rilles stretching more than 1,700 kilometers across Mare Sirenum. The vast amount of incoming data countered the notion that Mars was geologically inert. There was some speculation on the possibility of water having existed on the surface during an earlier period, but the spacecraft data could not provide any conclusive proof. By February 1972, the spacecraft had identified about twenty volcanoes, one of which, later named Olympus Mons, dwarfed any

The most conspicuous feature observed on Mars by Mariner 9 was the darkish spot located near the top of this picture. It was tentatively identified as Nix Olympica, a curious ring-shaped feature photographed by Mariners 6 and 7 in 1969 and a point which radar indicates is one of the highest on Mars. One possible explanation suggests a high mountain or plateau rising up through the bright dust surrounding the rest of the planet. The picture, one of a series of thirty-one recorded on the first tape-load during approach to Mars, was taken at 8:46 A.M. PST, 11 November 1971, at a range of about 408,000 miles. North is at the top. Mariner 9 was the first spacecraft to orbit another planet. The spacecraft was designed to continue the atmospheric studies begun by Mariners 6 and 7 and to map over 70 percent of the Martian surface from the lowest altitude (1,500 kilometers) and at the highest resolutions (1 kilometer per pixel to 100 meters per pixel) of any previous Mars mission. Mariner 9 was launched on 30 May 1971 and arrived on 14 November 1971.

similar feature on Earth. Olympus Mons, part of Nix Olympica—a "great volcanic pile" possibly formed by the eruption of hot magma from the planet's interior—is 25 kilometers high and has a base with a diameter of 600 kilometers. On 11 February 1972, NASA announced that Mariner 9 had achieved all its goals. By the time of last contact at 22:32 UT on 27 October 1972, the spacecraft had mapped 85 percent of the planet at a resolution of 1 to 2 kilometers, returning 7,329 photos.

128)
Apollo 15 Particle and Fields Subsatellite
Nation: U.S. (50)
Objective(s): lunar orbit
Spacecraft: Apollo 15 P&FS
Spacecraft Mass: 35.6 kg
Mission Design and Management: NASA MSC
Launch Vehicle: Apollo 15 CSM-112 (itself launched by Saturn V SA-510)
Launch Date and Time: 26 July 1971 / 13:34:00 UT (subsatellite ejection on 4 August 1971 / 20:13:19 UT)
Launch Site: ETR / launch complex 39A
Scientific Instruments:
1) magnetometer
2) S-band transponder
3) charged-particle detectors

Results: This small satellite was deployed by the Apollo 15 crew shortly before leaving lunar orbit. The probe was designed around a 35.6-centimeter-diameter hexagonal structure that was equipped with three instrument booms. Power supply came from solar panels and chemical batteries. The instruments measured the strength and direction of interplanetary and terrestrial magnetic fields, detected variations in the lunar gravity field, and measured proton and electron flux. The satellite confirmed Explorer 35's finding that while Earth's magnetic field deflects the incoming solar wind into a tail, the Moon acts as a physical barrier due to its weak field and creates a "hole" in the wind. An electronic failure on 3 February 1972 formally ended the mission. Although it originally had a one-year design life, all mission objectives were fulfilled.

129)
Luna 18
Nation: USSR (79)
Objective(s): lunar sample return
Spacecraft: Ye-8-5 (no. 407)
Spacecraft Mass: c. 5,750 kg
Mission Design and Management: GSMZ Lavochkin
Launch Vehicle: 8K82K + Blok D (Proton-K no. 256-01)
Launch Date and Time: 2 September 1971 / 13:40:40 UT
Launch Site: NIIP-5 / launch site 81P
Scientific Instruments:
1) stereo imaging system
2) remote arm for sample collection
3) radiation detector
4) radio altimeter

Results: This mission was the seventh Soviet attempt to recover soil samples from the surface of the Moon and the first after the success of Luna 16. After two midcourse corrections on 4 and 6 September 1971, Luna 18 entered a circular orbit around the Moon on 7 September at 100 kilometers altitude with an inclination of 35°. After several more orbital corrections, on 11 September, the vehicle began its descent to the lunar surface. Unfortunately, contact with the spacecraft was abruptly lost at 07:48 UT at the previously determined point of lunar landing. Impact coordinates were 3°34' north latitude and 56°30' east longitude, near the edge of the Sea of Fertility. Officially, the Soviets announced that "the lunar landing in the complex mountainous conditions proved to be unfavorable." Later, in 1975, the Soviets published data from Luna 18's continuous-wave radio altimeter that determined the mean density of the lunar topsoil.

130)
Luna 19
Nation: USSR (80)
Objective(s): lunar orbit
Spacecraft: Ye-8LS (no. 202)
Spacecraft Mass: c. 5,700 kg
Mission Design and Management: GSMZ Lavochkin
Launch Vehicle: 8K82K + Blok D (Proton-K no. 257-01)
Launch Date and Time: 28 September 1971 / 10:00:22 UT

Launch Site: NIIP-5 / launch site 81P
Scientific Instruments:
1) imaging system
2) gamma-ray spectrometer
3) radio altimeter
4) meteoroid detectors
5) magnetometer
6) cosmic-ray detectors
7) radiation detectors

Results: Luna 19 was the first of "advanced" lunar orbiters whose design was based upon the same Ye-8-class bus used for the lunar rovers and the sample collectors. For these orbiters, designated Ye-8LS, the basic "lander stage" was topped off by a wheelless Lunokhod-like frame that housed all scientific instrumentation in a pressurized container. Luna 19 entered orbit around the Moon on 2 October 1972 after two midcourse corrections on 29 September and 1 October. Initial orbital parameters were 140 x 140 kilometers at 40.58° inclination. Soon after, the spacecraft began its main imaging mission—to provide panoramic images of the mountainous region of the Moon between 30° and 60° south latitude and between 20° and 80° east longitude. Other scientific experiments included extensive studies on the shape and strength of the lunar gravitation field and the locations of mascons. Occultation experiments in May and June 1972 allowed scientists to determine the concentration of charged particles at an altitude of 10 kilometers. Additional studies of the solar wind were evidently coordinated with those performed by the Mars 2 and 3 orbiters and Veneras 7 and 8. Communications with Luna 19 were terminated sometime between 3 and 20 October 1972 after a year of operations, during more than 4,000 revolutions of the Moon.

1972

131)
Luna 20
Nation: USSR (81)
Objective(s): lunar sample return
Spacecraft: Ye-8-5 (no.408)
Spacecraft Mass: c. 5,750 kg
Mission Design and Management: GSMZ Lavochkin
Launch Vehicle: 8K82K + Blok D (Proton-K no. 258-01)
Launch Date and Time: 14 February 1972 / 03:27:59 UT
Launch Site: NIIP-5 / launch site 81P
Scientific Instruments:
1) stereo imaging system
2) remote arm for sample collection
3) radiation detector
4) radio altimeter

Results: This was the eighth Soviet spacecraft launched to return lunar soil to Earth. It was evidently sent to complete the mission that Luna 18 had failed to accomplish. After a 4.5-day flight to the Moon, which included a single midcourse correction on 15 February, Luna 20 entered orbit around the Moon on 18 February. Initial orbital parameters were 100 x 100 kilometers at 65° inclination. Three days later, at 19:13 UT, the spacecraft fired its main engine for 267 seconds to begin descent to the lunar surface. A second firing further reduced velocity before Luna 20 set down safely on the Moon at 19:19 UT on 21 February 1972 at coordinates 3°32' north latitude and 56°33' east longitude, only 1.8 kilometers from the crash site of Luna 18. After collecting a small sample of lunar soil, the spacecraft's ascent stage lifted off at 22:58 UT on 22 February and quickly accelerated to 2.7 kilometers per second velocity—sufficient to return to Earth. The small spherical capsule eventually parachuted down safely on an island in the Karkingir River, 40 kilometers north of the town of Dzhezkazgan in Kazakhstan, at 19:19 UT on 25 February 1972. The 55-gram soil sample differed from that collected by Luna 16 in that the majority (50 to 60 percent) of the rock particles in the newer sample were ancient anorthosite (which consists largely of feldspar) rather than the basalt of the earlier one (which contained about 1 to 2 percent of anorthosite). Like the Luna 16 soil, samples of the Luna 20 collection were shared with American and French scientists.

132)
Pioneer 10
Nation: U.S. (51)
Objective(s): Jupiter flyby
Spacecraft: Pioneer-F
Spacecraft Mass: 258 kg
Mission Design and Management: NASA ARC
Launch Vehicle: Atlas-Centaur (AC-27 / Atlas 3C no. 5007C / Centaur D-1A)

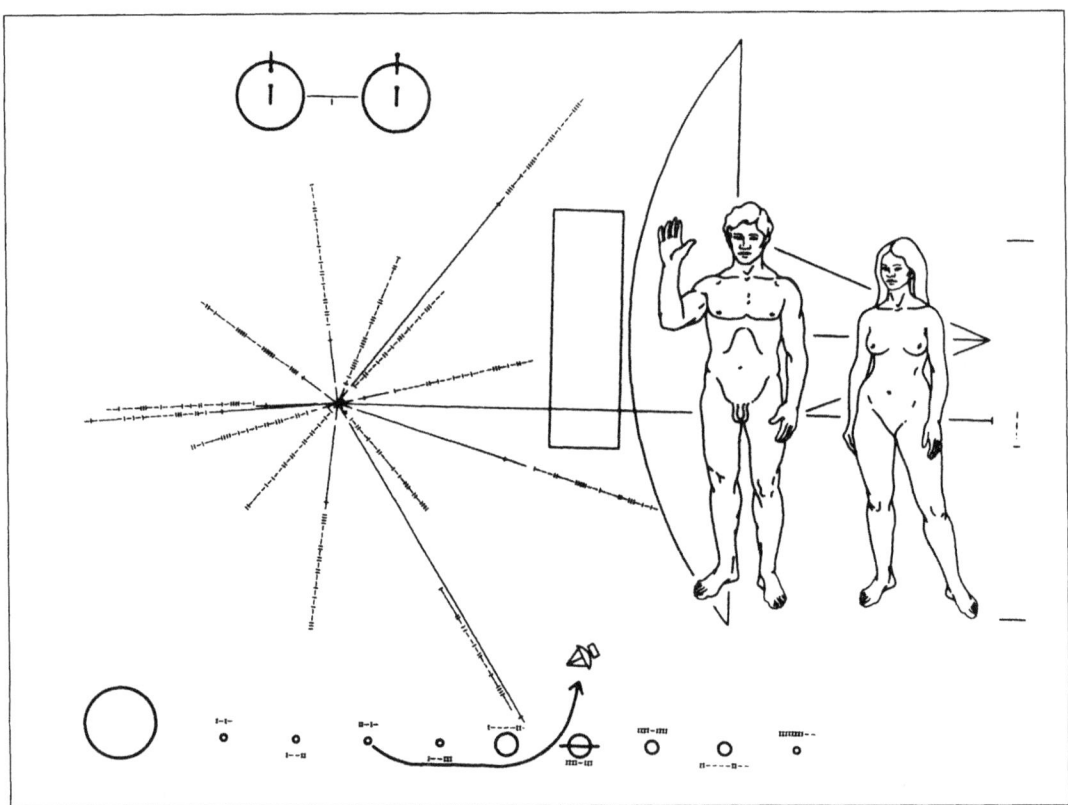

The Pioneer 10 and 11 spacecraft, which were the first humanmade objects to escape from the solar system into interstellar space, carried this pictorial plaque. It was designed to show scientifically educated inhabitants of other star systems, who might intercept it millions of years from now, when Pioneer was launched, from where, and by what kind of beings (with the hope that those who found the craft would not invade Earth). The design is etched into a 6-inch by 9-inch gold-anodized aluminum plate attached to the spacecraft's antenna support struts in a position to help shield it from erosion by interstellar dust. The radiating lines at left represents the positions of 14 pulsars, a cosmic source of radio energy, arranged to indicate our sun as the home star of our civilization. The "1-" symbols at the ends of the lines are binary numbers that represent the frequencies of these pulsars at the time of launch of Pioneers 10 and 11 relative of that to the hydrogen atom shown at the upper left with a "1" unity symbol. The hydrogen atom is thus used as a "universal clock," and the regular decrease in the frequencies of the pulsars will enable another civilization to determine the time that has elapsed since Pioneer was launched. Across the bottom are the planets, ranging outward from the Sun, with the spacecraft trajectory arching away from Earth, passing Mars, and swinging by Jupiter.

Launch Date and Time: 2 March 1972 / 01:49:04 UT
Launch Site: ETR / launch complex 36A
Scientific Instruments:
1) imaging photopolarimeter
2) magnetometer
3) infrared radiometer
4) plasma analyzer
5) ultraviolet photometer
6) charged-particle composition instrument
7) cosmic-ray telescope
8) Geiger tube telescopes
9) asteroid/meteoroid detector
10) Jovian trapped-radiation detector
11) meteoroid detector

Results: Pioneer 10, the first NASA mission to the outer planets, garnered a series of firsts perhaps unmatched by any other robotic spacecraft in the space era: the first vehicle placed on a trajectory to escape the solar system into interstellar space; the first spacecraft to fly beyond Mars; the first to fly through the asteroid belt; the first to fly past Jupiter; the first to use all-nuclear electrical power; and the first humanmade object to leave this solar system. After launch by a three-stage version of the Atlas-Centaur (with

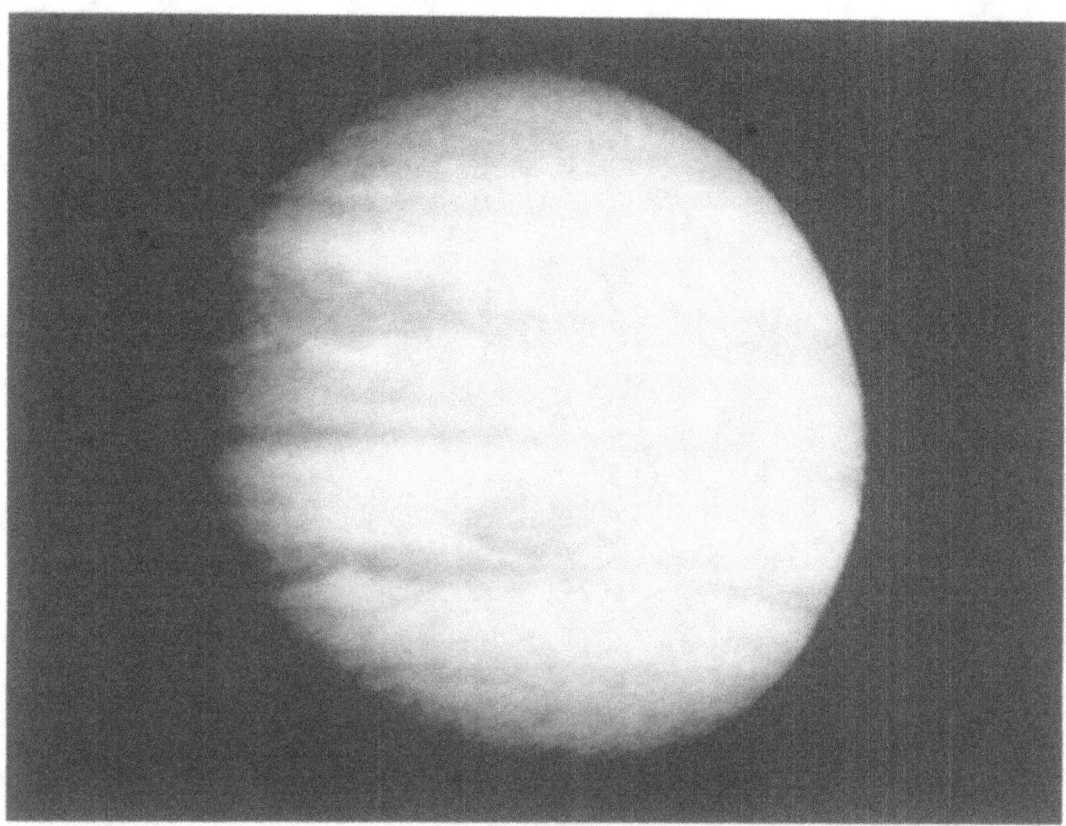

This view of Jupiter shows the giant planet's cloud tops taken by the Pioneer 10 spacecraft as it flew past Jupiter in December 1973. This view was taken from 2,695,000 kilometers away. It shows the 40,200-kilometer-long Great Red Spot, which is large enough to swallow up several Earths. Individual cloud formations are visible in some detail. The bright zones appear to become split up into the detailed flow patterns of Jupiter's atmosphere and clouds. The area surrounding the Spot in the bright South Tropical Zone suggests a flow pattern about the Spot that bulges toward the north by the Spot. The gigantic cloud swirls are thousands or more kilometers across. Pioneer 10 flew past Jupiter in December 1973. A sister spacecraft, Pioneer 11, reached Jupiter in December 1974. The Pioneer project was managed by NASA's Ames Research Center, Mountain View, California. The spacecraft was built by TRW Systems.

a TE-M-364-4 solid-propellant engine modified from the Surveyor lander), Pioneer 10 reached an initial speed of 51,800 kilometers per hour, faster than any previous humanmade object. There were some initial problems during the outbound voyage when direct sunlight caused heating problems. On 15 July 1972, the spacecraft entered the asteroid belt, emerging in February 1973 after a 435-million-kilometer voyage through the relatively densely packed rings. During this period, the spacecraft encountered some asteroid hits (although many fewer than expected) and also measured the density of Zodiacal light in interplanetary space. On 7 August, in conjunction with Pioneer 9 (in solar orbit), Pioneer 10 recorded details of one of the most violent solar storms in recent record. The spacecraft entered Jupiter's bow-shock wave (where the solar wind interacts with the planet's magnetic field) on 26 November, crossed the magnetopause, reentered the magnetic field on 1 December, and then crossed the magnetopause for the second time. By the following day, the spacecraft was returning better quality photos than possible with the best Earth-based telescopes—it had already begun imaging as early as 6 November 1973. Also during this period, Pioneer 10 took about 300 photos of Jupiter that included images of the planet's terminator and the Great Red Spot. Command-and-return time was up to 92 minutes by this time. Pioneer 10's closest approach to Jupiter was at 02:25 UT on 4 December

Mariner 10's first image of Mercury acquired on 24 March 1974. During its flight, Mariner 10's trajectory brought it behind the lighted hemisphere of Mercury, where this image was taken, in order to acquire important measurements with other instruments. This picture was acquired from a distance of 5,380,000 kilometers from the surface of Mercury. The diameter of Mercury (4,878 kilometers) is about one-third that of Earth. Images of Mercury were acquired in two steps, an inbound leg (images acquired before passing into Mercury's shadow) and an outbound leg (after exiting from Mercury's shadow). More than 2,300 useful images of Mercury were taken, both at moderate resolution (3–20 kilometers/pixel) color and at high resolution (better than 1 kilometer/pixel) black-and-white coverage.

1973, when the spacecraft raced by the planet at a range of 130,354 kilometers and a speed of 132,000 kilometers per hour. Of the spacecraft's eleven scientific instruments, six operated continuously through the encounter. The spacecraft passed by a series of Jovian moons, obtaining photos of Callisto, Ganymede, and Europa (but not Io). Pioneer 10 fulfilled all objectives except one (that one failure was due to false commands triggered by Jupiter's intense radiation). Based on incoming data, scientists identified plasma in Jupiter's magnetic field. The spacecraft crossed Saturn's orbit in February 1976, recording data that indicated that Jupiter's enormous magnetic tail, almost 800 million kilometers long, covered the whole distance between the two planets. Still operating nominally, Pioneer 10 crossed the orbit of Neptune (then the outermost planet) on 13 June 1983, thus becoming the first humanmade object to escape the solar system. Now the spacecraft is generally heading in the direction of the red star Aldebaran, a star that forms the eye of the Taurus constellation. It is expected to pass by Aldebaran in about two million years. In case of an intercept by intelligent life, Pioneer 10 carries an aluminum plaque with diagrams of a man and a woman, the solar system, and its location relative to fourteen pulsars. Pioneer 10 is heading out of the solar system in a direction very different from those of the two Voyager probes and Pioneer 11, that is, heading in an opposite direction toward the nose of the heliosphere in an upstream direction relative to the inflowing interstellar gas. NASA officially terminated routine contact with the vehicle at 19:35 UT on 31 March 1997 for budgetary reasons, although intermittent contact continues (as permitted by the onboard power source) with collection of data from the Geiger tube telescope and the charged-particle instrument. For example, ground control received a signal from the spacecraft on 28 April 2001. Pioneer 10 was the farthest humanmade object in existence until 17 February 1998, when Voyager 1 exceeded its range. By 1 July 2001, Pioneer 10 was 11.83 billion kilometers from Earth, traveling at 12.24 kilometers per second relative to the Sun.

133)
Venera 8
Nation: USSR (82)
Objective(s): Venus landing
Spacecraft: 3V (no. 670)
Spacecraft Mass: 1,184 kg
Mission Design and Management: GSMZ Lavochkin
Launch Vehicle: 8K78M
Launch Date and Time: 27 March 1972 / 04:15:01 UT
Launch Site: NIIP-5 / launch site 31
Scientific Instruments:
   Bus:
   1) cosmic-ray detector
   2) solar wind detector
   3) ultraviolet spectrometer
   Lander:
   1) thermometer
   2) barometer
   3) radio altimeter
   4) photometer
   5) gamma-ray spectrometer
   6) gas analyzer
   7) wind speed recorder
Results: Venera 8 was the first in another pair of Soviet spacecraft designed to explore Venus. Although similar in design to its predecessors, the 495-kilogram lander was substantially modified based on the Results from Venera 7. The new capsule was designed to withstand pressures of "only" 105 atmospheres (versus 180 atmospheres on Venera 7) and carried extra scientific instrumentation. After one midcourse correction on 6 April 1972, Venera 8's lander separated from the flyby bus and entered the Venusian atmosphere at 08:37 UT on 22 July 1972 at a velocity of 11.6 kilometers per second. Successful landing took place at 09:32 UT, about 500 kilometers from the morning terminator on the sunlit side of Venus. Landing coordinates were 10° south latitude and 335° longitude. The probe transmitted data for another 50 minutes 11 seconds from the hostile surface before succumbing to ground conditions. The transmitted information indicated that temperature and pressure at the landing site were 470 ± 8°C and 90 ± 1.5 atmospheres respectively. Wind speed was less than 1 kilometer per second below 10 kilometers altitude. The spacecraft also recorded a sharp change in illumination between 30 and 35 kilometers altitude. The data indicate that

visibility on the ground was about one kilometer at the time Venera 8 landed.

134)
Kosmos 482 / [Venera]
Nation: USSR (83)
Objective(s): Venus landing
Spacecraft: 3V (no. 671)
Spacecraft Mass: c. 1,180 kg
Mission Design and Management: GSMZ Lavochkin
Launch Vehicle: 8K78M
Launch Date and Time: 31 March 1972 / 04:02:33 UT
Launch Site: NIIP-5 / launch site 31
Scientific Instruments:
  Bus:
  1) cosmic-ray detector
  2) solar wind detector
  3) ultraviolet spectrometer
  Lander:
  1) thermometer
  2) barometer
  3) radio altimeter
  4) photometer
  5) gamma-ray spectrometer
  6) gas analyzer
  7) wind speed recorder

Results: This was the sister craft to Venera 8 (launched four days earlier). Unfortunately, the spacecraft never left Earth orbit. The Blok L escape stage's main engine prematurely cut off after only 125 seconds of firing due to a failure in the onboard timer. As a result, the spacecraft entered an elliptical orbit around Earth. Officially, the Soviets named the probe Kosmos 482 to disguise its true mission. The spacecraft reentered Earth's atmosphere in May 1981.

135)
Apollo 16 Particle and Fields Subsatellite
Nation: U.S. (52)
Objective(s): lunar orbit
Spacecraft: Apollo 16 P&FS
Spacecraft Mass: 42 kg
Mission Design and Management: NASA
Launch Vehicle: Apollo 16 CSM-113 (itself launched by Saturn V SA-511)
Launch Date and Time: 16 April 1972 / 17:54:00 UT (subsatellite ejection on 24 April 1972 / 09:56:09 UT)
Launch Site: ETR / launch complex 39A
Scientific Instruments:
  1) magnetometer
  2) S-band transponder
  3) charged-particle detectors

Results: Nearly identical to its predecessor, the Apollo 16 Particle and Fields Subsatellite was ejected from the Apollo 16 Command and Service Module about 4 hours prior to the crew's trans-Earth injection burn, which sent them home from the Moon. Because of problems with the Apollo CSM main engine, the crew was forced to release the subsatellite in a low lunar orbit of 100 x 100 kilometers at 10° inclination. Thus, the probe eventually crashed onto the lunar surface after thirty-four days in orbit rather than the planned one year. Impact point was at 10.2° north latitude and 112° east longitude at 21:00 UT on 29 May 1972. However, because of its low orbit, the spacecraft did return some valuable low-altitude data.

136)
no name / [N1 launch test]
Nation: USSR (84)
Objective(s): lunar orbit
Spacecraft: 7K-LOK (no. 6A)
Spacecraft Mass: c. 9,500 kg
Mission Design and Management: TsKBEM
Launch Vehicle: N1 (no. 15007)
Launch Date and Time: 23 November 1972 / 06:11:55 UT
Launch Site: NIIP-5 / launch site 110L
Scientific Instruments: unknown

Results: This was the fourth test launch of the giant Soviet N1 booster. The first two, launched in 1969, attempted to send rigged-up 7K-L1 ("Zond") spacecraft to lunar orbit. The third booster carried a payload mockup for tests in Earth orbit. All three failed. This fourth launch was intended to send a fully equipped 7K-LOK spacecraft (similar to a beefed-up Soyuz) on a robotic lunar orbiting mission during which the spacecraft would spend 3.7 days circling the Moon (over 42 orbits), taking photographs of future landing sites for piloted missions. The booster lifted off without problems, but a few seconds prior to first-stage cutoff, at T+107 seconds, a powerful explosion ripped apart the bottom of the first stage, destroying Soviet hopes of ever sending cosmonauts to the Moon. There was never a conclusive reason for the explosion; some suggested that there had been an engine failure, and others were convinced that the scheduled shutdown of six central engines had caused a structural shock wave that eventually caused the explosion.

1973

137)
Luna 21
Nation: USSR (85)
Objective(s): lunar roving operations
Spacecraft: Ye-8 (no. 204)
Spacecraft Mass: c. 5,950 kg
Mission Design and Management: GSMZ Lavochkin
Launch Vehicle: 8K82K + Blok D (Proton-K no. 259-01)
Launch Date and Time: 8 January 1973 / 06:55:38 UT
Launch Site: NIIP-5 / launch site 81L
Scientific Instruments:
1) imaging system (three low-resolution TVs and four high-resolution photometers)
2) x-ray spectrometer
3) penetrometer
4) laser reflector
5) radiation detectors
6) x-ray telescope
7) odometer/speedometer
8) visible/ultraviolet photometer
9) magnetometer
10) photodetector

Results: Luna 21 carried the second successful Soviet "8YeL" lunar rover, Lunokhod 2, and was launched less than a month after the last Apollo lunar landing. After a midcourse correction the day after launch, Luna 21 entered orbit around the Moon on 12 January 1973. Parameters were 100 x 90 kilometers at 60° inclination. On 15 January, the spacecraft deorbited and, after multiple engine firings, landed on the Moon at 22:35 UT the same day, inside the LeMonnier crater at 25°51' north latitude and 30°27' east longitude, between Mare Serenitatis and the Taurus Mountains. Less than 3 hours later, at 01:14 UT on 16 January, the rover disembarked onto the lunar surface. The 840-kilogram Lunokhod 2 was an improved version of its predecessor and was equipped with a third TV camera, an improved eight-wheel traction system, and additional scientific instrumentation. By the end of its first lunar day, Lunokhod 2 had already traveled further than Lunokhod 1 in its entire operational life. On 9 May, the rover inadvertently rolled into a crater and dust covered its solar panels, disrupting temperatures in the vehicle. Attempts to save the rover failed, and on 3 June, the Soviet news agency announced that its mission was over. Before last contact, the rover took 80,000 TV pictures and 86 panoramic photos and had performed hundreds of mechanical and chemical surveys of the soil. The Soviets later revealed that during a conference on planetary exploration in Moscow, 29 January to 2 February 1973 (that is, after the landing of Luna 21), an American scientist had given photos of the lunar surface around the Luna 21 landing site to a Soviet engineer in charge of the Lunokhod 2 mission. These photos, taken prior to the Apollo 17 landing, were later used by the "driver team" to navigate the new rover on its mission on the Moon.

138)
Pioneer 11
Nation: U.S. (53)
Objective(s): Jupiter flyby, Saturn flyby
Spacecraft: Pioneer-G
Spacecraft Mass: 258.5 kg
Mission Design and Management: NASA ARC
Launch Vehicle: Atlas-Centaur (AC-30 / Atlas 3D no. 5011D / Centaur D-1A)
Launch Date and Time: 6 April 1973 / 02:11 UT
Launch Site: ETR / launch complex 36B
Scientific Instruments:
1) imaging photopolarimeter
2) magnetometer
3) infrared radiometer
4) plasma analyzer
5) ultraviolet photometer
6) charged-particle composition instrument
7) cosmic-ray telescope
8) Geiger tube telescopes
9) asteroid/meteoroid detector
10) Jovian trapped radiation detector
11) meteoroid detector
12) fluxgate magnetometer

Results: Pioneer 11, the sister spacecraft to Pioneer 10, was the first humanmade object to fly past Saturn and also returned the first pictures of the polar regions of Jupiter. After two midcourse corrections (on 11 April 1973 and 7 November 1974), Pioneer 11 penetrated the Jovian bow shock on 25 November 1974. The spacecraft's closest approach to Jupiter occurred at 05:22 UT on 3 December 1974 at a range of 42,760 kilometers from the planet's cloud tops, three times closer than Pioneer 10. It was traveling faster than any humanmade object at the time—171,000 kilometers per hour. Because of its high speed during the encounter, the spacecraft's exposure to radiation was much less than that of its predecessor. Pioneer 11 repeatedly crossed Jupiter's bow shock, indicating that the Jovian magnetosphere changes its boundaries as it is buffeted by the solar wind. Pioneer 11 used Jupiter's massive gravitational field to swing back across the solar system to set itself on a flyby course with Saturn. After its Jupiter encounter, on 16 April 1975, the micrometeoroid detector was turned off because it was issuing spurious commands that were interfering with other instruments. Pioneer 11 detected Saturn's bow shock on 31 August 1979, about 1.5 million kilometers out from the planet, thus providing the first conclusive evidence of the existence of Saturn's magnetic field. The spacecraft crossed the planet's ring plane beyond the outer ring at 14:36 UT on 1 September 1979 and then passed by the planet at 16:31 UT for a close encounter at a range of 20,900 kilometers. It was moving at a relative speed of 114,100 kilometers per hour at the point of closest approach. Among Pioneer 11's many discoveries was a narrow ring outside the A ring named the "F" ring and a new satellite 200 kilometers in diameter. The spacecraft recorded the planet's overall temperature at –180°C and photographs indicated a more featureless atmosphere than that of Jupiter. Analysis of data suggested that the planet was primarily made of liquid hydrogen. After leaving Saturn, Pioneer 11 headed out of the solar system in a direction opposite to that of Pioneer 10—that is, to the center of galaxy in the general direction of Sagittarius. Pioneer 11 crossed the orbit of Neptune on 23 February 1990, thus becoming the fourth spacecraft (after Pioneer 10 and Voyagers 1 and 2) to do so. By 1995, twenty-two years after launch, two instruments were still operational on the vehicle. NASA Ames Research Center finally terminated routine contact with the spacecraft on 30 September 1995. Scientists received a few minutes of good engineering data on 24 November 1995 but lost final contact once Earth permanently moved out of view of the spacecraft's antenna. Like Pioneer 10, Pioneer 11 also carries a plaque with a message for any intelligent beings.

139)
Explorer 49
Nation: U.S. (54)
Objective(s): lunar orbit
Spacecraft: RAE-B
Spacecraft Mass: 330.2 kg
Mission Design and Management: NASA GSFC
Launch Vehicle: Delta 1913 (no. 95 / Thor no. 581)
Launch Date and Time: 10 June 1973 / 14:13:00 UT

Launch Site: ETR / launch complex 17B
Scientific Instruments:
1) galactic studies experiment
2) sporadic low-frequency solar radio bursts experiment
3) sporadic Jovian bursts experiment
4) radio emission from terrestrial magnetosphere experiment
5) cosmic source observation experiment

Results: This was the final U.S. lunar mission for twenty-one years (until Clementine in 1994). After launch on a direct ascent trajectory to the Moon and one midcourse correction on 11 June, Explorer 49 fired its insertion motor at 07:21 UT on 15 June to enter orbit around the Moon. Initial orbital parameters were 1,334 x 1,123 kilometers at 61.3° inclination. On 18 June, the spacecraft jettisoned its main engine and, using its Velocity Control Propulsion System, circularized its orbit. The spacecraft, with a partially deployed radio-antenna array measuring 183 meters from tip to tip, remains the largest spacecraft in physical dimensions to ever enter lunar orbit. Although the antennas did not deploy to full length, the mission goals were not affected. During its mission, Explorer 49 studied low-frequency radio emissions from the solar system (including the Sun and Jupiter) and other galactic and extra-galactic sources. It was placed in lunar orbit to avoid terrestrial radio interference. NASA announced completion of the mission in June 1975. Last contact was in August 1977.

140)
Mars 4
Nation: USSR (86)
Objective(s): Mars orbit
Spacecraft: M-73 (no. 52S)
Spacecraft Mass: 3,440 kg
Mission Design and Management: GSMZ Lavochkin
Launch Vehicle: 8K82K + Blok D (Proton-K no. 261-01)
Launch Date and Time: 21 July 1973 / 19:30:59 UT
Launch Site: NIIP-5 / launch site 81L
Scientific Instruments:
1) atmospheric radio-probing instrument
2) radiotelescope
3) infrared radiometer
4) spectrophotometer
5) narrow-band photometer
6) narrow-band interference-polarization photometer
7) imaging system
8) photometers
9) two polarimeters
10) ultraviolet photometer
11) scattered solar radiation photometer
12) gamma spectrometer
13) magnetometer
14) plasma traps
15) multichannel electrostatic analyzer

Results: Mars 4 was one of four Soviet spacecraft of the 3M (or M-73) series launched in 1973. Soviet planners were eager to preempt the American Viking missions planned for 1976 but were limited by the less advantageous positions of the planets that allowed the Proton boosters to launch limited payloads toward Mars. The Soviets thus separated the standard pair of orbiter-lander payload combinations into two orbiters and two landers. Less than four months prior to launch, ground testing detected a major problem with the 2T312 transistors used on all four vehicles. An analysis showed that the transistors' failure rate began to increase after 1.5 to 2 years of operation—that is, just about when the spacecraft would reach Mars. Despite the roughly 50-percent odds of success, the government decided to proceed with the missions. The first spacecraft, Mars 4, successfully left Earth orbit and headed toward Mars and accomplished a single midcourse correction on 30 July 1973, but soon two of three channels of the onboard computer failed due to the faulty transistors. As a result, the second midcourse correction could not be implemented. With no possibility for Mars orbit insertion, Mars 4 flew by the Red Planet at 15:34 UT on 10 February 1974 at a range of 1,844 kilometers. Ground control was able to command the vehicle to turn on its imaging system at 15:32:41 UT to begin a short photography session of the Martian surface during the flyby. During 6 minutes, cameras performed one regular cycle of imaging that included two panoramas of the surface. The spacecraft eventually entered heliocentric orbit.

141)
Mars 5
Nation: USSR (87)
Objective(s): Mars orbit
Spacecraft: M-73 (no. 53S)
Spacecraft Mass: 3,440 kg
Mission Design and Management: GSMZ Lavochkin
Launch Vehicle: 8K82K + Blok D (Proton-K no. 262-01)
Launch Date and Time: 25 July 1973 / 18:55:48 UT
Launch Site: NIIP-5 / launch site 81P
Scientific Instruments:
1) atmospheric radio-probing instrument
2) radiotelescope
3) infrared radiometer
4) spectrophotometer
5) narrow-band photometer
6) narrow-band interference-polarization photometer
7) imaging system
8) photometers
9) two polarimeters
10) ultraviolet photometer
11) scattered solar radiation photometer
12) gamma spectrometer
13) magnetometer
14) plasma traps
15) multichannel electrostatic analyzer

Results: Mars 5 was the sister Mars orbiter to Mars 4. After two midcourse corrections on 3 August 1973 and 2 February 1974, Mars 5 successfully fired its main engine at 15:44:25 UT to enter orbit around the planet. Initial orbital parameters were 1,760 x 32,586 kilometers at 35°19'17" inclination. Soon after orbital insertion, ground controllers detected the slow depressurization of the main instrument compartment on the orbiter—probably as a result of an impact with a particle during or after orbital insertion. Calculations showed that at the current rate of loss of air, the spacecraft would be operational for approximately three weeks. Scientists drew up a special accelerated science program that included imaging of the surface at 100 meters resolution. Five imaging sessions between 17 and 26 February 1974 produced a total of 180 frames of 43 usable photographs. Additionally, Mars 5 took five panoramas of the surface. The last communication with Mars 5, when the final panorama was transmitted back to Earth, took place on 28 February 1974, after which pressure in the spacecraft decreased to below working levels. Mars 5 photos, some of which were of comparable quality to those of Mariner 9, clearly showed surface features that indicated erosion caused by free-flowing water. Mars 5 was supposed to act as a data relay for the Mars 6 and Mars 7 landers but was obviously unable to do so.

142)
Mars 6
Nation: USSR (88)
Objective(s): Mars flyby and Mars landing
Spacecraft: M-73 (no. 50P)
Spacecraft Mass: 3,260 kg
Mission Design and Management: GSMZ Lavochkin
Launch Vehicle: 8K82K + Blok D (Proton-K no. 281-01)
Launch Date and Time: 5 August 1973 / 17:45:48 UT
Launch Site: NIIP-5 / launch site 81L
Scientific Instruments:
Bus:
1) magnetometer
2) plasma traps
3) cosmic-ray sensors
4) micrometeoroid detectors
5) Zhemo instrument for study of solar proton and electron fluxes

Lander:
1) thermometer
2) barometer
3) accelerometer
4) radio-altimeter
5) mass spectrometer
6) soil analyzer

Results: Mars 6 was one of two landers launched by the Soviet Union during the 1973 launch window. The landers were very similar in design to the Mars 2 and Mars 3 landers dispatched by the Soviets in 1971, except that the spacecraft was now composed of a flyby vehicle (instead of an orbiter) and a lander. Mars 6 completed its first midcourse correction en route to Mars on 13 August 1973. A few days later, there was a major failure in the telemetry system that transmitted scientific and operations data from the spacecraft. Only two channels remained operational, neither of which provided the ground with any data on the status of the flyby vehicle's systems. Amazingly, the flyby spacecraft automatically performed all its functions, and on 12 March 1974, the lander successfully separated from its mother ship at a distance of 48,000 kilometers from Mars. Three hours later, it entered the Martian atmosphere. The parachute system deployed correctly at an altitude of 20 kilometers, and scientific instruments began to record data as the probe descended. Data seemed to indicate that the lander was rocking back and forth under its parachute far more vigorously than expected. Moments before expected landing, the ground lost contact with the probe. The last confirmed data was information on ignition of the soft-landing engines at 08:58:20 UT. The probe landed at 09:11 UT at 23°54' south latitude and 19°25' west longitude. Later investigation never conclusively identified a single cause of loss of contact. Probable reasons included failure of the radio system or landing in a geographically rough area. All data from the Mars 6 lander was transmitted via the Mars 6 flyby bus, which also collected scientific information during its short flyby.

143)
Mars 7
Nation: USSR (89)
Objective(s): Mars flyby and Mars landing
Spacecraft: M-73 (no. 51P)
Spacecraft Mass: 3,260 kg
Mission Design and Management: GSMZ Lavochkin
Launch Vehicle: 8K82K + Blok D (Proton-K no. 281-02)
Launch Date and Time: 9 August 1973 / 17:00:17 UT
Launch Site: NIIP-5 / launch site 81P
Scientific Instruments:
   Bus:
   1) magnetometer
   2) plasma traps
   3) cosmic-ray sensors
   4) micrometeoroid detectors
   5) Zhemo instrument for study of solar proton and electron fluxes
   6) Stereo antenna
   Lander:
   1) thermometer
   2) barometer
   3) accelerometer
   4) radio-altimeter
   5) mass spectrometer
   6) soil analyzer

Results: Mars 7 was the last of the four Soviet spacecraft sent to Mars in the 1973 launch window (although it arrived at Mars prior to Mars 6). On its way to Mars, the spacecraft performed a single midcourse correction on 16 August 1973. En route to Mars, there were failures in the communications systems, and controllers were forced to maintain contact via the only remaining radio communications complex. On 9 March 1974, the flyby spacecraft ordered the lander capsule to separate for its entry into the Martian atmosphere. Although the lander initially refused to "accept" the command to separate, it eventually did accept it. Ultimately, the lander's main retro-rocket engine failed to fire to initiate entry into the Martian atmosphere. As a result, the lander flew by the planet at a range of 1,300 kilometers and eventually entered heliocentric orbit. The flyby probe did, however, manage to collect data during its short encounter with the Red Planet. The failures on both Mars 4 (computer failure) and Mars 7 (retro-rocket ignition failure) were probably due to the faulty transistors, installed in the circuits of the onboard computer, which were detected prior to launch.

144)
Mariner 10
Nation: U.S. (55)
Objective(s): Mercury flyby, Venus flyby
Spacecraft: Mariner-73J / Mariner-J
Spacecraft Mass: 502.9 kg
Mission Design and Management: NASA JPL
Launch Vehicle: Atlas-Centaur (AC-34 / Atlas 3D no. 5014D / Centaur D-1A)
Launch Date and Time: 3 November 1973 / 05:45:00 UT
Launch Site: ETR / launch complex 36B
Scientific Instruments:
   1) imaging system
   2) infrared radiometer
   3) ultraviolet airglow spectrometer
   4) ultraviolet occultation spectrometer
   5) two magnetometers
   6) charged-particle telescope
   7) plasma analyzer

Results: Mariner 10 was the first (and only) spacecraft sent to the planet Mercury, the first mission to explore two planets (Mercury and Venus) during a single mission, the first to use gravity-assist to change its flight path, the first to return to its target after an initial encounter, and the first to use the solar wind as a major means of spacecraft orientation during flight. The primary goal of Mariner 10 was to study the atmosphere (if any), surface, and physical characteristics of Mercury. Soon after leaving Earth orbit, the spacecraft returned photos of both Earth and the Moon as it sped to its first destination, Venus. During the coast, there were numerous technical problems, including malfunctions in the high-gain antenna and the attitude-control system. After midcourse corrections on 13 November 1973 and 21 January 1974, Mariner 10 approached Venus on 5 February 1974 and returned a total of 4,165 photos of the planet and collected important scientific data during its encounter. The closest flyby range was 5,768 kilometers at 17:01 UT. Assisted by Venusian gravity, the spacecraft now headed to the innermost planet, which it reached after another midcourse correction on 16 March 1974. As Mariner 10 approached Mercury, its photos began to show a very Moon-like surface with craters, ridges, and chaotic terrain. The spacecraft's magnetometers revealed a weak magnetic field. Radiometer readings suggested nighttime temperatures of –183°C and maximum daytime temperatures of 187°C. The closest encounter was at 20:47 UT on 29 March 1974 at a range of 703 kilometers. Having looped around the Sun, Mariner 10 flew by Mercury once more on 21 September 1974 at a more distant range of 48,069 kilometers. The spacecraft used solar pressure on its solar panels and high-gain antenna for attitude control. A third and final encounter, the closest to Mercury, took place on 16 March 1975 at a range of 327 kilometers. Contact with the spacecraft was terminated on 24 March 1975.

1974

145)
Luna 22
Nation: USSR (90)
Objective(s): lunar orbit
Spacecraft: Ye-6LS (no. 220)
Spacecraft Mass: 5,700 kg
Mission Design and Management: GSMZ Lavochkin
Launch Vehicle: 8K82K + Blok D (Proton-K no. 282-02)
Launch Date and Time: 29 May 1974 / 08:56:51 UT
Launch Site: NIIP-5 / launch site 81P
Scientific Instruments:
1) imaging system
2) gamma-ray spectrometer
3) radio-altimeter
4) meteoroid detectors
5) magnetometer
6) cosmic-ray detectors
7) radiation detectors

Results: Luna 22 was the second of two "advanced" lunar orbiters (the first being Luna 19) designed to conduct extensive scientific surveys from orbit. Launched about a year after the termination of Lunokhod 2 operations on the lunar surface, Luna 20 performed a single midcourse correction en route the Moon on 30 May before entering lunar orbit on 2 June 1974. Initial orbital parameters were 219 x 222 kilometers at 19°35' inclination. In addition to its primary mission of surface photography, Luna 22 also performed investigations to determine the chemical composition of the lunar surface, recorded meteoroid activity, searched for a lunar magnetic field, measured solar and cosmic radiation flux, and continued studies of the irregular magnetic field. Through various orbital changes, Luna 22 performed without any problems and continued to return photos fifteen months into the mission, although its primary mission had ended by 2 April 1975. The spacecraft's maneuvering propellant was finally depleted on 2 September, and the highly successful mission was formally terminated in early November 1975. Luna 21 remains the final Soviet or Russian lunar orbiter.

146)
Luna 23
Nation: USSR (91)
Objective(s): lunar sample return
Spacecraft: Ye-8-5M (no. 410)
Spacecraft Mass: c. 5,800 kg
Mission Design and Management: GSMZ Lavochkin
Launch Vehicle: 8K82K + Blok D (Proton-K no. 285-01)
Launch Date and Time: 28 October 1974 / 14:30:32 UT
Launch Site: NIIP-5 / launch site 81P
Scientific Instruments:
1) stereo imaging system

2) improved drill for sample collection
3) radiation detector
4) radio-altimeter

Results: Luna 23 was the first modified lunar sample return spacecraft, designed to return a deep core sample of the Moon's surface (hence the change in index from Ye-8-5 to Ye-8-5M). While Luna 16 and 20 had returned samples from a depth of 0.3 meters, the new spacecraft was designed to dig to 2.5 meters. After a mid-course correction on 31 October, Luna 23 entered orbit around the Moon on 2 November 1974. Parameters were 104 x 94 kilometers at 138° inclination. Following several more changes to the orbit, the spacecraft descended to the lunar surface on 6 November and landed in the southernmost portion of Mare Crisium. Landing coordinates were 13° north latitude and 62° east longitude. During landing in "unfavorable" terrain, the lander's drilling device was evidently damaged, preventing fulfillment of the primary mission, the return of lunar soil to Earth. Scientists devised a makeshift plan to conduct a limited science exploration program with the stationary lander. Controllers maintained contact with the spacecraft until 9 November 1974.

147)
Helios 1
Nation: Federal Republic of Germany and U.S. (1)
Objective(s): heliocentric orbit
Spacecraft: Helios-A
Spacecraft Mass: 370 kg
Mission Design and Management: DFVLR and NASA GSFC
Launch Vehicle: Titan IIIE-Centaur (TC-2 / Titan no. 23E-2 / Centaur D-1T)
Launch Date and Time: 10 November 1974 / 07:11:02 UT
Launch Site: ETR / launch complex 41

Scientific Instruments:
1) plasma detector
2) two flux gate magnetometers
3) plasma and radio wave experiment
4) cosmic-ray detectors
5) electron detector
6) zodiacal light photometer
7) micrometeoroid analyzer
8) celestial mechanics experiment

Results: Helios 1 was a joint German-American deep space mission to study the main solar processes and solar-terrestrial relationships. Specifically, the spacecraft's instruments were designed to investigate phenomena such as solar wind, magnetic and electric fields, cosmic rays, and cosmic dust in regions between Earth's orbit and approximately 0.3 AU from the Sun. It was the largest bilateral project to date for NASA, with Germany paying about $180 million of the total $260-million cost. Germany provided the spacecraft and NASA the launch vehicles. After a successful launch, Helios 1 passed within 47 million kilometers of the Sun at a speed of 238,000 kilometers per hour on 15 March 1975, the closest any humanmade object had been to our nearest star. During its mission, the spacecraft spun once every second to evenly distribute the heat coming from the Sun, 90 percent of which was reflected by optical surface mirrors. Its data indicated the presence of fifteen times more micrometeorites close to the Sun than there are near Earth. Helios 1's data was correlated with the Interplanetary Monitoring Platform (IMP) Explorers 47 and 50 in Earth orbit, the Pioneer solar orbiters, and Pioneers 10 and 11 while leaving the solar system. Control was maintained from a German center outside of Munich. Data was received until late 1982.

1975

148)
Venera 9
Nation: USSR (92)
Objective(s): Venus orbit and landing
Spacecraft: 4V-1 (no. 660)
Spacecraft Mass: 4,936 kg
Mission Design and Management: NPO Lavochkin
Launch Vehicle: 8K82K + Blok D (Proton-K no. 286-01)
Launch Date and Time: 8 June 1975 / 02:38:00 UT
Launch Site: NIIP-5 / launch site 81P
Scientific Instruments:

Orbiter:
1) imaging system
2) infrared radiometer
3) ultraviolet imaging spectrometer
4) magnetometer
5) photopolarimeter
6) ion/electron detectors
7) optical spectrometer

Lander:
1) panoramic imaging system
2) thermometer
3) barometer
4) mass spectrometer
5) anemometer
6) photometers
7) nephelometer
8) gamma-ray spectrometer
9) radiation densitometer
10) accelerometers

Results: Venera 9 was the first of a new generation of Soviet space probes ("4V") designed to explore Venus. Launched by the more powerful Proton launch booster, the new spacecraft were nearly five times heavier than their predecessors. Each spacecraft comprised both an orbiter and a lander. The 2,300-kilogram orbiters (at Venus orbit insertion) were designed to spend their missions photographing the planet in ultraviolet light and conducting other scientific investigations. The landers, of a completely new design, employed aerodynamic braking during Venusian atmospheric entry and contained a panoramic photometer to take images of the surface. Without any apparent problems and with two trajectory corrections (on 16 June and 15 October), Venera 9's lander separated from its parent on 20 October 1975, and two days later, it hit Venus's turbulent atmosphere at a speed of 10.7 kilometers per hour. After using a series of parachutes, the lander set down on the planet's day side at 05:13 UT on 22 October. Landing coordinates were 32° north latitude and 291° longitude at the base of a hill near Beta Regio. During its 53 minutes of transmissions from the surface, Venera 9 took and transmitted the very first picture of the Venusian surface from a height of 90 centimeters. These were, in fact, the very first photos received of the surface of another planet. The lander was supposed to transmit a full 360° panorama, but because one of the two covers on the camera failed to release, only a 180° panorama was received. Illumination was akin to that of a cloudy day on Earth. The image clearly showed flat rocks strewn around the lander. The Venera 9 orbiter meanwhile entered a 1,500 x 111,700-kilometer orbit around the planet at 34°10' inclination and acted as a communications relay for the lander. It became the first spacecraft to go into orbit around Venus. The Soviets announced on 22 March 1976 that the orbiter's primary mission, which included using French-made ultraviolet cameras to obtain photographs in 1,200-kilometer swaths, had been fulfilled.

149)
Venera 10
Nation: USSR (93)
Objective(s): Venus orbit and landing
Spacecraft: 4V-1 (no. 661)
Spacecraft Mass: 5,033 kg
Mission Design and Management: NPO Lavochkin
Launch Vehicle: 8K82K + Blok D (Proton-K no. 285-02)
Launch Date and Time: 14 June 1975 / 03:00:31 UT
Launch Site: NIIP-5 / launch site 81P
Scientific Instruments:
  Orbiter:
  1) imaging system
  2) infrared radiometer
  3) ultraviolet imaging spectrometer
  4) magnetometer
  5) photopolarimeter
  6) ion/electron detectors
  7) optical spectrometer
  Lander:
  1) panoramic imaging system
  2) thermometer
  3) barometer
  4) mass spectrometer
  5) anemometer
  6) photometers
  7) nephelometer
  8) gamma-ray spectrometer
  9) radiation densitometer
  10) accelerometers
Results: Venera 10, like its sister craft Venera 9, fully accomplished its mission to soft-land on Venus and return data from the surface. The spacecraft followed an identical mission to that of its twin, arriving only a few days later after two trajectory corrections on 21 June and 18 October 1975. The 660-kilogram lander separated from its parent on 23 October and entered the atmosphere two days later at 01:02 UT. During reentry, the lander survived gravity acceleration as high as 168 g and temperatures as high 12,000°C. It performed its complex landing procedures without fault and landed without incident at 02:17 UT approximately 2,200 kilometers from the Venera 9 landing site. Landing coordinates were 16° north latitude and 291° longitude. Venera 10 transmitted for a record 65 minutes from the surface, although it was designed to last only 30 minutes. A photo of the Venera 10 landing site showed a smoother surface than that of its twin. Like Venera 9, the Venera 10 lander was supposed to take a 360° panorama but covered only 180° of the surroundings because of a stuck lens cover. Meanwhile, the Venera 10 orbiter entered a 1,400 x 114,000-kilometer orbit around Venus inclined at 29°30'. Soviet officials later revealed that the termination of data reception from both Veneras 9 and 10 was not caused by the adverse surface conditions but by the flying out of view of the orbiter relays for both spacecraft. Gamma-ray spectrometer and radiation densitometer data indicated that the surface layer was akin to basalt rather than granite as hinted by the information from Venera 8.

150)
Viking 1
Nation: U.S. (56)
Objective(s): Mars landing and orbit
Spacecraft: Viking-B
Spacecraft Mass: 3,527 kg
Mission Design and Management: NASA LaRC (overall) and NASA JPL (Orbiter)
Launch Vehicle: Titan IIIE-Centaur (TC-4 / Titan no. E-4 / Centaur D-1T)
Launch Date and Time: 20 August 1975 / 21:22:00 UT
Launch Site: ETR / launch complex 41
Scientific Instruments:
  Orbiter:
  1) imaging system
  2) atmospheric water detector
  3) infrared thermal mapper

Lander:
1) imaging system
2) gas chromatograph mass spectrometer
3) seismometer
4) x-ray fluorescence
5) biological laboratory
6) weather instrument package (temperature, pressure, wind velocity)
7) remote sampler arm

Aeroshell:
1) retarding potential analyzer
2) upper-atmosphere mass spectrometer

Results: Viking 1 was the first of a pair of complex deep space probes that were designed to reach Mars and collect evidence on the possibility (or lack thereof) for life on Mars. Each spacecraft was composed of two primary elements, an Orbiter (2,339 kilograms) and a Lander (978 kilograms). The Orbiter design heavily borrowed from the Mariner buses, while the Lander looked superficially like a much larger version of the Surveyor lunar lander. Prior to launch, the batteries of the first spacecraft were discharged, prompting NASA to replace the original first spacecraft with the second, which was launched as Viking 1. After three midcourse corrections (on 27 August 1975 and 10 and 15 June 1976), the spacecraft entered orbit around Mars on 19 June 1976. Initial orbital parameters were 1,500 x 50,300 kilometers. The following day, when the Orbiter began transmitting back photos of the primary landing site in the Chryse region, scientists discovered that the area was rougher than expected. Using the new photos, scientists targeted the lander to a different site on the western slopes of Chryse Planitia. The Lander separated from the Orbiter, and after a complex atmospheric entry sequence, during which the probe took air samples, Viking 1 Lander set down safely at 22.483° north latitude and 47.94° west longitude at 11:53:06 UT on 20 July 1976. Once down, the spacecraft began taking high-quality photographs (in three colors) of its surroundings. Instruments recorded temperatures ranging from –86°C (before dawn) to –33°C (in the afternoon). The seismometer on the Lander was inoperable. On 28 July, the lander's robot arm scooped up the first soil samples and deposited them into a special biological laboratory that included a gas chromatograph mass spectrometer. While some data could be construed as indicating the presence of life, a major test for organic compounds gave negative Results. The Lander continued to return daily (and then eventually weekly) weather reports until loss of contact on 1 February 1983. Further attempts to regain contact proved unsuccessful. The Orbiter was shut down on 7 August 1980, after it ran out of attitude-control propellant.

151)
Viking 2
Nation: U.S. (57)
Objective(s): Mars landing and orbit
Spacecraft: Viking-A
Spacecraft Mass: 3,527 kg
Mission Design and Management: NASA LaRC (overall) and NASA JPL (Orbiter)
Launch Vehicle: Titan IIIE-Centaur (TC-3 / Titan no. E-3 / Centaur no. D-1T)
Launch Date and Time: 9 September 1975 / 18:39:00 UT
Launch Site: ETR / launch complex 41
Scientific Instruments:

Orbiter:
1) imaging system
2) atmospheric water detector
3) infrared thermal mapper

Lander:
1) imaging system
2) gas chromatograph mass spectrometer
3) seismometer
4) x-ray fluorescence
5) biological laboratory
6) weather instrument package (temperature, pressure, wind velocity)
7) remote sampler arm

Aeroshell:
1) retarding potential analyzer
2) upper-atmosphere mass spectrometer

Results: Viking-A was scheduled to be launched before Viking-B but had to be launched second due to a problem with its batteries that had to be repaired. After a successful launch and a midcourse correction on 19 September 1975, Viking 2 entered orbit around Mars on 7 August 1976, nearly a year after launch. As with Viking 1, photographs

The boulder-strewn field of red rocks reaches to the horizon nearly two miles from Viking 2 on Mars's Utopian Plain. Scientists believe that the colors of the Martian surface and sky in this photo represent their true colors. Fine particles of red dust have settled on spacecraft surfaces. The salmon color of the sky is caused by dust particles suspended in the atmosphere. Color calibration charts for the cameras are mounted at three locations on the spacecraft. Note the blue starfield and red stripes of the flag. The circular structure at top is the high-gain antenna, pointed toward Earth. Viking 2 landed on 3 September 1976, some 4,600 miles from its twin, Viking 1, which touched down on 20 July.

of the original landing site indicated rough terrain, prompting mission planners to select a different site at Utopia Planitia near the edge of the polar ice cap where water was located, that is, where there was a better chance of finding signs of life. The Lander separated from the Orbiter without incident on 3 September 1976 and, after atmospheric entry, landed safely at 22:37:50 UT about 6,460 kilometers from the Viking 1 landing site. Touchdown coordinates were 47.968° north latitude and 225.71° west longitude Photographs of the area showed a rockier, flatter site than that of Viking 1. The Lander was in fact tilted 8.5° to the west. The biology experiments with scooped-up soil produced similar results to that of its twin—inconclusive on the question of whether life exists or ever has existed on the surface of Mars. Scientists believed that Martian soil contained reactants created by ultraviolet bombardment of the soil that could produce characteristics of organisms living in Earth soil. The Orbiter continued its successful imaging mission, approaching as close as 28 kilometers to the Martian moon Deimos in May 1977. A series of leaks prompted the termination of Orbiter 2 operations on 24 July 1978, while Lander 2 continued to transmit data until 12 April 1980. In total, the two Orbiters returned 51,539 images of Mars at 300 meters resolution, that is, about 97 percent of the surface. The Landers returned 4,500 photos of the two landing sites.

152)
no name / [Luna]
Nation: USSR (94)

Objective(s): lunar sample return
Spacecraft: Ye-8-5M (no. 412)
Spacecraft Mass: c. 5,800 kg
Mission Design and Management: NPO Lavochkin
Launch Vehicle: 8K82K + Blok D (Proton-K no. 287-02)
Launch Date and Time: 16 October 1975 / 04:04:56 UT
Launch Site: NIIP-5 / launch site 81L

Scientific Instruments:
1) stereo imaging system
2) improved drill for sample collection
3) radiation detector
4) radio-altimeter

Results: This was the second attempt by the Soviet Union to send an "advanced" lunar sample return craft to the Moon, equipped with the capability to dig for a deeper core. The first spacecraft (Luna 23) was damaged during landing on the Moon in October 1974. On this mission, the first three stages of the Proton-K launch vehicle worked without fault, but the Blok D stage, during its first burn for insertion into Earth orbit, failed. The expensive payload burned up in Earth's atmosphere without ever reaching Earth orbit.

1976

153)
Helios 2
Nation: Federal Republic of Germany and U.S. (2)
Objective(s): solar orbit
Spacecraft: Helios-B
Spacecraft Mass: 370 kg
Mission Design and Management: DFVLR and NASA GSFC
Launch Vehicle: Titan IIIE-Centaur (TC-5 / Titan no. E-5 / Centaur D-1T)
Launch Date and Time: 15 January 1976 / 05:34:00 UT
Launch Site: ETR / launch complex 41
Scientific Instruments:
  1) plasma detector
  2) two flux gate magnetometers
  3) search-coil magnetometer
  4) plasma and radio wave experiment
  5) cosmic-ray detectors
  6) electron detectors
  7) zodiacal light photometer
  8) micrometeoroid analyzer
  9) celestial mechanics experiment
  10) Faraday rotation experiment
  11) occultation experiment

Results: Helios 2 was the second spacecraft launched to investigate solar processes as part of a cooperative project between the Federal Republic of Germany and the United States in which the former provided the spacecraft and the latter the launch vehicle. Like its twin, the spacecraft was put into heliocentric orbit. In contrast to Helios 1, however, Helios 2 flew three million kilometers closer to the Sun, achieving perihelion on 17 April 1976 at a distance of 0.29 AU (or 43.432 million kilometers). As a result, the spacecraft was exposed to 10 percent more heat than was its predecessor. The spacecraft provided important information on solar plasma, the solar wind, cosmic rays, and cosmic dust, and also performed magnetic field and electrical field experiments.

154)
Luna 24
Nation: USSR (95)
Objective(s): lunar sample return
Spacecraft: Ye-8-5M (no. 413)
Spacecraft Mass: c. 5,800 kg
Mission Design and Management: NPO Lavochkin
Launch Vehicle: 8K82K + Blok DM (Proton-K no. 288-02)
Launch Date and Time: 9 August 1976 / 15:04:12 UT
Launch Site: NIIP-5 / launch site 81L
Scientific Instruments:
  1) stereo imaging system
  2) improved drill for sample collection
  3) radiation detector
  4) radio-altimeter

Results: Luna 24 was the third attempt to recover a sample from the unexplored Mare

Crisium (after Luna 23 and a launch failure in October 1975), the location of a large lunar mascon. After a trajectory correction on 11 August 1976, Luna 24 entered orbit around the Moon three days later. Initial orbital parameters were 115 x 115 kilometers at 120° inclination. After further changes to its orbit, Luna 24 set down safely on the lunar surface at 06:36 UT on 18 August 1976 at 12°45' north latitude and 62°12' east longitude, not far from where Luna 23 had landed. After appropriate commands from ground control, the Lander deployed its sample arm and pushed its drilling head about 2 meters into the nearby soil. The sample was safely stowed in the small return capsule, and after nearly a day on the Moon, Luna 24 lifted off successfully from the Moon at 05:25 UT on 19 August 1976. After an uneventful return trip, Luna 24's capsule entered Earth's atmosphere and parachuted down to Earth safely at 05:55 UT on 23 August 1976, about 200 kilometers southeast of Surgut in western Siberia. Study of the recovered 170.1 grams of soil indicated a laminated type structure, as if laid down in successive deposits. Tiny portions of the sample were shared with NASA in December 1976. Luna 24 remains the last Soviet or Russian probe to the Moon. An American spacecraft (Clementine) returned to the Moon over fourteen years later.

1977

155)
Voyager 2
Nation: U.S. (58)
Objective(s): Jupiter flyby, Saturn flyby, Uranus flyby, Neptune flyby
Spacecraft: Voyager-2
Spacecraft Mass: 2,080 kg (822 kg mission module)
Mission Design and Management: NASA JPL
Launch Vehicle: Titan IIIE-Centaur (TC-7 / Titan no. 23E-7 / Centaur D-1T)
Launch Date and Time: 20 August 1977 / 14:29:44 UT
Launch Site: ETR / launch complex 41
Scientific Instruments:
1) imaging system
2) ultraviolet spectrometer
3) infrared spectrometer
4) planetary radio astronomy experiment
5) photopolarimeter
6) magnetometers
7) plasma particles experiment
8) low-energy charged-particles experiment
9) plasma waves experiment
10) cosmic-ray telescope

Results: Although launched after Voyager 1, Voyager 2, the second in a pair of spacecraft designed to explore the outer planets, exited the Asteroid Belt after its twin and then followed it to Jupiter and Saturn. Its primary radio transmitter failed on 5 April 1978, and the spacecraft has used its backup ever since. Voyager 2 began transmitting images of Jupiter on 24 April 1979 for time-lapse movies of atmospheric circulation. During its encounter, it relayed back spectacular photos of the entire Jovian system, including its moons Amalthea, Io, Callisto, Ganymede, and Europa, all of which had already been surveyed by Voyager 1. Voyager 2's closest encounter with Jupiter was at 22:29 UT on 9 July 1979 at a range of 645,000 kilometers. It transmitted new data on the planet's clouds and its newly discovered four moons and ring system.

Following a midcourse correction 2 hours after its closest approach to Jupiter, Voyager 2 sped to Saturn. Its encounter with the sixth planet began on 22 August 1981, two years after leaving the Jovian system, with imaging of the moon Iapetus. Once again, Voyager 2 repeated the photographic mission of its predecessor, although it actually flew 23,000 kilometers closer to Saturn. The closest encounter was at 01:21 UT on 26 August 1981 at a range of 101,000 kilometers. The spacecraft provided more detailed images of the ring spokes and kinks, as well as the F-ring and its shepherding moons. Voyager 2's data suggested that Saturn's A-ring was perhaps only 300 meters thick. It also photographed the Saturn moons Hyperion, Enceladus, Tethys, and Phoebe.

The little spacecraft that could, Voyager, which flew on a "grand tour" of the outer planets during the latter 1970s and early 1980s and is now departing the solar system.

This Voyager 2 view, focusing on Saturn's C-ring (and to a lesser extent, the B-ring at top and left) was compiled from three separate images taken through ultraviolet, clear, and green filters. On 23 August 1981, when it acquired these frames, Voyager 2 was 2.7 million kilometers from the planet. In general, C-ring material is very bland and gray, the color of dirty ice. Color differences between this ring and the B-ring indicate differing surface compositions for the material composing these complex structures. More than sixty bright and dark ringlets are evident here; the small, bland squares are caused by the removal of reseau (reference) marks during processing.

Although Voyager 2 had fulfilled its primary mission goals with the two planetary encounters, mission planners directed the veteran spacecraft to Uranus on a 4.5-year journey, during which it covered 33 AU. The geometry of the Uranus encounter was defined by the possibility of a future encounter with Neptune: Voyager 2 had only 5.5 hours of close study during its flyby, the first of any human-made spacecraft past the planet Uranus. Long-range observations of the planet began on 4 November 1985, when signals took approximately 2.5 hours to reach Earth. Light conditions were 400 times less than terrestrial conditions. The closest approach to Uranus took place at 17:59 UT on 24 January 1986 at a range of 71,000 kilometers. During its flyby, Voyager 2 discovered ten new moons, two new rings in addition to the "older" nine, and a magnetic field tilted at 55° off-axis and off-center. The spacecraft found that wind speeds in the atmosphere of Uranus were as high as 724 kilometers per hour and found evidence of a boiling ocean of water some 800 kilometers below the top cloud surface. Voyager 2 also returned spectacular photos of Miranda, Oberon, Ariel, Umbriel, and Titania, five larger moons of Uranus.

Following the Uranus Encounter, the spacecraft performed a single midcourse correction on 14 February 1986 to set it on a precise course to Neptune. Voyager 2's encounter with Neptune capped a 7-billion-kilometer journey when on 25 August 1989, at 03:56 UT, it flew 4,500 kilometers over the cloud tops of the giant planet, the closest of its four flybys. It was the first humanmade object to fly by the planet. Its ten instruments were still in working order at the time. During the encounter, the spacecraft discovered five new moons and four new rings. The planet itself was found to be more active than previously believed, with 1,100-kilometer winds. Hydrogen was found to be the most common atmospheric element, although the abundant methane gives the planet its blue appearance. Voyager data on Triton, Neptune's largest moon, revealed the coldest known planetary body in the solar system and a nitrogen ice "volcano" on its surface. Once past the Neptune system, Voyager 2 followed a course below the elliptic plane and out of the solar system. Approximately 56 million kilometers past the encounter, Voyager 2 instruments were put in low-power mode to conserve energy. After the Neptune encounter, NASA formally renamed the entire project the Voyager Interstellar Mission (VIM). In November 1998, twenty-one years after launch, nonessential instruments were permanently turned off, leaving seven instruments still operating. By 1 June 2001, the spacecraft was 9.6 billion kilometers from Earth and traveling at 15.75 kilometers per second (relative to the Sun). NASA's JPL continues to receive regular ultraviolet and fields/particles data. For example, on 12 January 2001, an immense shock wave that had blasted out of the outer heliosphere on 14 July 2000 finally reached Voyager 2. During the six-month journey, the shock wave had ploughed through the solar wind, sweeping up and accelerating charged particles. The spacecraft provided important information on high-energy shock-energized ions. Data from the operating instruments could be received as late as 2020, when power levels are expected to reduce to the minimum 230 watts.

156)
Voyager 1
Nation: U.S. (57)
Objective(s): Jupiter flyby, Saturn flyby
Spacecraft: Voyager-1
Spacecraft Mass: 2,080 kg (822 kg mission module)
Mission Design and Management: NASA JPL
Launch Vehicle: Titan IIIE-Centaur (TC-6 / Titan no. 23E-6 / Centaur D-1T)
Launch Date and Time: 5 September 1977 / 12:56:01 UT
Launch Site: ETR / launch complex 41
Scientific Instruments:
1) imaging system
2) ultraviolet spectrometer
3) infrared spectrometer
4) planetary radio astronomy experiment
5) photopolarimeter
6) magnetometers
7) plasma particles experiment
8) low-energy charged-particles experiment
9) plasma waves experiment
10) cosmic-ray telescope

Results: The two-spacecraft Voyager missions were designed to replace original plans for a "Grand Tour" of the planets that would have used four complex spacecraft to explore the five outer planets during the late 1970s. NASA canceled the plan in 1972 and instead proposed to send two spacecraft to Jupiter and Saturn in 1977. The two spacecraft were designed to explore the two gas giants in more detail than the two Pioneers (Pioneers 10 and 11) that preceded them. Each of the two spacecraft was equipped with slow-scan color TV to take live television images from the planets, and each also carried an extensive suite of instruments to record magnetic, atmospheric, lunar, and other data about the planets. The original design of

This picture of Neptune was produced from the last whole planet images taken through the green and orange filters on the Voyager 2 narrow-angle camera. The images were taken at a range of 7.1 million kilometers from the planet, 4 days and 20 hours before closest approach. The picture shows the Great Dark Spot and its companion bright smudge; on the west limb, the fast-moving bright feature called Scooter and the little dark spot are visible. These clouds were seen to persist for as long as Voyager's cameras could resolve them. North of these, a bright cloud band similar to the south polar streak may be seen. Years later, when the Hubble telescope was focused on the planet, these atmospheric features had changed, indicating that Neptune's atmosphere is dynamic.

the spacecraft was based on that of the older Mariners. Power was provided by three plutonium oxide radioisotope thermoelectric generators (RTGs) mounted at the end of a boom.

Voyager 1 was launched after Voyager 2, but because of a faster route, it exited the asteroid belt earlier than its twin. It began its Jovian imaging mission in April 1978 at a range of 265 million kilometers from the planet; images sent back by January the following year indicated that Jupiter's atmosphere was more turbulent than during the Pioneer flybys in 1973 and 1974. On 10 February 1979, the spacecraft crossed into the Jovian moon system, and in early March, it had already discovered a thin (less than 30 kilometers thick) ring circling Jupiter. Flying past Amalthea, Io, Europa, Ganymede, and Callisto (in that order) on 5 March, Voyager 1 returned spectacular photos of their terrain, opening up a completely new world for planetary scientists. The most interesting find was on Io, where images showed a bizarre yellow, orange, and brown world with at least eight active volcanoes spewing material into space, making it one of the most (if not the most) geologically active planetary bodies in the solar system. The spacecraft also discovered two new moons, Thebe and Metis. Voyager 1's closest encounter with Jupiter was at 12:05 UT on 5 March 1979 at a range of 280,000 kilometers.

Following the Jupiter encounter, Voyager 1 completed a single course correction on 9 April 1979 in preparation for its rendezvous with Saturn. A second correction on 10 October 1979 ensured that the spacecraft would not hit Saturn's moon Titan. Its flyby of the Saturn system in November 1979 was as spectacular as its previous encounter. Voyager 1 found five new moons and a ring system consisting of thousands of bands, discovered a new ring (the "G-ring"), and found "shepherding" satellites on either side of the F-ring satellites that keep the rings well defined. During its flyby, the spacecraft photographed Saturn's moons Titan, Mimas, Enceladus, Tethys, Dione, and Rhea. Based on incoming data, all the moons appeared to be largely composed of water ice. Perhaps the most interesting target was Titan, which Voyager 1 passed at 05:41 UT on 12 November at a range of 4,000 kilometers. Images showed a thick atmosphere that completely hid the surface.

The spacecraft found that the Moon's atmosphere was composed of 90 percent nitrogen. Pressure and temperature at the surface was 1.6 atmospheres and –180° C, respectively. Voyager 1's closest approach to Saturn was at 23:45 UT on 12 November 1980 at a range of 124,000 kilometers.

Following the encounter with Saturn, Voyager 1 headed on a trajectory escaping the solar system at a speed of about 3.5 AU per year, 35° out of the ecliptic plane to the north, in the general direction of the Sun's motion relative to nearby stars. Because of the specific requirements for the Titan flyby, the spacecraft was not directed to Uranus and Neptune. The official goal of the Voyager Interstellar Mission (VIM), as the dual Voyager flights have been called since 1989, is to extend NASA's exploration of the solar system beyond the neighborhood of the outer planets to the outer limits of the Sun's sphere of influence, and possibly beyond. Specific goals include collecting data on the heliopause boundary, the outer limits of the Sun's magnetic field, and the outward flow of the solar wind. As with Voyager 2, there are seven instruments that remain operational on Voyager 1 and continue to transmit data regularly back to Earth. On 17 February 1998, Voyager 1 became the most distant human-made object in existence when it surpassed Pioneer 10's range from Earth. By 1 June 2001, Voyager 1 was 12.033 billion kilometers from Earth and traveling at 17.25 kilometers per second relative to the Sun.

1978

157)
Pioneer Venus 1
Nation: U.S. (60)
Objective(s): Venus orbit
Spacecraft: Pioneer Venus Orbiter
Spacecraft Mass: 582 kg
Mission Design and Management: NASA ARC
Launch Vehicle: Atlas-Centaur (AC-50 / Atlas no. 5030D)
Launch Date and Time: May 20 1978 / 13:13:00 UT
Launch Site: ETR / launch complex 36A
Scientific Instruments:
1) charged-particle retarding potential analyzer
2) charged-particle mass spectrometer
3) thermal electron temperature Langmuir probe
4) neutral-particle mass spectrometer
5) cloud photopolarimeter/imaging system
6) temperature sounding infrared radiometer
7) magnetic field fluxgate magnetometer
8) solar wind plasma analyzer
9) surface radar mapper
10) electric field experiment
11) transient gamma-ray burst experiment
12) gas and plasma environment experiment
13) radio occultation experiment
14) atmospheric and solar corona turbulence experiment
15) drag measurements experiment
16) internal density distribution experiment
17) celestial mechanics experiment

Results: The Pioneer Venus project comprised two spacecraft to explore the atmosphere and surface of Venus. Both spacecraft used a basic cylindrical bus. Pioneer Venus 1, the orbiter, was designed to spend an extended period in orbit around Venus mapping the surface using a radar package. The orbiter entered an elliptical orbit around Venus on 4 December 1978 after a 6.5-month journey. The initial orbital period was 23.4 hours, which was altered within two orbits to the desired 24 hours—a maneuver that would allow the orbit's high and low points (about 150 kilometers) to occur at the same time each Earth day. Data from the radar mapper allowed scientists to produce a topographical map of most of the Venusian surface between 73° north and 63° south latitude at a resolution of 75 kilometers. The data indicated that Venus was much smoother and more spherical than Earth. The orbiter identified the highest point on Venus as Maxwell Montes, which rises 10.8 kilometers above the mean surface. Infrared observations revealed a clearing in the planet's atmosphere over the north pole. In addition, ultraviolet light photos showed dark markings that covered the clouds in the visible hemisphere. Cameras also detected almost continuous lightning activity in the atmosphere. The spacecraft confirmed that Venus has little, if any, magnetic field. Although the mapping radar was switched off on 19 March 1981, it was reactivated again in 1991, thirteen years after launch, to explore the previously inaccessible southern portions of the planet. In May 1992, Pioneer Venus 1 began the final phase of its mission, maintaining its periapsis between 150 and 250 kilometers until propellant depletion. The last transmission was received at 19:22 UT on 8 October 1992, as its decaying orbit no longer permitted communications. The spacecraft burned in the atmosphere soon after, ending a successful fourteen-year mission that was planned to last only eight months.

158)
Pioneer Venus 2
Nation: U.S. (61)
Objective(s): Venus impact
Spacecraft: Pioneer Venus Multiprobe
Spacecraft Mass: 904 kg
Mission Design and Management: NASA ARC
Launch Vehicle: Atlas-Centaur (AC-51 / Atlas no. 5031D)
Launch Date and Time: 8 August 1978 / 07:33 UT
Launch Site: ETR / launch complex 36A
Scientific Instruments:
  Bus:
  1) neutral mass spectrometer
  2) ion mass spectrometer
  3) differential long baseline interferometry experiment
  4) atmospheric propagation experiment
  5) atmospheric turbulence experiment
  Large probe:
  1) neutral mass spectrometer
  2) solar flux radiometer
  3) gas chromatograph
  4) infrared radiometer
  5) cloud particle size spectrometer
  6) atmospheric structure experiment
  Small probes (each):
  1) atmospheric structure experiment
  2) cloud particles experiment
  3) net flux radiometer

Results: Pioneer Venus 2, the twin to Pioneer Venus 1, comprised a main bus, a large probe (316.5 kilograms), and three identical small probes, all of which were designed to collect data during independent atmospheric entry into Venus. Each probe was shaped like a cone and not designed to survive past surface impact. After a course correction on 16 August 1978, Pioneer Venus 2 released the 1.5-meter-diameter large probe on 16 November 1978, at about 11.1 million kilometers from the planet. Four days later, the bus released the three small probes while 9.3 million kilometers from Venus. All five components reached the Venusian atmosphere on 9 December 1978, with the large probe entering first. Using a combination of air drag and a parachute, the large probe descended through the atmosphere until it impacted on the Venusian surface at 4.4° north latitude and 304.0° longitude at a speed of 32 kilometers per hour. Transmissions ceased at impact as expected. The three 76-centimeter-diameter small probes arrived in the atmosphere within minutes of the bigger one and descended rapidly through the atmosphere without the benefit of parachutes. Amazingly, two of three probes survived the hard impact. The so-called Day Probe transmitted data from the surface for 67.5 minutes before succumbing to the high temperatures and power depletion. All three small probes suffered instrument failures, but none significant enough to jeopardize their main missions. Their landing coordinates were 59.3° north latitude and 4.8° longitude (North Probe); 31.3° south latitude and 317.0° longitude (Day Probe); and 28.7° south latitude and 56.7° longitude (Night Probe). The main bus, meanwhile, burned up in the atmosphere at an altitude of 120 kilometers—about 1.5 hours after the other probes—and provided key data on higher regions. Data from the probes indicated that between 10 and 50 kilometers, there is almost no convection in the atmosphere. Below a haze layer at 30 kilometers, the atmosphere appears to be relatively clear.

159)
ISEE-3
Nation: U.S. (62)
Objective(s): Earth-Sun L1 Libration Point, Comet Giacobini-Zinner flyby, lunar flybys

Spacecraft: ISEE-C
Spacecraft Mass: 479 kg
Mission Design and Management: NASA GSFC
Launch Vehicle: Delta 2914 (no. 144 / Thor no. 633)
Launch Date and Time: 12 August 1978 / 15:12 UT
Launch Site: ETR / launch complex 17B
Scientific Instruments:
1) solar wind plasma experiment
2) magnetometer
3) low-energy cosmic-ray experiment
4) medium-energy cosmic-ray experiment
5) high-energy cosmic-ray experiment
6) plasma waves experiment
7) protons experiment
8) cosmic-ray electrons experiment
9) x-rays and electrons experiment
10) radio mapping experiment
11) plasma composition experiment
12) high-energy cosmic-rays experiment
13) ground-based solar studies experiment

Results: ISEE-3 was the third of three International Sun-Earth Explorers (ISEE) designed and operated by NASA in cooperation with the European Space Agency. NASA built the first and third spacecraft, while ESA built the second. The three spacecraft were to simultaneously investigate a wide range of phenomena in interplanetary space. After launch, on 20 November 1978, ISEE-3 was successfully placed at Libration Point 1 (L1) on the Sunward side of Earth, a point 1.5 million kilometers from Earth, where the gravitational forces of Earth and the Sun are exactly counterbalanced. ISEE 3 became not only the first spacecraft to be put into orbit around a Libration Point, but also the first spacecraft to monitor the solar wind approaching Earth. ISEE-3 completed its primary mission in 1981, but Goddard Space Flight Center scientists proposed sending the spacecraft first through Earth's magnetic tail and second into position to intercept a comet. By 10 June 1982, the spacecraft began to use its thrusters to move into the geotail. ISEE-3 completed the first deep survey of Earth's tail and detected a huge plasmoid of electrified gas that was ejected from Earth's magnetosphere. Subsequently, after a series of five complex flybys of the Moon (the last on 22 December 1983 at a range of only 120 kilometers), ISEE-3 was sent on a trajectory to encounter the Comet Giacobini-Zinner. At this point, the spacecraft was renamed the International Cometary Explorer (ICE). On 11 September 1985 at 11:02 UT, ICE passed within 7,862 kilometers of the comet's core, becoming the first spacecraft to fly past a comet. The spacecraft returned excellent data on the comet's tail, confirming theories that comets are essentially "dirty snowballs" of ice, with surface material sleeting off during motion. ICE also flew to 40.2 million kilometers of the sunward side of Comet Halley on 28 March 1986 and provided upstream solar wind data. ICE remains in heliocentric orbit at about 1 AU; it continued to return information until NASA authorized termination of operations on 5 May 1997. On 10 August 2014, ICE will return to the vicinity of Earth, where it could possibly be captured for analysis of its exterior for dust impacts. If it is recovered, NASA will donate the spacecraft to the Smithsonian Institution for display.

160)
Venera 11
Nation: USSR (96)
Objective(s): Venus flyby and landing
Spacecraft: 4V-1 (no. 360)
Spacecraft Mass: 4,450 kg
Mission Design and Management: NPO Lavochkin
Launch Vehicle: 8K82K + Blok DM (Proton-K no. 296-01 / Blok DM no. 3L)
Launch Date and Time: 9 September 1978 / 03:25:39 UT
Launch Site: NIIP-5 / launch site 81L
Scientific Instruments:
Flyby bus:
1) plasma spectrometer
2) Konus gamma-ray detector
3) Sneg-2MZ gamma- and x-ray burst detector
4) ultraviolet spectrometer
5) magnetometer
6) solar wind detectors
7) cosmic-ray detectors
Lander:
1) imaging system
2) Sigma gas chromatograph
3) mass spectrometer
4) gamma-ray spectrometer

5) Groza lightning detector
6) temperature and pressure sensors
7) nephelometer
8) anemometer
9) optical spectrophotometer
10) remote soil collector
11) x-ray fluorescence cloud aerosol analyzer
12) Arakhis x-ray fluorescence spectrometer and drill

Results: Venera 11 was one of two identical probes (the other being Venera 12) that followed up on the highly successful Soviet missions to Venus in 1975. Veneras 11 and 12 differed from their predecessors principally in the fact each carried a flyby bus/lander combination instead of the previous orbiter/lander combination. Engineers reverted to the flyby combination partly because of the weight limitations of the 1978 launch window, but also because flyby probes afforded better transmission time for landers. Several of the scientific instruments were also modified and new ones added. Venera 11 arrived at Venus after two course corrections on 16 September and 17 December 1978. On 23 December 1978, the lander separated from the flyby probe and entered the Venusian atmosphere two days later. The lander probe safely landed on Venus at 03:24 UT on 15 December 1978 and then relayed 95 minutes of data from the surface. Landing coordinates were 14° south latitude and 299° longitude. The point of cutoff was determined by the range of visibility of the flyby probe. A soil-drilling instrument collected soil for chemical and physical analysis, but soil analysis was unsuccessful because the soil was not properly deposited to an examination container for analysis (probably due to leaking air that disturbed the soil). The lander also failed to take color panoramas of the Venusian surface due to a failure of the lens covers of the camera system to open. While extensive atmospheric data was later released, the Soviets have published relatively little data from surface measurements. The flyby probe entered heliocentric orbit after flying past the planet at a range of 35,000 kilometers.

161)
Venera 12

Nation: USSR (97)
Objective(s): Venus flyby and landing
Spacecraft: 4V-1 (no. 361)
Spacecraft Mass: 4,461 kg
Mission Design and Management: NPO Lavochkin
Launch Vehicle: 8K82K + Blok DM (Proton-K no. 296-02 / Blok DM no. 4L)
Launch Date and Time: 14 September 1978 / 02:25:13 UT
Launch Site: NIIP-5 / launch site 81P
Scientific Instruments:
  Flyby bus:
  1) plasma spectrometer
  2) Konus gamma-ray detector
  3) Sneg-2MZ gamma- and x-ray burst detector
  4) ultraviolet spectrometer
  5) magnetometer
  6) solar wind detectors
  7) cosmic-ray detectors
  Lander:
  1) imaging system
  2) Sigma gas chromatograph
  3) mass spectrometer
  4) gamma-ray spectrometer
  5) Groza lightning detector
  6) temperature and pressure sensors
  7) nephelometer
  8) anemometer
  9) optical spectrophotometer
  10) remote soil collector
  11) x-ray fluorescence cloud aerosol analyzer
  12) Arakhis x-ray fluorescence spectrometer and drill

Results: Venera 12 was the identical sister craft to Venera 11. Launched successfully towards Venus, the spacecraft performed two midcourse corrections on 21 September and 14 December 1978. As with its twin, two days prior to the planetary encounter, the flyby probe released its lander. On 21 December, the lander entered the Venusian atmosphere at a velocity of 11.2 kilometers per second and performed a descent profile almost identical to that of the earlier Veneras 9 and 10 in 1975. The lander safely touched down at 03:30 UT on 21 December 1978 after a descent lasting about an hour. Landing coordinates were 7° south latitude and 294° longitude, about 800 kilometers from its twin. From the ground, the probe relayed data for a record 110 minutes, although like Venera 11, the spacecraft suffered two major failures: its soil sample delivery instrument failed to deposit the soil appropriately for scientific analysis; and lens covers on the imaging system failed to release, effectively rendering the color imaging system useless. The flyby probe passed by the planet at a range of 35,000 kilometers after performing its data transmission mission and then entered heliocentric orbit.

1981

162)
Venera 13
Nation: USSR (98)
Objective(s): Venus flyby and landing
Spacecraft: 4V-1M (no. 760)
Spacecraft Mass: 4,363 kg
Mission Design and Management: NPO Lavochkin
Launch Vehicle: 8K82K + Blok DM (Proton-K no. 311-01 / Blok DM no. 5L)
Launch Date and Time: 30 October 1981 / 06:04 UT
Launch Site: NIIP-5 / launch site 200P
Scientific Instruments:
Flyby bus:
1) magnetometer
2) cosmic-ray detector
3) solar wind detectors
4) Signe-2MS3 gamma-ray burst detector

Lander:
1) x-ray fluorescence spectrometer and drill
2) x-ray fluorescence spectrometer for aerosols
3) imaging system
4) pressure and temperature sensors
5) mass spectrometer
6) Groza-2 lightning detector
7) gas chromatograph
8) nephelometer
9) spectrophotometer
10) accelerometer
11) humidity sensor
12) prop soil mechanical/electrical probe
13) seismometer

Results: Venera 13 was one of the third pair of heavy Venus flyby/lander probes launched towards Venus by the Soviet Union in the 1970s (after Venera 9/10 and Venera 11/12). The Soviets picked the landing site for Venera 13 based on information passed on by NASA from the Pioneer Venus Orbiter vehicle. The Venera 13/14 combination had an improved set of instruments (such as the spectrophotometer, the gas chromatograph, and the mass spectrometer), including a redesigned soil sampler. After two midcourse corrections on 10 November 1981 and 21 February 1982, the Venera 13 lander separated from its parent on 27 February 1982. The capsule entered the Venusian atmosphere and began relaying atmospheric data back to the flyby probe, which continued to fly past the planet after a 36,000-kilometer-range encounter. After a roughly 1-hour-long descent, the lander set down on the Venusian surface at 03:57:21 UT on 1 March 1982. Landing coordinates were 7.5° south latitude and 303° longitude. The probe continued to transmit for another additional 127 minutes, far beyond the planned lifetime of 32 minutes. The probe found temperature and pressure to be 465°C and 89.5

atmospheres, respectively. Venera 13 repeated the attempts at color surface photography (using red, green, and blue filters) that failed on Veneras 11 and 12 and succeeded by relaying to Earth the first color photographs of the surface of Venus. Venera 13 returned eight successive panoramas showing a field of orange-brown angular rocks and loose soil. Successful soil analysis (which failed on Veneras 11 and 12) showed soil similar to terrestrial leucitic basalt with a high potassium content. The flyby module entered heliocentric orbit. Its engine was fired on 10 June 1982 as part of a test for the anticipated Halley's Comet flyby.

163)
Venera 14
Nation: USSR (99)
Objective(s): Venus flyby and landing
Spacecraft: 4V-1M (no. 761)
Spacecraft Mass: 4,363.5 kg
Mission Design and Management: NPO Lavochkin
Launch Vehicle: 8K82K + Blok DM (Proton-K no. 311-02 / Blok DM no. 6L)
Launch Date and Time: 4 November 1981 / 05:31 UT
Launch Site: NIIP-5 / launch site 200L
Scientific Instruments:
  Flyby bus:
  1) magnetometer
  2) cosmic-ray detector
  3) solar wind detectors
  4) Signe-2MS3 gamma-ray burst detector
  Lander:
  1) x-ray fluorescence spectrometer and drill
  2) x-ray fluorescence spectrometer for aerosols
  3) imaging system
  4) pressure and temperature sensors
  5) mass spectrometer
  6) Groza-2 lightning detector
  7) gas chromatograph
  8) nephelometer
  9) spectrophotometer
  10) accelerometer
  11) humidity sensor
  12) prop soil mechanical/electrical probe
  13) seismometer

Results: Venera 14 was identical to its twin, Venera 13. The spacecraft carried out three midcourse corrections on the way to Venus: on 14 November 1981, 23 November 1981, and 25 February 1982. Russian sources indicate that one of the corrections was incorrect (probably the first) and could have jeopardized the mission. The lander probe separated from its flyby parent on 3 March 1982 before the entry cycle began. The probe's main parachute opened at an altitude of 62 to 63 kilometers, thus activating the atmospheric instruments. The parachute was released at an altitude of 47 kilometers, and the 760-kilogram lander fell to the surface using only the atmosphere as a retarding medium. The probe made safe contact with the Venusian surface at 07:00:10 UT on 3 March 1982 and continued with 57 minutes of transmissions. Landing coordinates were 13.25° south latitude and 310° longitude, about 1,000 kilometers from the Venera 13 landing site. As with its twin, Venera 14 returned color photographs of its surroundings and examined a soil sample (about 1 cubic centimeter taken from a 30-millimeter-deep sample). Soil was deposited in a chamber sealed off from the outside environment and was then progressively transferred through a series of chambers by blowing air until the sample was deposited in its final chamber with a temperature of only 30°C. Here it was examined by the x-ray fluorescence spectrometer. Temperature and pressure outside were considerably higher than at the Venera 13 site: 470°C and 93.5 atmospheres, respectively. The flyby probe, meanwhile, passed Venus at a range of 36,000 kilometers and entered heliocentric orbit, continuing to provide data on solar x-ray flares. It performed one trajectory change on 14 November 1982.

1983

164)
Venera 15
Nation: USSR (100)
Objective(s): Venus orbit
Spacecraft: 4V-2 (no. 860)
Spacecraft Mass: 5,250 kg
Mission Design and Management: NPO Lavochkin
Launch Vehicle: 8K82K + Blok DM (Proton-K no. 321-01 / Blok DM no. 8L)
Launch Date and Time: 2 June 1983 / 02:38:39 UT
Launch Site: NIIP-5 / launch site 200L
Scientific Instruments:
   1) Polyus-V side-looking radar
   2) Omega radiometric system
   3) Radio occultation experiment
   4) infrared spectrometer
   5) cosmic-ray detectors
   6) solar wind detectors

Results: Venera 15 and Venera 16 were a pair of dedicated radar mappers designed to extend the studies begun by the American Pioneer Venus Orbiter in constructing a detailed map of the surface down to a resolution of about 1 to 2 kilometers. For these missions, Soviet engineers lengthened the central bus of the earlier Veneras (by 1 meter), installed much larger solar batteries, and attached a large side-looking radar antenna in place of the descent lander module on the earlier spacecraft. Venera 15 carried out two midcourse corrections (on 10 June 1983 and 1 October 1983) before successfully entering orbit around Venus at 03:05 UT on 10 October. Initial orbital parameters were 1,000 x 65,000 kilometers at 87° inclination—that is, a near-polar orbit. The spacecraft's mapping operations began six days after entering orbit over the north pole. Because of the nature of the spacecraft's orbit, the two orbiters mapped only the area from 30° north latitude to the pole—about 115 million square kilometers—before the mission was completed on 10 July 1984.

165)
Venera 16
Nation: USSR (101)
Objective(s): Venus orbit
Spacecraft: 4V-2 (no. 861)
Spacecraft Mass: 5,300 kg
Mission Design and Management: NPO Lavochkin
Launch Vehicle: 8K82K + Blok DM (Proton-K no. 321-02 / Blok DM no. 9L)
Launch Date and Time: 7 June 1983 / 02:32 UT
Launch Site: NIIP-5 / launch site 200P
Scientific Instruments:
   1) Polyus-V side-looking radar
   2) Omega radiometric system
   3) Radio occultation experiment
   4) infrared spectrometer
   5) cosmic-ray detectors
   6) solar wind detectors

Results: Venera 16 arrived at Venus at 06:22 UT on 14 October 1983 after en route course corrections on 15 June and 5 October 1983. It began its mapping operations six days later in its 24-hour-period near-polar orbit. Mapping resolution of both Veneras 15 and 16 was comparable to that possible with the 300-meter dish at Arecibo in Puerto Rico, although the Soviet orbiters provided coverage over latitudes higher than 30°, too far north for Earth-based observations. Both spacecraft also used an East German infrared spectrometer to map the planet in infrared wavelengths in order to provide a "heat atlas" of the atmosphere. Although the primary missions of both spacecraft were fulfilled by 10 July 1984, at least one of the pair was still operational in November 1984. If there were plans to change its orbit to provide coverage of lower latitudes, these were never carried out.

1984

166)
Vega 1
Nation: USSR (102)
Objective(s): Venus atmospheric entry and landing, Halley's Comet flyby
Spacecraft: 5VK (no. 901)
Spacecraft Mass: c. 4,920 kg
Mission Design and Management: NPO Lavochkin
Launch Vehicle: 8K82K + Blok DM (Proton-K no. 329-01 / Blok DM no. 11L)
Launch Date and Time: 15 December 1984 / 09:16:24 UT
Launch Site: NIIP-5 / launch site 200L
Scientific Instruments:
  Lander:
  1) Malakhit mass spectrometer
  2) Sigma-3 gas chromatograph
  3) VM-4 hygrometer
  4) GS-15-SCV gamma-ray spectrometer
  5) UV spectrometer
  6) BDRP-AM25 x-ray fluorescence spectrometer and drill
  7) ISAV nephelometer/scatterometer
  8) temperature and pressure sensors
  9) IFP aerosol analyzer
  Balloon:
  1) temperature and pressure sensors
  2) vertical wind anemometer
  3) nephelometer
  4) light level/lighting detector
  Bus:
  1) imaging system
  2) infrared spectrometer
  3) ultraviolet, visible, infrared imaging spectrometer
  4) shield penetration detector
  5) dust detectors
  6) dust mass spectrometer
  7) neutral gas mass spectrometer
  8) APV-V plasma energy analyzer
  9) energetic-particle analyzer
  10) magnetometer
  11) wave and plasma analyzers

Results: The twin-spacecraft Vega project was perhaps the most ambitious deep space Soviet mission to date. The mission had three major goals: to place advanced lander modules on the surface of Venus, to deploy balloons (two each) in the Venusian atmosphere, and, by using Venusian gravity, to fly the remaining buses past the Comet Halley. The entire mission was a cooperative effort among the Soviet Union (who provided the spacecraft and launch vehicle) and Austria, Bulgaria, Hungary, the German Democratic Republic (East Germany), Poland, Czechoslovakia, France, and the Federal Republic of Germany (West Germany). Although the landers were similar to ones used before for exploring Venus, the balloon gondolas were completely new French-made vehicles that carried American-French nephelometers to measure aerosol distribution in the atmosphere. The cometary flyby probes, which contained a 120-kilogram scientific package for investigations, were protected against high-velocity impacts from dust particles. After a successful flight to Venus, Vega 1 released its 1,500-kilogram descent module on 9 June 1985, two days before atmospheric entry. At 61 kilometers altitude, as the lander descended, it released the first helium-inflated plastic balloon with a hanging gondola underneath it. Mass was around 20.8 kilograms. As the balloon drifted through the Venusian atmosphere (controlled partly by ballast), it transmitted important data on the atmosphere back to a network of tracking antennas on Earth. Balloon 1 survived for 46.5 hours, eventually terminating operations because of battery failure. The lander set down safely on the ground at 03:02:54 UT on 11 June 1985 at 7.2° north latitude and 177.8° longitude, on the night side of Venus in the Mermaid Plain north of Aphrodite, and transmitted from the surface for 56 minutes. Having deployed before it reached the surface, the soil sample drill failed to complete its soil analysis, but the mass spectrometer returned important data.

The Vega 1 bus flew by Venus at a range of 39,000 kilometers and then headed for its encounter with Halley. After a course correction on 10 February 1986, the spacecraft began its formal studies of the comet on 4 March, when it was 14 million kilometers from its target. During the 3-hour encounter on 6 March 1986, the spacecraft approached to within 8,889 kilometers (at 07:20:06 UT) of Halley. Vega 1 took more than 500 pictures via different filters as it flew through the gas cloud around the coma. Although the spacecraft was battered by dust, none of the instruments were disabled during the encounter. Vega 1 collected a wealth of information on Halley, including data on its nucleus, its dust production rate, its chemical composition, and its rotational rate. After subsequent imaging sessions on 7 and 8 March 1986, Vega 1 headed out to deep space.

167)
Vega 2
Nation: USSR (103)
Objective(s): Venus atmospheric entry, Halley's Comet flyby
Spacecraft: 5VK (no. 902)
Spacecraft Mass: 4,920 kg
Mission Design and Management: NPO Lavochkin
Launch Vehicle: 8K82K + Blok DM (Proton-K no. 325-02 / Blok DM no. 12L)
Launch Date and Time: 21 December 1984 / 09:13:52 UT
Launch Site: NIIP-5 / launch site 200P
Scientific Instruments:
　Lander:
　1) Malakhit mass spectrometer
　2) Sigma-3 gas chromatograph
　3) VM-4 hygrometer
　4) GS-15-SCV gamma-ray spectrometer
　5) UV spectrometer
　6) BDRP-AM25 x-ray fluorescence spectrometer and drill
　7) ISAV nephelometer/scatterometer
　8) temperature and pressure sensors
　9) IFP aerosol analyzer
　Balloon:
　1) temperature and pressure sensors
　2) vertical wind anemometer
　3) nephelometer
　4) light level/lighting detector
　Bus:
　1) imaging system
　2) infrared spectrometer
　3) ultraviolet, visible, infrared imaging spectrometer
　4) shield penetration detector
　5) dust detectors
　6) dust mass spectrometer
　7) neutral gas mass spectrometer
　8) plasma energy analyzer
　9) energetic-particle analyzer
　10) magnetometer
　11) wave and plasma analyzers
Results: Vega 2 was the sister spacecraft to Vega 1 and essentially performed a near-identical mission to its twin. The main lander probe set down without problems at 03:00:50 UT on 15 June 1985 in the northern region of Aphrodite, about 1,500 kilometers southeast of Vega. Landing coordinates were 6.45° south latitude and 181.08° longitude. The spacecraft transmitted from the surface for 57 minutes.

Unlike its twin, the Vega 2 lander was able to collect and investigate a soil sample; the experiment identified an anorthosite-troctolite rock—rarely found on Earth, but present in the lunar highlands. According to the lander's data, the area was probably the oldest explored by any Venera vehicle. The mass spectrometer did not return any data. The balloon, released upon entry into the atmosphere, flew through the Venusian atmosphere, collecting data like its twin, and survived for 46.5 hours of data transmission.

After releasing its lander, the flyby probe continued on its flight to Comet Halley. The spacecraft initiated its encounter on 7 March 1986 by taking 100 photos of the comet from a distance of 14 million kilometers. Vega 2's closest approach to Halley was at 07:20 UT two days later when the spacecraft was traveling at a speed of 76.8 kilometers per second (slightly lower than Vega 1's 79.2 kilometers per second). During the encounter, Vega 2 took 700 images of the comet—of much better resolution than those from the spacecraft's twin, partly due to the presence of less dust outside of the coma during this transit. Ironically, Vega 2 sustained an 80-percent power loss during the encounter (as compared to Vega 1's 40 percent). Seven instruments between the two spacecraft were partially damaged, although no instrument on both was incapacitated. After further imaging sessions on 10 and 11 March 1986, Vega 2 finished its primary mission and headed out into heliocentric orbit.

1985

168)
Sakigake
Nation: Japan (1)
Objective(s): Halley's Comet flyby
Spacecraft: MS-T5
Spacecraft Mass: 138.1 kg
Mission Design and Management: ISAS
Launch Vehicle: Mu-3S-II (no. 1)
Launch Date and Time: 7 January 1985 / 19:26 UT
Launch Site: Kagoshima / launch complex M1
Scientific Instruments:
 1) solar wind ion detector
 2) plasma wave probe
 3) magnetometer

Results: The MS-T5 spacecraft (named Sakigake after launch) was the first deep space spacecraft launched by any country apart from the Soviet Union and the United States (the two German Helios probes had been launched by NASA). Japan's goal had been to launch a single modest probe to fly past Halley. As part of a test to prove out the technologies and mission operations of the actual mission, the country's Institute of Space and Astronautical Sciences (ISAS) launched this test spacecraft known as MS-T5, nearly identical to the "actual" vehicle launched later. The spin-stabilized spacecraft was launched by a new Japanese launch vehicle, the Mu-3S-II. Following two course corrections on 10 January and 14 February 1985, Sakigake was sent on a long-range encounter (about 7.6 million kilometers) with Halley. The spacecraft served as a reference vehicle to permit scientists to eliminate Earth atmospheric and ionospheric contributions to the variations in Giotto's transmissions from within the coma. The spacecraft's closest approach to Halley was at 04:18 UT on 11 March 1986, when it was 6.99 million kilometers from the comet. Nearly six years after the Halley encounter, Sakigake flew by Earth on 8 January 1992 at a range of 88,790 kilometers. After two more distant flybys through Earth's magnetic tail (in June 1993 and July 1994), Sakigake maintained weekly contact with the ground until telemetry was lost on 15 November 1995, although the ground continued to receive a beacon signal until all contact was terminated on 7 January 1999.

169)
Giotto
Organization: European Space Agency (1)
Objective(s): Halley's Comet flyby
Spacecraft: Giotto
Spacecraft Mass: 960 kg
Mission Design and Management: ESA
Launch Vehicle: Ariane 1 (V14)
Launch Date and Time: 2 July 1985 / 11:23:16 UT
Launch Site: Kourou / ELA-1

Scientific Instruments:
1) neutral mass spectrometer
2) ion mass spectrometer
3) dust mass spectrometer
4) dust impact detector system
5) plasma analysis 1 experiment
6) plasma analysis 2 experiment
7) energetic-particle analyzer
8) magnetometer
9) optical probe experiment
10) color imaging system

Results: Giotto was the first deep space probe launched by the European Space Agency (ESA). Because the cylindrical spacecraft was designed to approach closer to Halley than any other probe, it was equipped with two dust shields separated by 23 centimeters; the first would bear the shock of impact and spread the impact energy over larger areas of the second, thicker rear sheet. The design of the spacecraft was based on the spin-stabilized magnetospheric Geos satellites launched in 1977 and 1978. After course corrections on 26 August 1985, 12 February 1986, and 12 March 1986, Giotto was put on a 500-kilometer flyby to the comet's core. Data on its trajectory was based upon tracking information from the Soviet Vega 1 and 2 probes. The spacecraft eventually passed by Halley on 14 March 1986. Closest encounter was at a range of 605 kilometers at 00:03:02 UT. At a range of 137.6 million kilometers from Earth, just 2 seconds before closest approach, telemetry stopped due to impact with a heavy concentration of dust that probably knocked the spacecraft's high-gain antenna out of alignment with Earth. Fortunately, data transmission was restored within 32 minutes. On average, Giotto had been hit 100 times a second by particles weighing up to 0.001 grams. By the end of its encounter with Halley, the spacecraft was covered in at least 26 kilograms of dust. Giotto returned 2,000 images of Halley. After the encounter, ESA decided to redirect the vehicle for a flyby of Earth. The spacecraft was officially put in hibernation mode on 2 April 1986. Course corrections on 19 March, 20 March, and 21 March 1986, however, set it on a 22,000-kilometer flyby of Earth on 2 July 1990 for a gravity-assist (the first time that Earth had been used for such a purpose) to visit a new target: Giotto successfully flew by Comet Grigg-Skjellerup at 15:30 UT on 10 July 1992 at range of approximately 200 kilometers. Eight experiments provided extensive data on a wide variety of cometary phenomena during this closest ever flyby of a comet. After formal termination of the encounter on 23 July 1992, Giotto was put in hibernation. In September 1999, ESA scientists revealed that a second comet or cometary fragment may have been accompanying Grigg-Skjellerup during the encounter in 1992. The spacecraft repeated a flyby of Earth at 02:40 UT on 1 July 1999 at range of 219,000 kilometers.

170)
Suisei
Nation: Japan (2)
Objective(s): Halley's Comet flyby
Spacecraft: Planet-A
Spacecraft Mass: 139.5 kg
Mission Design and Management: ISAS
Launch Vehicle: Mu-3S-II (no. 2)
Launch Date and Time: 18 August 1985 / 23:33 UT
Launch Site: Kagoshima / launch complex M1
Scientific Instruments:
1) ultraviolet imaging system
2) solar wind experiment

Results: Planet-A (named Suisei after launch), was the second of two Japanese probes launched towards Halley during the 1986 encounter. The cylindrical spacecraft was launched directly on a deep space trajectory without entering intermediate-Earth orbit. The main payload of the spacecraft was an ultraviolet-based imaging system that could study the huge hydrogen corona around the comet. After a course correction on 14 November 1985, Suisei flew within 152,400 kilometers of the comet's nucleus on 8 March 1986 at 13:06 UT, returning ultraviolet images of the 20-million-kilometer-diameter hydrogen gas coma. Even at that relatively large distance from the comet, the spacecraft was hit by at least two dust particles, each 1 millimeter in diameter. After the Halley Encounter, in 1987, ISAS decided to send the spacecraft through an elaborate trajectory for an encounter with the Comet Giacobini-Zinner on 24 November 1998, thirteen years after launch. Suisei performed a series of trajectory corrections between 5 and

10 April 1987 in order to send it on a gravity-assist around Earth on 20 August 1992 at a range of 60,000 kilometers. Unfortunately, hydrazine for further corrections had been depleted by 22 February 1991. The planned encounter with Giacobini-Zinner (as well as a far-distance flyby of Comet Tempel-Tuttle) had to be canceled on 28 February 1998; the cancellation formally ended the mission.

1988

171)
Fobos 1
Nation: USSR (104)
Objective(s): Mars flyby, Phobos encounter
Spacecraft: 1F (no. 101)
Spacecraft Mass: 6,220 kg
Mission Design and Management: NPO Lavochkin
Launch Vehicle: 8K82K + Blok D-2 (Proton-K no. 356-02 / Blok D-2 no. 2L)
Launch Date and Time: 7 July 1988 / 17:38:04 UT
Launch Site: NIIP-5 / launch site 200L
Scientific Instruments:
  Planetary studies (on Orbiter):
  1) VSK videospectrometric system
  2) ISM infrared spectrometer
  3) GS-14 gamma-emission spectrometer
  4) IPNM neutron detector
  5) RLK radar system
  6) LIMA-D laser mass spectrometric analyzer
  7) DION secondary ion mass analyzer
  8) ISO optical radiation spectrometer
  Plasma studies:
  1) MAGMA magnetometer
  2) FGMM magnetometer
  3) APV-F plasma wave analyzer
  4) ASPERA scanning energy-mass spectrometer
  5) SOVIKOMS energy-mass charge spectrometer
  6) TAUS proton and alpha-particle spectrometer
  7) HARP ion and electron spectrometer
  8) SLED energetic charged-particle spectrometer
  Solar studies:
  1) IPHIR solar photometer
  2) TEREK solar telescope/coronograph
  3) RF-15 x-ray photometer
  4) SUFR ultrasound spectrometer
  5) LILAS gamma-burst spectrometer
  6) VGS gamma-burst spectrometer

Results: Fobos 1 and 2 were part of an ambitious mission to Mars and its 27-kilometer-diameter moon Phobos that was the culmination of a decade-long program of development. Each spacecraft comprised a Mars Orbiter for long-term studies of the planet and a Long-Term Automated Lander (DAS) that would land on Phobos to study its geological and climatic conditions. After each spacecraft entered orbit around Mars, it would make close flybys of Phobos, sample surface material using an innovative onboard laser spectrometer, and also deploy the Lander. Laser beams would prepare small samples of material for analysis. Each spacecraft, with a newly designed bus, carried twenty-four experiments provided by thirteen countries and the European Space

Agency. Fobos 1 performed a course correction en route to Mars on 16 July 1988. On 29 August 1988, due to a programming error, a command was issued to turn off the orientation and stabilization system (instead of a routine command to switch on the gamma-ray spectrometer). As a result, the spacecraft lost proper solar orientation and began to lose power. There was no word from Fobos 1 at the next scheduled communications session on 2 September. Continuing attempts to establish contact failed, and on 3 November 1988, the Soviets officially announced that there would be no further attempts at contact. The spacecraft flew by Mars without entering orbit (scheduled for 23 January 1989) and eventually entered heliocentric orbit.

172)
Fobos 2
Nation: USSR (105)
Objective(s): Mars flyby, Phobos encounter
Spacecraft: 1F (no. 102)
Spacecraft Mass: 6,220 kg
Mission Design and Management: NPO Lavochkin
Launch Vehicle: 8K82K + Blok D-2 (Proton-K no. 356-01 / Blok D-2 no. 1L)
Launch Date and Time: 12 July 1988 / 17:01:43 UT
Launch Site: NIIP-5 / launch site 200P
Scientific Instruments:
  Planetary studies (on Orbiter):
  1) VSK videospectrometric system
  2) KRFM infrared radiometer/spectrometer
  3) ISM infrared spectrometer
  4) Thermoscan scanning infrared radiometer
  5) GS-14 gamma-emission spectrometer
  6) RLK radar system
  7) LIMA-D laser mass spectrometric analyzer
  8) DION secondary ion mass analyzer
  9) ISO optical radiation spectrometer
  Plasma studies:
  1) MAGMA magnetometer
  2) FGMM magnetometer
  3) APV-F plasma wave analyzer
  4) ASPERA scanning energy-mass spectrometer
  5) SOVIKOMS energy-mass charge spectrometer
  6) TAUS proton and alpha-particle spectrometer
  7) HARP ion and electron spectrometer
  8) SLED energetic charged-particle spectrometer
  Solar studies:
  1) IPHIR solar photometer
  2) RF-15 x-ray photometer
  3) SUFR ultrasound spectrometer
  4) LILAS gamma-burst spectrometer
  5) VGS gamma-burst spectrometer

Results: Fobos 2 had the same mission as its twin Fobos 1 but had an additional payload on board, a 110-kilogram "hopper" designed to make up to ten 20-meter jumps across the Phobos surface to gather surface data on the tiny Martian moon. The orbiter also had a slightly different instrument complement. Fobos 2 carried out two en route course corrections on 21 July 1988 and 23 January 1989, despite some major problems. One of the two radio transmitters failed when there were spuriously generated commands in one channel of its computer. At 12:55 UT on 29 January 1989, the spacecraft fired its engine to enter orbit around Mars. Initial orbital parameters were 819 x 81,214 kilometers at 1.5° inclination. After four further orbital corrections, its trajectory was put on an encounter course with Phobos. Fobos 2 took high-resolution photos of the moon on 23 February (at a range of 860 kilometers), 28 February (320 kilometers), and 25 March 1989 (191 kilometers). Release of its lander was scheduled for 4–5 April 1989, but on 27 March, during a regularly planned communications session at 15:58 UT, there was no word from the spacecraft. A weak signal was received between 17:51 and 18:03 UT, but there was no telemetry information. The nature of the signal indicated that the spacecraft had lost all orientation. Future attempts to regain communication were unsuccessful, and the mission was declared lost on 15 April 1989. The most probable cause of failure was simultaneous malfunctions in both channels of the onboard computer (due to insufficiently robust software) that put the spacecraft into an improper tumble.

1989

173)
Magellan
Nation: U.S. (63)
Objective(s): Venus orbit
Spacecraft: Magellan
Spacecraft Mass: 3,445 kg
Mission Design and Management: NASA JPL
Launch Vehicle: STS-30R *Atlantis*
Launch Date and Time: 4 May 1989 / 18:47:00 UT
Launch Site: ETR / launch complex 39B
Scientific Instruments:
1) synthetic aperture radar
2) gravimetry experiment
3) Magellan radio science occultation experiment

Results: Magellan was the first deep space probe launched by the United States in almost eleven years, and it was also the first launched by the Space Shuttle. The spacecraft was designed to use a synthetic aperture radar (SAR) to map 70 percent of the Venusian surface down to a resolution of 120 to 300 meters. Magellan was deployed by the STS-30R crew and released at 01:01 UT on 5 May 1989 from the payload bay of *Atlantis*. One hour later, a two-stage Inertial Upper Stage (IUS) fired to send the spacecraft on a trajectory to rendezvous with Venus. After three en route trajectory corrections (the first two on 21 May 1989 and 13 March 1990), Magellan arrived in Venus orbit on 10 August 1990. Orbital parameters were 297 x 8,463 kilometers at 85.5° inclination. Six days after entering orbit, Magellan suffered a communications outage lasting 15 hours. After a second 17-hour interruption on 21 August, the ground sent up new preventative software to reset the system in case of such anomalies. Beginning 15 September 1990, the spacecraft began returning high-quality radar images of the Venusian terrain that showed evidence of vulcanism, tectonic movement, turbulent surface winds, kilometers of lava channels, and pancake-shaped domes. Magellan completed its first 243-day cycle (the time it took for Venus to rotate once under Magellan's orbit) of radar mapping on 15 May 1991, providing the first clear views of 83.7 percent of the surface. The spacecraft returned 1,200 gigabits of data, far exceeding the 900 gigabits of data from all NASA planetary missions combined at the time. The spacecraft's second mapping cycle, already beyond the original goals of the mission, ended on 15 January 1992, raising coverage to 96 percent. A third cycle that focused on stereo imaging ended on 13 September 1992 and finished coverage at 98 percent. Further investigations focused on obtaining gravimetric data and performing aerobraking exercises (in 1993). Contact was lost after 10:04 UT on 12 October 1994 as the spacecraft was commanded to plunge into the

The hemispheric view of Venus, as revealed by more than a decade of radar investigations culminating in the 1990–94 Magellan mission, is centered at 180° east longitude. The Magellan spacecraft imaged more than 98 percent of Venus at a resolution of about 100 meters; the effective resolution of this image is about 3 kilometers. A mosaic of the Magellan images (most with illumination from the west) forms the image base. Gaps in the Magellan coverage were filled with images from the Earth-based Arecibo radar in a region centered roughly on 0° latitude and longitude, and with a neutral tone elsewhere (primarily near the south pole). The composite image was processed to improve contrast and to emphasize small features, and it was color-coded to represent elevation. Gaps in the elevation data from the Magellan radar altimeter were filled with altimetry from the Venera spacecraft and the U.S. Pioneer Venus missions. An orthographic projection was used, simulating a distant view of one hemisphere of the planet. The Magellan mission was managed for NASA by the Jet Propulsion Laboratory (JPL), Pasadena, CA.

atmosphere to gather aerodynamic data. The spacecraft burned up in the Venusian atmosphere the following day at about 08:00 UT, after one of the most successful deep space missions. Magellan found that at least 85 percent of the Venusian surface is covered with volcanic flows. Despite the high surface temperatures (475°C) and high atmospheric pressures (92 atmospheres), the complete lack of water makes erosion an extremely slow process. As a result, surface features can persist for hundreds of millions of years.

174)
Galileo
Nation: U.S. (64)
Objective(s): Jupiter orbit and atmospheric entry, Venus flyby, two Earth flybys, flybys of Gaspra and Ida asteroids
Spacecraft: Galileo
Spacecraft Mass: 2,561 kg
Mission Design and Management: NASA JPL
Launch Vehicle: STS-34R *Atlantis*
Launch Date and Time: 18 October 1989 / 16:53:40 UT
Launch Site: ETR / launch complex 39B
Scientific Instruments:
  Orbiter:
  1) imaging system
  2) near-infrared mapping spectrometer
  3) ultraviolet spectrometer
  4) photopolarimeter-radiometer
  5) magnetometer
  6) energetic-particles detector
  7) plasma detector
  8) plasma wave
  9) heavy ion counter
  10) radio system
  Atmospheric entry probe:
  1) atmospheric structure instrument
  2) neutral mass spectrometer
  3) helium abundance detector
  4) net flux radiometer
  5) nephelometer
  6) lightning/energetic-particles experiment

Results: Galileo, one of NASA's most ambitious deep space exploration projects, was the result of plans dating back to the early 1980s to deploy a Jupiter orbiter and probe. In its final configuration, the orbiter was a 4.6-meter-tall spacecraft designed to operate for twenty-two months in Jovian orbit using ten instruments/experiments to study the planet's atmosphere, satellites, and magnetosphere. Galileo carried a 337-kilogram probe designed to return data as it entered the Jovian atmosphere to identify atmospheric materials and conditions that cannot be detected from outside. Because of limitations of a Space Shuttle/IUS combination, NASA decided to use a complex multiple-gravity-assist scheme that required three flybys (two of Earth and one of Venus) on its way to Jupiter. The STS-34R crew released the spacecraft 6.5 hours after launch; an hour later, the two-stage IUS fired to send Galileo on its way. Galileo flew past Venus at 05:58:48 UT on 10 February 1990 at a range of 16,106 kilometers; as it did so, it conducted an extensive survey of the planet (including imaging). Having gained 8,030 kilometers per hour in speed, the spacecraft flew by Earth twice, the first time at a range of 960 kilometers at 20:34:34 UT on 8 December 1990, when it clearly detected traces of life in atmospheric trace elements on our home planet. The spacecraft also conducted lunar observations. A major problem occurred on 11 April 1991, when the high-gain antenna failed to fully deploy, thus eliminating the possibility of data transmission during its flyby of the asteroid Gaspra. Becoming the first humanmade object to fly past an asteroid, Galileo approached the minor planet to a distance of 1,604 kilometers at 22:37 UT on 29 October 1991. The encounter provided much data, including 150 images of the asteroid. Galileo then sped to its second encounter with the Earth-Moon system, with a flyby of Earth at 303.1 kilometers at 15:09:25 UT on 8 December 1992, adding 3.7 kilometers per second to its cumulative speed. Despite extensive attempts to salvage the high-gain antenna, ground controllers eventually had to restructure the mission to use only the low-gain antenna, which would allow about 70 percent of the originally planned scientific return (using software and hardware improvements on Earth). Galileo flew by a second asteroid, Ida, at 16:51:59 UT on 28 August 1993 at a range of 2,410 kilometers, thus providing further data on minor planets. Later, in July 1994, as it was speeding toward Jupiter, Galileo provided astronomers' only direct observations of

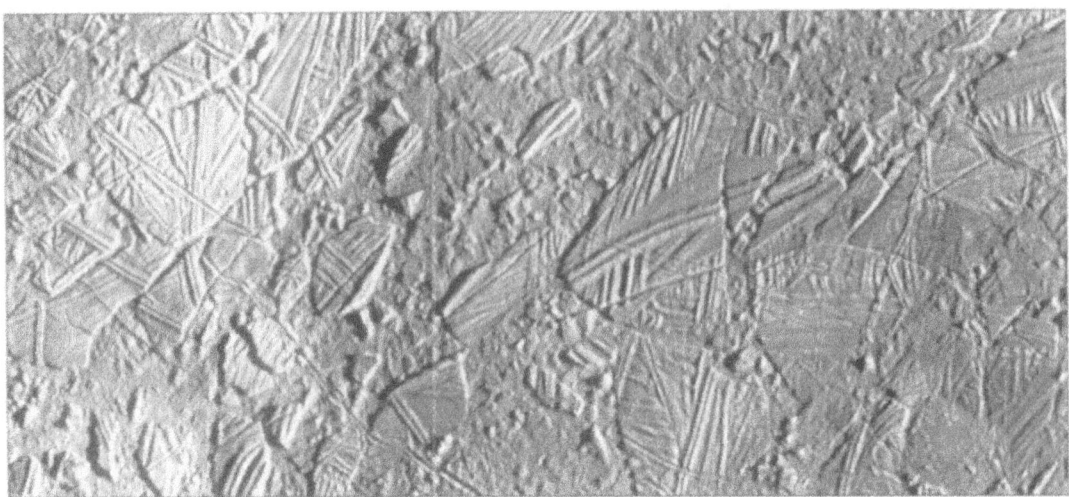

This is an image of a small region of the thin, disrupted ice crust in the Conamara region of Jupiter's moon Europa. The lighter areas on the left of the image (actual color, white and blue) show areas that have been blanketed by a fine dust of ice particles ejected at the time of formation of the large crater Pwyll, approximately 1,000 kilometers to the south. A few small craters of less than 500 meters in diameter can be seen associated with these regions. These craters were probably formed at the same time as the blanketing occurred, by large, intact blocks of ice thrown up in the impact explosion that formed Pwyll. The areas on the right (actual color, reddish brown) constitute an unblanketed surface that has been painted by mineral contaminants carried and spread by water vapor released from below the crust. The image covers an area approximately 70 kilometers by 30 kilometers and combines data taken by the Solid State Imaging system on the Galileo spacecraft during three of its orbits through the Jovian system in September and December 1996 and February 1997.

Comet Shoemaker-Levy 9's impact with the Jovian atmosphere.

Galileo's atmospheric entry probe was finally released on 13 July 1995, when the spacecraft was still 80 million kilometers from Jupiter. The probe hit the atmosphere at 6.5° north latitude and 4.4° west longitude at 22:04 UT on 7 December 1995 and returned valuable data for 57 minutes as it plunged into the Jovian cauldron. Data, originally transmitted to its parent craft and then later transmitted back to Earth, indicated an intense radiation belt 50,000 kilometers above Jupiter's clouds, few organic compounds, and winds as high as 640 meters per second. The Galileo orbiter, meanwhile, fired its engine at 00:27 UT on 8 December, becoming Jupiter's first humanmade satellite. Its orbital period was 198 days. Soon after, Galileo began its planned eleven tours over twenty-two months, exploring the planet and its moons, beginning with a first encounter with Ganymede on 27 June 1996 and ending with a flyby of Europa on 6 November 1997 (which also included flybys of Callisto). Having fulfilled the mission's original goals, NASA implemented a two-year extension (later extended four years to 31 January 2000) with the Galileo Europa Mission (GEM), during which the spacecraft conducted numerous flybys of Jupiter's moons, each encounter yielding a wealth of scientific data. These included flybys of Europa nine times (eight between December 1997 and February 1999 and one in January 2000), Callisto four times (between May 1999 and September 1999), and Io three times (in October 1999, November 1999, and February 2000). On the last flyby of Io, Galileo flew only 198 kilometers from the surface and sent back the highest resolution photos yet of the volcanically active moon. On 8 March 2000, NASA announced plans to extend Galileo's mission further to the end of the year, renaming the flight the Galileo Millennium Mission. Galileo coordinated investigations of Jupiter and its environs with the Cassini spacecraft (on its way to Saturn) in December 2000. Earlier, under the new Millennium Mission, Galileo flew by Ganymede, the largest moon in the solar

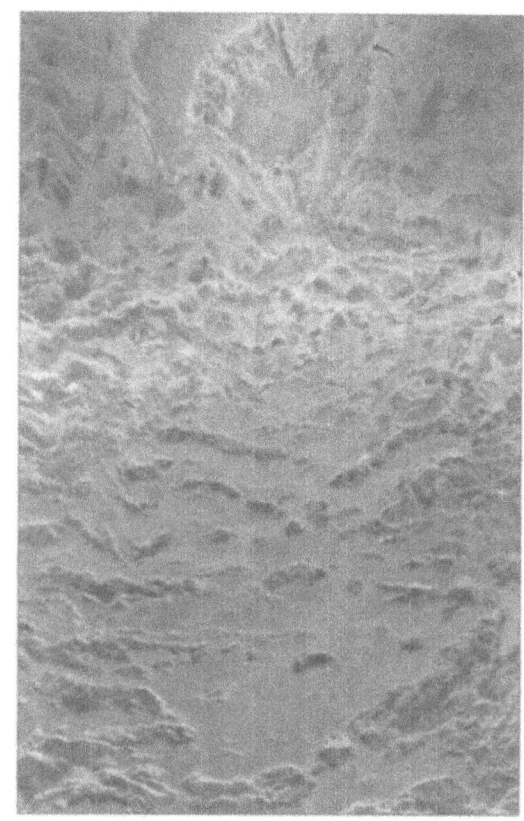

This perspective view of Venus, generated by computer from Magellan data and color-coded with emissivity, is a look westward across the Fortuna Tessera toward the slopes of Maxwell Montes. The tessera terrain of both Fortuna and the slopes of Maxwell is characterized by roughly parallel north-south trending ridges. With a maximum elevation of roughly 11 kilometers above the planetary reference surface (which has a radius of 6,051 kilometers), Maxwell is the highest mountain on Venus. The circular feature on the slope of Maxwell is the crater Cleopatra, which has a diameter of approximately 100 kilometers. Before the high-resolution Magellan images were available, Cleopatra was thought to be a volcanic feature because of its mountainous location and the visible lava flow emanating from the crater and flooding the troughs of the foreground terrain. The Magellan images, however, clearly show an ejecta blanket characteristic of an impact origin around Cleopatra. Other Venusian craters have associated outflow features, but these do not resemble the flow from Cleopatra. The difference may be the result of unique target conditions (high elevation, and perhaps high subsurface temperatures if Maxwell is still actively being supported by activity in the interior of Venus) or may simply be the consequence of the formation of the crater on an unusually steep slope.

---

system, on 20 May 2000 at a range of 809 kilometers. It completed a second flyby of the same moon on 28 December 2000.

On 15 March 2001, NASA extended the Galileo mission a third time by planning five more flybys of the planet's moons: Callisto (in May 2001), Io (in August and October 2001 and January 2002), and Amalthea (in November 2002). During the 25 May 2001 encounter with Callisto, a heavily cratered moon about the size of Mercury, the spacecraft flew by the surface at a scant 138 kilometers, closer than any previous encounter.

In December 2000, the National Research Council of the National Academy of Sciences approved plans for ending the Galileo mission. After finishing its imaging mission in 2002, Galileo will continue studies of Jupiter's massive magnetic field with seven instruments. After a final orbit shaped like an elongated loop, the spacecraft will hurtle back into the Jovian atmosphere in December 2003.

In its six-year exploration of the Jovian system, Galileo has discovered far less lightning activity (about 10 percent of that found in an equal area on Earth) than anticipated, helium abundance in Jupiter very nearly the same as in the Sun (24 percent compared to 25 percent), extensive resurfacing of Io's surface due to continuing volcanic activity since the Voyagers flew by in 1979, and evidence for a liquid water ocean under Europa's surface. Galileo has also discovered organic compounds on Callisto, Ganymede, Europa, and even Io. The spacecraft has also discovered the first internal magnetic field of a moon. Ganymede's intrinsic magnetic field actually produces a "mini magnetosphere" embedded within Jupiter's huge magnetosphere. By March 2000, the spacecraft had returned about 14,000 images back to Earth.

1990

175)
Hiten/Hagomoro
Nation: Japan (3)
Objective(s): lunar flyby and lunar orbit
Spacecraft: Muses-A and Muses-A subsatellite
Spacecraft Mass: 197.4 kg
Mission Design and Management: ISAS
Launch Vehicle: Mu-3S-II (no. 5)
Launch Date and Time: 24 January 1990 / 11:46 UT
Launch Site: Kagoshima / launch complex M1
Scientific Instruments:
   Hiten:
   1)   cosmic dust detector

Results: This two-module Japanese spacecraft was designed to fly past the Moon and release an orbiter. It was the first Japanese lunar mission and also the first robotic lunar probe since the flight of the Soviet Luna 24 in 1976. Muses-A (for Mu-launched Space Engineering Satellite) was launched into a highly elliptical orbit that intersected the Moon's orbit. After launch, the spacecraft, which was renamed Hiten, returned technical data on trajectory and optical navigation from an onboard computer. The cosmic dust experiment was jointly designed with Germany. On 19 March 1990, the spacecraft approached the Moon to a range of 16,472 kilometers and then released a small 12-kilogram orbiter satellite named Hagomoro into lunar orbit. Initial orbital parameters were 22,000 x 9,000 kilometers. Although the maneuver successfully demonstrated the use of the swingby technique to enter lunar orbit, communication with Hagomoro was lost shortly after release. Hiten, on the other hand, continued on its trajectory, simulating the orbital path of the proposed Geotail spacecraft. On 19 March 1991, Hiten flew by Earth at a range of 126 kilometers during a gravity-assist maneuver that slowed it by 1.7 meters per second—the first aerobraking maneuver by a deep space probe. During its eleventh flyby of the Moon on 15 February 1992, Hiten swung into lunar orbit and eventually impacted on 10 April 1993.

176)
Ulysses
Organization/Nation: ESA and U.S. (1)
Objective(s): heliocentric orbit
Spacecraft: Ulysses
Spacecraft Mass: 371 kg
Mission Design and Management: ESA and NASA JPL
Launch Vehicle: STS-41 *Atlantis*
Launch Date and Time: 6 October 1990 / 11:47:16 UT
Launch Site: ETR / launch complex 39B
Scientific Instruments:
   1)   BAM solar wind plasma experiment
   2)   GLG solar wind ion composition experiment
   3)   HED magnetic fields experiment

This montage of the nine planets and four large moons of Jupiter in our solar system are set against a false-color view of the Rosette Nebula. The light emitted from the Rosette Nebula results from the presence of hydrogen, oxygen, and sulfur. Most of the planetary images in this montage were obtained by NASA's planetary missions, which have dramatically changed our understanding of the solar system.

4) KEP energetic-particle composition/neutral gas experiment
5) LAN low-energy charged-particle composition/anisotropy experiment
6) SIM cosmic rays and solar particles experiment
7) STO radio/plasma waves experiment
8) HUS solar x-rays and cosmic gamma-ray bursts experiment
9) GRU cosmic dust experiment

Results: The Ulysses mission was an outgrowth of the abandoned International Solar Polar Mission (ISPM) that involved two spacecraft flying over opposite solar poles to investigate the Sun in three dimensions. Eventually, ESA built a single spacecraft for launch on the Space Shuttle. The vehicle was designed to fly a unique trajectory that would use a gravity-assist from Jupiter to take it below the elliptic plane, past the solar south pole, and then above the elliptic to fly over the north pole. Eventually, thirteen years after ESA's science council had originally approved the mission, Ulysses was sent on its way via a Shuttle/PAM-S motor combination. Escape velocity was 15.4 kilometers per second, higher than had been achieved by either of the Voyagers or Pioneers, and the fastest velocity ever achieved by a human-made object. After a midcourse correction on 8 July 1991, Ulysses passed within 378,400 kilometers of Jupiter at 12:02 UT on 8 February 1992. After a seventeen-day period passing through and studying the Jovian system, the spacecraft headed downwards and back to the Sun. From about mid-1993 on, Ulysses was constantly in the region of space dominated by the Sun's southern pole, as indicated by the constant negative polarity measured by the magnetometer. South polar observations extended from 26 June to 6 November 1994, when the vehicle was above 70° solar latitude. It reached a maximum of

80.2° in September 1994. Its instruments found that the solar wind blows faster at the south pole than at the equatorial regions. Flying up above the solar equator on 5 March 1995, Ulysses passed over the north polar regions between 19 June and 30 September 1995 (maximum latitude of 80.2°). The closest approach to the Sun was on 12 March 1995 at a range of 200 million kilometers. ESA officially extended Ulysses's mission on 1 October 1995, renaming this portion as the Second Solar Orbit. The spacecraft made a second pass over the south pole between September 2000 and January 2001, and it made a pass over the northern pole in October 2001. In October 2000, ESA announced that Ulysses had discovered the most distant gamma-ray burst yet recorded, about 11 billion light years from Earth. At that time, the Sun was at the peak of its eleven-year cycle. ESA's Science Programme Committee, during a meeting on 5–6 June 2000, agreed to extend the Ulysses mission from the end of 2001 to 30 September 2004. NASA was expected to approve the plan by mid-2001.

1992

177)
Mars Observer
Nation: U.S. (65)
Objective(s): Mars orbit
Spacecraft: Mars Observer
Spacecraft Mass: 2,573 kg
Mission Design and Management: NASA JPL
Launch Vehicle: Titan III (CT-4)
Launch Date and Time: 25 September 1992 / 17:05:01 UT
Launch Site: ESMC / launch complex 40
Scientific Instruments:
1) imaging system
2) thermal emission spectrometer
3) pressure modulator infrared radiometer
4) laser altimeter
5) magnetometer/electron reflectometer
6) gamma-ray spectrometer
7) radio science experiment
8) Mars balloon relay receiver

Results: Mars Observer was designed to carry out a high-resolution photography mission of the Red Planet over the course of a Martian year (687 days) from a 378 x 350-kilometer polar orbit. It carried a suite of instruments to investigate Martian geology, atmosphere, and climate in order to fill in gaps in our knowledge of planetary evolution. A mere 31 minutes after launch, the new Transfer Orbit Stage (TOS) fired to boost the spacecraft on an encounter trajectory with Mars. After a 725-million-kilometer voyage lasting eleven months, just two days prior to planned entry into Mars orbit, the spacecraft suddenly fell silent at 01:00 UT on 22 August 1993. Despite vigorous efforts to regain contact, Mars Observer remained quiet. When the spacecraft did not reestablish command as a result of a stored program that was designed to do so in case of five days of silence, mission planners finally gave up hope on salvaging the mission. The results of a five-month investigation proved to be inconclusive, but one likely cause of the catastrophic failure may have been a fuel line rupture that could have damaged the spacecraft's electronics, throwing the vehicle into a spin.

1994

178)
Clementine
Nation: U.S. (66)
Objective(s): lunar orbit
Spacecraft: Clementine
Spacecraft Mass: 424 kg
Mission Design and Management: BMDO and NASA
Launch Vehicle: Titan IIG (no. 23G-11)
Launch Date and Time: 25 January 1994 / 16:34 UT
Launch Site: WSMC / SLC-4W
Scientific Instruments:
1) ultraviolet/visible camera
2) near-infrared camera
3) long-wave infrared camera
4) high-resolution camera
5) two star tracker cameras
6) laser altimeter
7) bistatic radar experiment
8) gravity experiment
9) charged-particle telescope

Results: Clementine was the first U.S. spacecraft launched to the Moon in over twenty years (since Explorer 49 in June 1973). The spacecraft, also known as the Deep Space Program Science Experiment (DSPSE), was designed and built to demonstrate a set of lightweight technologies such as small-imaging sensors for future low-cost missions flown by the Department of Defense. Clementine carried fifteen advanced flight-test components and ten science instruments. After launch, the spacecraft remained in a temporary orbit until 3 February 1994, at which time a solid-propellant rocket ignited to send the vehicle to the Moon. After two subsequent Earth flybys on 5 February and 15 February, Clementine successfully entered an elliptical polar orbit on 19 February with a period of 5 days and a perilune of 400 kilometers. In the following two months, it transmitted about 1.6 million digital images of the lunar surface; in the process, it provided scientists with their first look at the total lunar landscape, including polar regions. After completing its mission goals over 297 orbits around lunar orbit, controllers fired Clementine's thrusters on 3 May to inject it on a rendezvous trajectory in August 1994 with the asteroid 1620 Geographos. Due to a computer problem at 14:39 UT on 7 May that caused a thruster to fire and use up all propellant, the spacecraft was put into an uncontrollable tumble at about 80 rpm with no spin control. Controllers were forced to cancel the asteroid flyby and return the vehicle to the vicinity of Earth. A power supply problem on 20 July further diminished the operating capacity of the vehicle. Eventually, lunar gravity took control of Clementine and propelled it into heliocentric orbit. The mission was terminated in June 1994 when falling power supply levels no longer allowed clear telemetry exchange. On

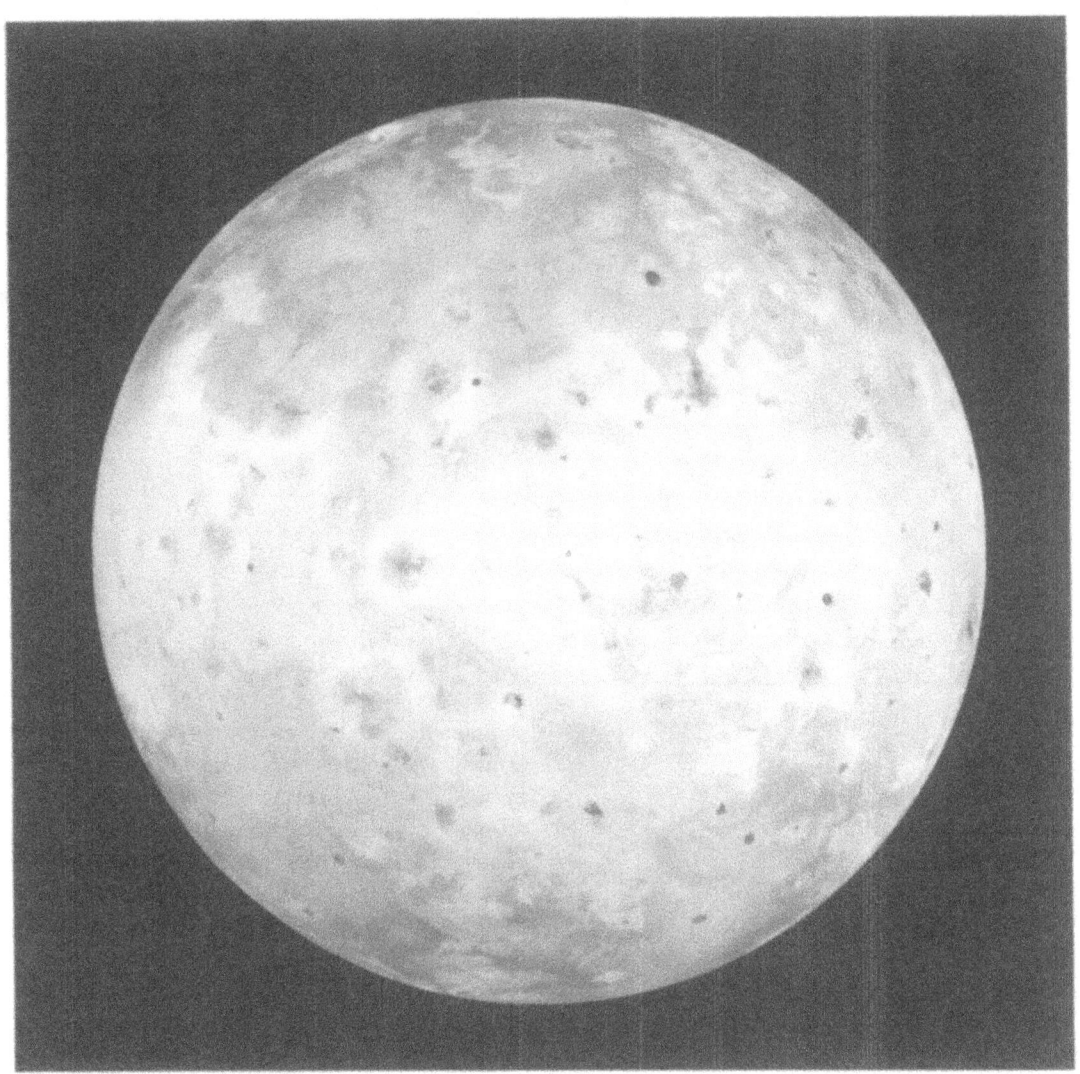

NASA's Galileo spacecraft acquired its highest resolution images of Jupiter's moon Io on 3 July 1999, during its closest pass to Io since orbit insertion in late 1995. This color mosaic uses the near-infrared, green, and violet filters (slightly more than the visible range) of the spacecraft's camera and approximates what the human eye would see. Most of Io's surface has pastel colors, punctuated by black, brown, green, orange, and red units near the active volcanic centers. A false-color version of the mosaic has been created to enhance the contrast of the color variations. The improved resolution reveals small-scale color units that had not been recognized previously and that suggest that the lavas and sulfurous deposits are composed of complex mixtures. Some of the bright (whitish), high-latitude (near the top and bottom) deposits have an ethereal quality like a transparent covering of frost. Bright red areas were seen previously only as diffuse deposits. However, they are now seen to exist as both diffuse deposits and sharp linear features like fissures. Some volcanic centers have bright and colorful flows, perhaps due to flows of sulfur rather than silicate lava. In this region, bright, white material can also be seen to emanate from linear rifts and cliffs. Comparison of this image to previous Galileo images reveals many changes due to the ongoing volcanic activity. North is toward the top of the picture, and the Sun illuminates the surface from almost directly behind the spacecraft. This illumination geometry is good for imaging color variations but poor for imaging topographic shading. However, some topographic shading can be seen here due to the combination of relatively high resolution (1.3 kilometers per picture element) and the rugged topography over parts of Io. The image is centered at 0.3° north latitude and 137.5° west longitude. The resolution is 1.3 kilometers per picture element. The images were taken on 3 July 1999 at a range of about 130,000 kilometers by the Solid State Imaging (SSI) system on NASA's Galileo spacecraft during its twenty-first orbit.

3 December 1996, DoD announced that Clementine data indicated that there was ice in the bottom of a permanently shadowed crater on the lunar south pole. Scientists estimated the deposit to be approximately 60,000 to 120,000 cubic meters in volume—comparable to a small lake that is 4 football fields in surface area and 5 meters deep. This estimate was very uncertain, however, due to the nature of the data.

179)
Wind
Nation: U.S. (67)
Objective(s): orbit around L1 Libration Point, lunar flybys
Spacecraft: Wind
Spacecraft Mass: 1,250 kg
Mission Design and Management: NASA GSFC
Launch Vehicle: Delta 7925-10 (no. D227)
Launch Date and Time: 1 November 1994 / 09:31:00 UT
Launch Site: ESMC / launch complex 17B
Scientific Instruments:
1) WAVES radio and plasma wave experiment
2) three low-energy matrix telescopes
3) electron isotope telescope
4) suprathermal energetic-particle telescope
5) solar wind experiment
6) solar wind ion composition spectrometer
7) high-mass-resolution spectrometer
8) suprathermal ion composition spectrometer
9) two fluxgate magnetometers
10) 3-D plasma and energetic-particle analyzer
11) transient gamma-ray spectrometer
12) Konus gamma-ray burst studies experiment

Results: Wind is part of the twelve-satellite Inter-Agency Solar-Terrestrial Physics (IASTP) Program, a joint project among the United States, Japan, Russia, the Czech Republic, and ESA to study the behavior of the solar-terrestrial system. The first of two NASA-sponsored Global Geospace Science Program vehicles, the Wind spacecraft carries eight instruments (including one each from France and Russia) to investigate the solar wind's encounters with Earth's magnetosphere and ionosphere in order to determine the origins and three-dimensional characteristics of the solar wind. Wind initially operated in a unique figure-eight-shaped elliptical orbit around Earth at 28,000 x 1.6 million kilometers, partially maintained by regular "double flybys" of the Moon. The closest of nineteen flybys of the Moon between 1 December 1994 and 17 November 1998 was on 27 December 1994, at a range of 11,834 kilometers. By November 1996, Wind was in a "halo orbit" around the Earth-Sun Libration Point, where the solar and terrestrial gravity are approximately equal. On 17 November 1998, it began to move into a series of "petal" orbits designed to take it out of the elliptical plane. Wind's trips above and below the elliptic (up to 60°) allowed the spacecraft to sample regions of interplanetary space and the magnetosphere that had not been previously studied. All of its instruments were operational in July 2001.

1995

180)
SOHO
Organization/Nation: ESA and U.S. (2)
Objective(s): L1 Libration Point
Spacecraft: SOHO
Spacecraft Mass: 1,864 kg
Mission Design and Management: ESA and NASA
Launch Vehicle: Atlas-Centaur IIAS (AC-121 / Atlas IIAS no. 8206 / Centaur II)
Launch Date and Time: 2 December 1995 / 08:08:01 UT
Launch Site: ESMC / launch complex 36B
Scientific Instruments:
1) SUMER solar-ultraviolet emitted radiation experiment
2) CDS coronal diagnostic spectrometer
3) EIT extreme ultraviolet imaging telescope
4) UVCS ultraviolet coronograph spectrometer
5) LASCO white light/spectrometric coronograph
6) SWAN solar wind anisotropies experiment
7) CELIAS charge, element/isotope analysis experiment
8) COSTEP suprathermal/energetic-particle analyzer
9) ERNE energetic-particle analyzer
10) GOLF global oscillations at low frequencies experiment
11) VIRGO variability of solar irradiance experiment
12) MDI Michelson Doppler imager

Results: The ESA-sponsored Solar and Heliospheric Observatory (SOHO) carries twelve scientific instruments to study the solar atmosphere, helioseismology, and solar wind. Information from the mission allows scientists to learn more about the Sun's internal structure and dynamics, the chromosphere, the corona, and solar particles. The SOHO and Cluster missions, part of ESA's Solar Terrestrial Science Programme (STSP), are ESA's contributions to the Inter-Agency Solar Terrestrial Physics (IASTP) program. NASA contributed three instruments on SOHO as well as launch and flight operations support. About two months after launch, on 14 February 1996, SOHO was placed at a distance of 1.5 million kilometers from Earth at the L1 Libration Point. The spacecraft returned its first image on 19 December 1995 and was fully commissioned for operations by 16 April 1996. SOHO finished its planned two-year study of the Sun's atmosphere, surface, and interior in April 1998. Communications with the spacecraft were interrupted for four months beginning on 24 June 1998, but, after intensive search efforts, controllers managed to regain full control by 16 September.

Barring three instruments, the spacecraft was functional and was declared fully operational once again by mid-October 1998. SOHO's original lifetime was three years (to 1998), but ESA and NASA jointly decided to prolong the mission to 2003, thus enabling the spacecraft to compare the Sun's behavior during low dark sunspot activity (1996) to the peak (around 2000). One of SOHO's most important discoveries has been locating the origin of the fast solar wind at the corners of honeycomb-shaped magnetic fields surrounding the edges of large bubbling cells located near the Sun's poles. SOHO remains in its halo orbit, circling L1 once every six months.

1996

181)
NEAR
Nation: U.S. (68)
Objective(s): multiple asteroid flybys
Spacecraft: NEAR
Spacecraft Mass: 805 kg
Mission Design and Management: NASA GSFC and Johns Hopkins University Applied Physics Laboratory
Launch Vehicle: Delta 7925-8 (no. D232)
Launch Date and Time: 17 February 1996 / 20:43:27 UT
Launch Site: ESMC / launch complex 17B
Scientific Instruments:
1) MSI multispectral imager
2) MAG magnetometer
3) NIS near infrared spectrometer
4) XRS-GRS x-ray/gamma-ray spectrometer
5) NLR laser rangefinder
6) radio science and gravimetry experiment

Results: Near Earth Asteroid Rendezvous (NEAR) is the first mission flown under NASA's new Discovery program, a series of low-cost (less than $150 million) planetary science projects. NEAR's primary goal was to rendezvous with the minor planet 433 Eros (an S-class asteroid), approximately 355 million kilometers from Earth, and gather data on its composition and physical properties (mineralogy, morphology, internal mass distribution, and magnetic field). The spacecraft is the first probe to rely on solar cells for power during operations beyond Mars orbit. On the way to its primary mission, NEAR performed a 25-minute flyby of the asteroid 253 Mathilde on 27 June 1997. The closest approach to 1,200 kilometers was at 12:56 UT. During the encounter, the spacecraft photographed 60 percent of the minor planet from a range of 1,200 kilometers. The collected information indicated that the 4.5-billion-year-old asteroid is covered with craters and is less dense than previously believed. After a midcourse correction on 3 July 1997, NEAR flew by Earth on 23 January 1998 at 07:23 UT for a gravity-assist on its way to Eros. The closest approach was 540 kilometers. After the Earth flyby encounter, NEAR's previously planned mission profile had to be revised in the light of an aborted engine burn on 20 December 1998 that prevented a critical trajectory correction to meet up with Eros a month later. Instead, NEAR was put on a backup trajectory that afforded a different flyby than originally planned. As part of this new plan, the spacecraft first flew past Eros on 23 December 1998 at 18:41:23 UT at a range of 3,827 kilometers (distance measured from the center of mass), at which time it observed about 60 percent of the asteroid and discovered that the minor planet was smaller than expected. NEAR also found that the asteroid has two medium-sized

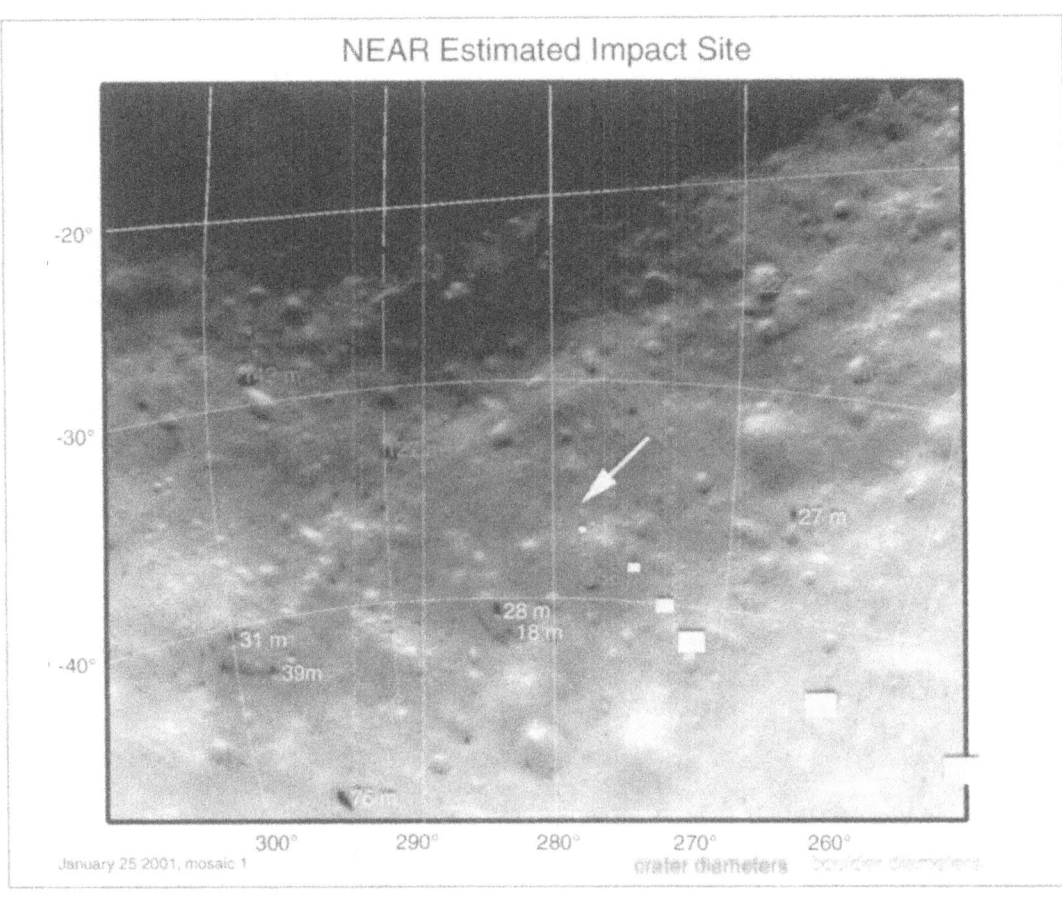

This map projection of NEAR Shoemaker images shows locations and sizes of landmarks surrounding the spacecraft's planned landing site. Diameters of craters are shown in red, and diameters of boulders are shown in yellow. Diameters are given in units of meters (1 meter is about 3.3 feet). Coordinates along the left side of the map are degrees south latitude and coordinates along the bottom are degrees west longitude. The six yellow "footprint" boxes represent approximate image size at 500, 1,000, 1,500, 2,000, 2,500, and 3,000 meters above the surface during descent. The spacecraft will take pictures continuously between spots. The arrow marks the estimated touchdown site. The mosaic is made from images taken 25 January 2001 from an altitude of about 25 kilometers.

craters, a long surface ridge, and a density similar to that of Earth's crust. After several more trajectory adjustments, NEAR finally moved into orbit around Eros at 15:33 UT on 14 February 2000, roughly a year later than intended. Orbital parameters were 321 x 366 kilometers. NEAR was the first humanmade object to orbit an asteroid. Through 2000, NEAR's orbit has been shifted in stages to permit scientific research programs. There were a few problems before the landing on the asteroid. For example, on 13 May 2000, controllers had to turn off the NEAR Infrared Spectrometer because of an excessive power surge. By 30 April, the spacecraft was in its operational orbit at an altitude of about 50 kilometers from the center of Eros. Later on 13 July, Eros entered an even lower orbit at 35 kilometers that brought the vehicle as close as 19 kilometers from the surface. After about ten days, it moved back into a higher orbit. On 26 October, NEAR performed another close flyby of the surface, this time to just 5.3 kilometers. In anticipation of the actual landing, the spacecraft conducted a flyby in January 2001 down to a range of 2.7 kilometers and, in the process, returned more spectacular pictures.

The historic landing phase began at 15:32 UT on 12 February 2001, when Eros fired its engines to begin controlled descent. After a total of four thruster firings, at 20:01: 52 UT on 12 February, the spacecraft gingerly landed on the surface of Eros at a gentle 1.6 meters per

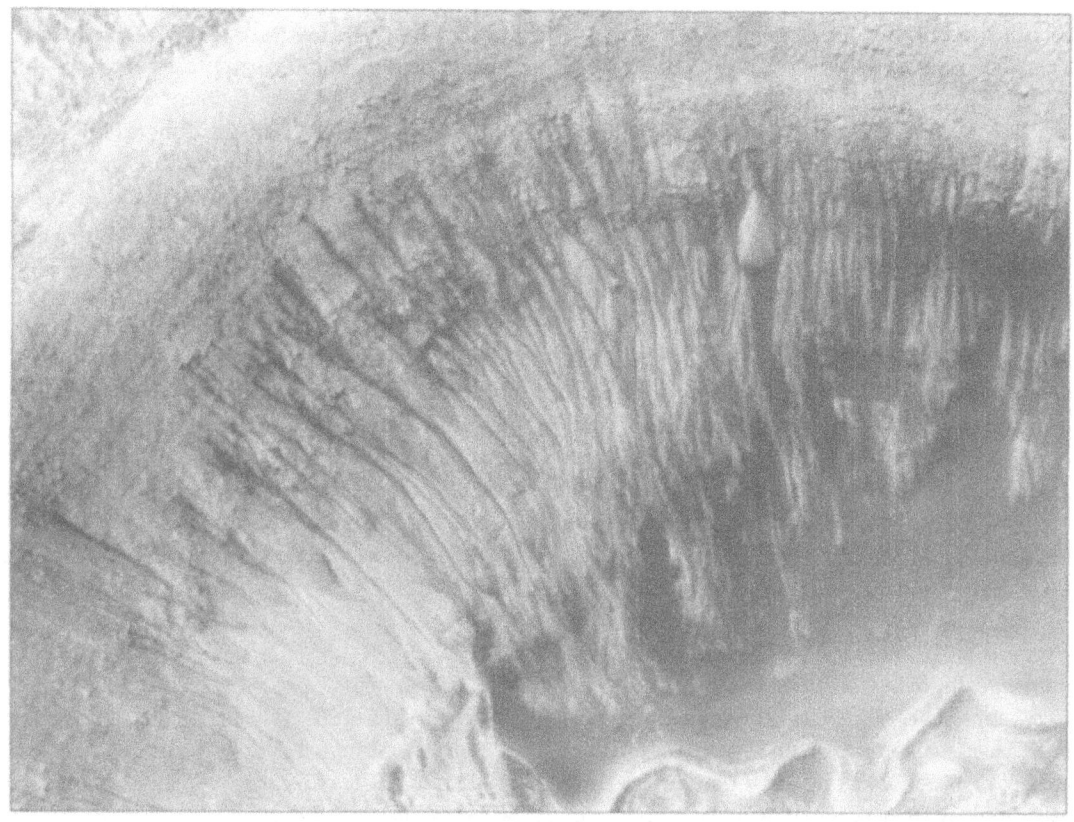

This image from Mars Global Surveyor shows channeled aprons in a small crater within Newton Crater, a large basin formed by an asteroid impact that probably occurred more than 3 billion years ago. It is approximately 287 kilometers across. The picture shown here (top) highlights the north wall of a specific, smaller crater located in the southwestern quarter of Newton Crater (above). The crater of interest was also formed by an impact; it is about 7 kilometers across, which is about 7 times bigger than the famous Meteor Crater in northern Arizona in North America. The north wall of the small crater has many narrow gullies eroded into it. These are to have been formed by flowing water and debris. Debris transported with the water created lobed and finger-like deposits at the base of the crater wall where it intersects the floor (bottom center). Many of the finger-like deposits have small channels, indicating that a liquid—most likely water—flowed in these areas. Hundreds of individual water and debris flow events might have occurred to create the scene shown here. Each outburst of water from higher up on the crater slopes would have constituted a competition among evaporation, freezing, and gravity.

second. During its entire descent, NEAR snapped a series of 69 spectacular photographs, the last one being a mere 120 meters from the surface. Touchdown was in an area just outside a saddle-shaped depression known as Himeros. Eros was 196 million miles from Earth at the time. Although the NEAR spacecraft was not designed to survive landing, its instruments remained operational. Immediately after landing, NASA approved a ten-day extension that was lengthened to fourteen days in order to use the gamma-ray spectrometer. The last transmission from the spacecraft was at 00:00 UT on 1 March 2001. During the mission, NEAR collected ten times more data than had been originally planned and returned approximately 160,000 images. On 14 March 2000, a month after entering asteroid orbit, NASA renamed the NEAR spacecraft NEAR Shoemaker in honor of renowned geologist Eugene Shoemaker.

182)
Mars Global Surveyor
Nation: U.S. (69)
Objective(s): Mars orbit
Spacecraft: MGS
Spacecraft Mass: 1,062.1 kg
Mission Design and Management: NASA JPL
Launch Vehicle: Delta 7925 (no. D239)
Launch Date and Time: 7 November 1996 / 17:00:49 UT

Launch Site: ESMC / launch complex 17A
Scientific Instruments:
1) MOC Mars orbital camera
2) MOLA Mars orbital laser altimeter
3) TES thermal emission spectrometer
4) MAG/ER magnetometer/electron reflectometer
5) RS radio science experiment
6) MR Mars relay antenna for future spacecraft

Results: Mars Global Surveyor was the first spacecraft in NASA's new Mars Surveyor program that was designed to inaugurate a new generation of American space probes to explore Mars every twenty-six months from 1996 to 2005. The Mars Surveyor program (formulated in 1994) was intended to economize costs and maximize returns by involving a single industrial partner with the Jet Propulsion Laboratory to design, build, and deliver a flightworthy vehicle for Mars every two years. The Mars Global Surveyor spacecraft carries five instruments similar to those carried by the lost Mars Observer probe that fell silent in 1993. After midcourse corrections on 21 November 1996 and 20 March 1997, Mars Global Surveyor entered orbit around Mars on 12 September 1997 after engine ignition at 01:17 UT. Initial orbital parameters were 258 x 54,021 kilometers. Commencement of its planned two-year mission was delayed because one of its two solar panels (-Y) had not fully deployed soon after launch, prompting mission planners to reconfigure the aerobraking process required to place the vehicle in its intended orbit. The solar panels were designed to act as atmospheric brakes to change orbit. The modified aerobraking maneuver altered the planned orbit from an afternoon pass over the equator to a nighttime pass and also delayed the mission by a year and shortened its projected lifetime. The spacecraft's revised aerobraking maneuvers were finally completed on 4 February 1999 with a major burn from its main engine. A subsequent firing on 19 February finally put Mars Global Surveyor into a Sun-synchronous orbit, and on 9 March 1999, its mapping mission formally began. Despite the early problems, Mars Global Surveyor began to send back impressive data and images of Mars during its movement to its new orbit. The spacecraft tracked the evolution of a dust storm, gathered information on the Martian terrain, found compelling evidence indicating the presence of liquid water at or near the surface (formally announced by NASA on 22 June 2000), and photographed the infamous "face on Mars" that some believed was an artificial formation. During its mission, the Mars Global Surveyor also produced the first three-dimensional profiles of Mars's north pole using laser altimeter readings. By mid-2000, the spacecraft had taken tens of thousands of high-resolution photos of the Red Planet. Operations were expected to end by 31 January 2001, but the good health of onboard systems allowed scientists to continue the mission. All scientific instruments remain operational as of mid-2001 and are expected to continue to at least April 2002.

183)
Mars 8 / Mars-96
Nation: Russia (106)
Objective(s): Mars orbit and landing
Spacecraft: M1 (no. 520)
Spacecraft Mass: 6,200 kg
Mission Design and Management: NPO Lavochkin
Launch Vehicle: 8K82K + Blok D-2 (Proton-K no. 392-02)
Launch Date and Time: 16 November 1996 / 20:48:53 UT
Launch Site: GIIK-5 / launch site 200L
Scientific Instruments:
  Orbiter:
  1) ASPERA-C energy-mass experiment
  2) FONEMA omni non-scanning energy-mass ion analyzer
  3) DYMIO omni ionosphere energy mass spectrometer
  4) MARIPROB ionosphere plasma spectrometers
  5) MAREMF electron analyzer/ magnetometer
  6) ELISMA wave complex experiment
  7) SLED-2 low-energy charged-particle spectrometer
  8) PGS precision gamma spectrometer
  9) LILAS-2 cosmic and solar gamma-burst spectrometer
  10) EVRIS stellar oscillations photometer
  11) RADIUS-MD dosimeter

12) MORION-S science data acquisition instrument
13) ARGUS imaging system
14) TERMOSCAN mapping radiometer
15) SVET mapping spectrometer
16) SPICAM multichannel spectrometer
17) UVS-M ultraviolet spectrometer
18) LWR longwave radar
19) NEUTRON-S neutron spectrometer
20) PFS infrared Fourier spectrometer
21) PHOTON gamma spectrometer
22) MAK quadruple mass spectrometer

Small autonomous stations (each):
1) MIS meteorology instrument system
2) DPI three-component accelerometer
3) APX alpha-particle proton and x-ray spectrometer
4) OPTIMIZM seismometer/magnetometer/inclinometer
5) PanCam panoramic camera
6) DesCam descent phase camera

Penetrators (each):
1) TV camera
2) MECOM meteorological unit
3) PEGAS gamma-ray spectrometer
4) ANGSTREM x-ray spectrometer
5) ALPHA alpha/proton spectrometer
6) NEUTRON-P neutron spectrometer
7) GRUNT accelerometers
8) TERMOZOND temperature probes
9) Kamerton seismometer
10) IMAP-6 magnetometer

Results: Mars 8, the only Soviet/Russian lunar or planetary probe in twelve years (1988 to 2000), was an ambitious mission to investigate the evolution of the Martian atmosphere, its surface, and its interior. The entire spacecraft comprised an orbiter, two small autonomous stations, and two independent penetrators. The three-axis stabilized orbiter carried two platforms for pointing several optical instruments for studying the Martian surface and atmosphere. After an initial period in low orbit lasting three to four weeks acting as a relay to the landers, the orbiter would have spent approximately two Earth years in a 250 x 18,000-kilometer orbit at 101° inclination mapping Mars. The orbiter would have released the two small autonomous stations four to five days before entering orbit. The small stations would have landed on the Martian surface, cushioned by an inflatable shell that was to split open after landing. The stations were to have transmitted data daily (initially) and then every three days for about 20 minutes each session. The stations would have studied soil characteristics and taken photos on the surface. The two 75-kilogram (each) penetrators, meanwhile, would have impacted the Martian surface at a speed of 76 meters per second to reach about 6 to 8 meters in depth. The orbiter would have released them after entering Martian orbit (between seven and twenty-eight days after entering orbit). During the mission's one-year lifetime, the penetrators would have served as nodes of a seismic network. The Proton-K launch vehicle successfully delivered the payload to Earth orbit (after the first firing of the Blok D-2 upper stage). At that point, the Blok D-2 was to fire once again to place Mars 8 into an elliptical orbit, after which the Fregat propulsion module would have sent the spacecraft on a Martian encounter trajectory. The Blok D-2 engine, however, shut down prematurely after only 20 seconds as a result of a command from the payload, thus putting its precious payload into an incorrect orbit of 145.7 x 171.1 kilometers. Mars 8 and its Fregat module then automatically separated from the Blok D-2. The latter seems to have fired (as planned earlier), placing Mars 8 in an 87 x 1,500-kilometer orbit that deposited the planetary probe in Earth's atmosphere. Reports at the time suggested that debris from Mars 8 may have fallen in Chile or Bolivia, contaminating areas with its plutonium power source. Mars 8 was scheduled to arrive in Mars orbit on 23 September 1997.

184)
Mars Pathfinder
Nation: U.S. (70)
Objective(s): Mars landing and roving operations
Spacecraft: Mars Pathfinder
Spacecraft Mass: 870 kg
Mission Design and Management: NASA JPL
Launch Vehicle: Delta 7925 (no. D240)
Launch Date and Time: 4 December 1996 / 06:58:07 UT
Launch Site: ESMC / launch complex 17B
Scientific Instruments:
Pathfinder lander:
1) IMP imaging system (included magnets and wind socks)

In the summer of 1997, the Mars Pathfinder excited people around the globe as its tiny Rover, "Sojourner," set about exploring the Red Planet.

2) APXS alpha/proton/x-ray spectrometer
3) ASI/MET atmospheric structure/meteorology package

Sojourner rover:
1) imaging system (three cameras)
2) laser stripers
3) accelerometers
4) potentiometers

Results: Mars Pathfinder was an ambitious mission to send a lander and a separate, remote-controlled rover to the surface of Mars, the second of NASA's Discovery missions. Launched one month after Mars Global Surveyor, Pathfinder was sent on a slightly shorter seven-month trajectory designed for earlier arrival. The main spacecraft included a 10.6-kilogram, six-wheeled rover known as Sojourner capable of traveling 500 meters from the main ship at top speeds of 1 centimeter per second. The mission's primary goal was not only to demonstrate innovative, low-cost technologies, but also to return geological, soil, magnetic property, and atmospheric data. After a seven-month traverse and four trajectory corrections (on 10 January, 3 February, 6 May, and 25 June 1997), Pathfinder arrived at Mars on 4 July 1997. The spacecraft entered the atmosphere and was then slowed by aerobraking, retro-rockets, and a parachute before bouncing on the surface using cushioned landing bags that had deployed 8 seconds before impact. Pathfinder landed at 16:56:55 UT on 4 July 1997 at 19.30° north latitude and 33.52° west longitude in Ares Vallis, about 19 kilometers southwest of the original target. Impact speed was about 10.5 meters per second; the spacecraft bounced several times before coming to a complete stop. The next day, Pathfinder deployed the Sojourner rover on the Martian surface via landing ramps. Sojourner was the first wheeled vehicle to be used on any other planet of the solar system. During its eighty-three-day mission, the rover covered hundreds of square meters, returned 550 photographs, and performed chemical analyses at sixteen different locations near the lander. The latter, meanwhile, transmitted more than 16,500 images and 8.5 million measurements of atmospheric pressure, temperature, and windspeed. Data from the rover suggested that rocks at the landing site resembled terrestrial volcanic types with high silicon content, specifically a rock type known as andesite. Although the planned lifetimes of Pathfinder and Sojourner were expected to be one month and one week, respectively, these times were exceeded by three and twelve times, respectively. Final contact with Pathfinder was at 10:23 UT on 27 September 1997. Although mission planners tried to reestablish contact for the next five months, the highly successful mission was officially declared terminated on 10 March 1998. After landing, Mars Pathfinder was renamed the Sagan Memorial Station after the late astronomer and planetologist Carl Sagan.

1997

185)
ACE
Nation: U.S. (71)
Objective(s): L1 Libration Point
Spacecraft: ACE
Spacecraft Mass: 752 kg
Mission Design and Management: NASA GSFC
Launch Vehicle: Delta 7920-8 (no. D247)
Launch Date and Time: 25 August 1997 / 14:39 UT
Launch Site: ESMC / launch complex 17A
Scientific Instruments:
1) SWIMS solar wind ion mass spectrometer
2) SWICS solar wind ion composition spectrometer
3) ULEIS ultra-low-energy isotope spectrometer
4) SEPICA solar energetic-particle ionic charge analyzer
5) SIS solar isotope spectrometer
6) CRIS cosmic-ray isotope spectrometer
7) SWEPAM solar wind electron, proton, and alpha monitor
8) EPAM electron, proton, and alpha-particle monitor
9) MAG magnetometer
10) RTSW real-time solar wind experiment

Results: The Advanced Composition Explorer (ACE) spacecraft was designed to study space-borne energetic particles from the L1 Libration Point, about 1.4 million kilometers from Earth. Specifically, the spacecraft was launched to investigate the matter ejected from the Sun to establish the commonality and interaction among the Sun, Earth, and the Milky Way galaxy. In addition, ACE also provides real-time space weather data and advanced warning of geomagnetic storms. ACE's nine instruments have a collecting power that is 10 to 10,000 times greater than anything previously flown. After launch, the spacecraft's Delta 2 launch vehicle's second stage reignited (for 4 hours) to insert the satellite into a 177 x 1.37-million-kilometer orbit. After reaching apogee a month after launch, ACE inserted itself into its halo orbit around the L1 point. The spacecraft was declared operational on 21 January 1998, with a projected two- to five-year lifetime. With the exception of the SEPICA solar energetic-particle ionic charge analyzer, all instruments on ACE were operational as of June 2001.

186)
Cassini/Huygens
Nation/Organization: U.S., ESA, and the ASI (1)
Objective(s): Saturn orbit and Titan landing
Spacecraft: Cassini and Huygens
Spacecraft Mass: 5,655 kg
Mission Design and Management: NASA JPL and ESA

Launch Vehicle: Titan 401B-Centaur (TC-21 / Titan 401 no. 4B-33)
Launch Date and Time: 15 October 1997 / 08:43 UT
Launch Site: ESMC / launch complex 40
Scientific Instruments:
Cassini:
1) VIMS visual infrared mapping spectrometer
2) ISS imaging system
3) RADAR instrument
4) ion neutral mass spectrometer
5) plasma/radio wave spectrometer
6) plasma spectrometer
7) ultraviolet spectrometer/imager
8) magnetospheric imaging instrument
9) dual technique magnetometer
10) RF instrument subsystem
11) composite infrared spectrometer

Huygens:
1) HASI atmospheric structure instrument
2) GCMS gas chromatograph neutral mass spectrometer
3) ACP aerosol collector/pyrolyser
4) DISR descent imager/spectral radiometer
5) SSP surface science package
6) DWE Doppler wind experiment

Results: The Cassini-Huygens project is the result of plans at NASA dating from the early 1980s. The cooperative project with ESA involves a NASA-supplied spacecraft, Cassini, which is on a 3.2-billion-kilometer journey to Saturn orbit, and a lander, Huygens, supplied by ESA (with major participation by the Italian Space Agency), which will descend into the atmosphere of Titan, Saturn's largest moon. During its scheduled four-year mission near Saturn, Cassini will use a large complement of instruments (including radar and optical imagers expected to return up to 300,000 images) to explore both Saturn and its many moons. The 3,132-kilogram orbiter, with a design life of eleven years, is powered by three RTGs. The 335-kilogram probe, during its descent, will determine Titan's atmosphere's chemical properties and measure winds, temperature, and pressure profiles from 170 kilometers down to the surface. Although the probe is not designed to survive past landing, scientists hope that Huygens might return data after touchdown. Cassini's trip to Saturn includes four gravity-assists. Seven months after launch, the spacecraft passed Venus on 26 April 1988 at a range of 284 kilometers, gaining 26,280 kilometers per hour. Cassini performed a second flyby of Venus on 24 June 1999 at a range of 600 kilometers and one of Earth at 03:28 UT on 18 August 1999 at a range of 1,171 kilometers; it then headed to Jupiter. During this portion of the traverse, Cassini passed by the asteroid 2685 Masursky on 23 January 2000, coming close to a distance of 1.5 million kilometers at 09:58 UT. During the encounter, Cassini used its remote-sensing instruments to investigate the asteroid's size and dimensions and albedo. During the Jupiter encounter, on 30 December 2000, Cassini performed simultaneous observations of the planet with the Galileo probe. Once past Jupiter, Cassini's trajectory will be set up for a Saturn encounter beginning 1 July 2004. Cassini is scheduled to go into a 147-day orbit around Saturn eleven days later. Parameters are expected to be 1.3 x 176 RS with a 17° inclination. About four months after entering orbit, on 6 November 2004, Cassini will release the Huygens probe and continue on its numerous flybys. The orbiter is expected to fly by Titan during number 33 of its 63-orbit mission with a closest approach of 950 kilometers. The spacecraft will also perform close flybys of the other moons (including Iapetus, Enceladus, Dione, and Rhea) and more distant encounters with Tethys, Mimas, and Hyperion. The orbiter's mission is scheduled to end formally on 30 June 2008. Meanwhile, the European Huygens probe will enter Titan's atmosphere on 27 November 2004. During its 2.5-hour descent, the spacecraft will deploy a main parachute for stabilization while it relays data back to the orbiter for subsequent transmission back to Earth.

187)
Asiasat 3 / "HGS 1"
Organization: Asia Satellite Telecommunications Co. (1)
Objective(s): geostationary orbit
Spacecraft: Asiasat 1
Spacecraft Mass: 3,465 kg

Mission Design and Management:
Launch Vehicle: 8K82K + Blok DM3 (Proton-K no. 394-01 / Blok DM3 no. 5L)
Launch Date and Time: 24 December 1997 / 23:19 UT
Launch Site: GIIK-5 / launch site 81L
Scientific Instruments: none
Results: Asiasat 3 was a communications satellite, launched by the Russians for Asia Satellite Telecommunications Company, that ended up in an incorrect orbit after a failure of the Blok DM3 upper stage. Because of the improper second firing of the Blok DM3, the satellite ended up in a useless 203 x 36,000-kilometer orbit and was written off as a loss by Asiasat. Insurance underwriters subsequently signed an agreement with Hughes Global Systems (who also built the satellite) to salvage the vehicle and bring it to its originally intended geostationary orbit by using as little propellant as possible. Using eleven carefully planned burns beginning 12 April 1998, controllers raised the orbit's apogee to 321,000 kilometers. Then, with the twelfth firing on 7 May 1998, the spacecraft was sent on a nine-day round trip around the Moon, approaching as close as 6,200 kilometers to its surface on 13 May. Using this gravity-assist, Asiasat 3 hurtled back into a usable orbit. By 16 May 1998, perigee had been raised to 42,000 kilometers and inclination reduced from 51° to 18°. A second circumlunar mission began on 1 June and culminated in a 34,300-kilometer flyby of the Moon. After four more engine firings, the satellite was finally in a 24-hour orbit by 17 June 1998, above 153°. The satellite, now owned by Hughes, has been renamed HGS 1.

1998

188)
Lunar Prospector
Nation: U.S. (72)
Objective(s): lunar orbit
Spacecraft: Lunar Prospector
Spacecraft Mass: 300 kg
Mission Design and Management: NASA ARC
Launch Vehicle: Athena-2 (LM-004)
Launch Date and Time: 7 January 1998 / 02:28:44 UT
Launch Site: WSMC / SLC-46
Scientific Instruments:
1) MAG magnetometer
2) ER electron reflectometer
3) GRS gamma-ray spectrometer
4) NS neutron spectrometer
5) APS alpha particle spectrometer
6) DGE Doppler gravity experiment (using S-band antenna)

Results: Lunar Prospector was the third mission selected as part of NASA's Discovery program of low-cost missions. The spacecraft was designed to create the first complete compositional and gravity maps of the Moon during its one-year mission. After two midcourse corrections, Lunar Prospector entered orbit around the Moon 105 hours after launch. Initial parameters were 92 x 153 kilometers. After two further corrections on 13 and 15 January, the spacecraft entered its operational 100- x 100-kilometer orbit at 90° inclination. Perhaps of most interest to scientists was continued investigation into the signs of water ice on the Moon as found by the Clementine probe. Lunar Prospector's data showed an estimated six billion tons of water ice trapped in the shadows of lunar polar regions. The spacecraft also detected strong localized magnetic fields; mapped the global distribution of major rock types; and discovered signs of a tiny, iron-rich core. On 10 December 1998, Lunar Prospector's orbit was lowered to 40 kilometers to perform high-resolution studies. A subsequent maneuver on 28 January 1999 changed the orbit to 15 x 45 kilometers and ended the space probe's primary mission. Lunar Prospector was deliberately landed on a shadowed crater on the lunar surface at 09:52:02 UT on 31 July 1999. During the descent, the spacecraft failed to find any observable signature of water. The vehicle carried the cremated remains of geologist Eugene Shoemaker to the lunar surface.

189)
Nozomi
Nation: Japan (4)
Objective(s): Mars orbit, lunar flybys
Spacecraft: Planet-B
Spacecraft Mass: 536 kg
Mission Design and Management: ISAS
Launch Vehicle: M-5 (no. 3)
Launch Date and Time: 3 July 1998 / 18:12 UT
Launch Site: Kagoshima / launch complex M-5

Scientific Instruments:
1) MIC visible camera
2) MGF magnetometer
3) ESA energetic electrons experiment
4) ISA energetic ions experiment
5) IMI energetic ion mass experiment
6) EIS high-energy particles experiment
7) TPA thermal ion drift experiment
8) PET electro, UVS ultraviolet spectrometer
9) PWS sounder/HF waves experiment
10) LFA plasma waves experiment
11) NMS neutral gas mass spectrometer
12) MDC dust counter
13) XUV EUV spectrometer
14) USO ultra-stable oscillator/radio science experiment

Results: Nozomi, Japan's fourth "deep space" probe, was also its first planetary spacecraft. The spacecraft was slated to enter a highly elliptical orbit around Mars on 11 October 1999. Its mission is to conduct long-term investigations of the planet's upper atmosphere and its interactions with the solar wind and to track the escape trajectories of oxygen molecules from Mars' thin atmosphere. The spacecraft is expected to take pictures of the planet and its moons from its operational orbit of 300 x 47,500 kilometers. During perigee, Nozomi will perform remote sensing of the atmosphere and surface; while close to apogee, the spacecraft will study ions and neutral gas escaping from the planet. Although designed and built by Japan, the spacecraft carries a set of fourteen instruments from Japan, Canada, Germany, Sweden, and the United States. After entering an elliptical parking orbit around Earth, Nozomi was sent on an interplanetary trajectory that involved two gravity-assist flybys of the Moon on 24 September and 18 December 1998 (at 2,809 kilometers), and one of Earth on 20 December 1998 (at 1,003 kilometers). Due to insufficient velocity imparted during the Earth flyby and two trajectory correction burns on 21 December 1998 that used more propellant than intended, Nozomi's originally planned mission had to be completely reconfigured. The spacecraft, currently in heliocentric orbit, is now planned to arrive in Mars orbit in December 2003, four years after its original schedule. A nominal mission is planned for two Earth years but may be extended to three to five years depending on the state of the spacecraft.

190)
Deep Space 1
Nation: U.S. (73)
Objective(s): asteroid flyby
Spacecraft: DS 1
Spacecraft Mass: 489 kg
Mission Design and Management: NASA JPL
Launch Vehicle: Delta 7326-9.5 (no. D261)
Launch Date and Time: 24 October 1998 / 12:08:00 UT
Launch Site: ESMC / launch complex 17A
Scientific Instruments:
1) MICAS miniature integrated camera-spectrometer
2) PEPE plasma experiment for planetary exploration technology

Results: Deep Space 1 (DS 1) was designed to test innovative technologies appropriate for future deep space and interplanetary missions. It is the first in a new series of technology demonstration missions under NASA's New Millennium program. The spacecraft's main goals are to test such technologies as ion propulsion, autonomous optical navigation, a solar power concentration array, a miniature camera, and an imaging spectrometer during a flyby of the asteroid 1992 KD (renamed 9969 Braille). A month after launch, on 24 November 1998, controllers fired the Deep Space 1's ion propulsion system (fueled by xenon gas) while the spacecraft was 4.8 million kilometers from Earth. The engine ran continuously for 14 days and demonstrated a specific impulse of 3,100 seconds, as much as ten times higher than possible with conventional chemical propellants. DS 1 passed by the near-Earth asteroid 9669 Braille at 04:46 UT on 29 July 1999 at a range of only 26 kilometers at a speed of 15.5 kilometers per second. It was the closest asteroid flyby to date. Photographs taken and other data collected during the encounter were transmitted back to Earth in the following few days. DS 1 found Braille to be 2.2 kilometers at its longest and 1 kilometer at its shortest. Once the very successful primary mission was over on 18 September 1999, NASA formulated an extended mission. Originally, the plan had been to make DS 1 fly by the dormant Comet

This artist's conception of the New Millennium Deep Space 1 mission illustrates the new technologies to be validated for future missions.

Wilson-Harrington in January 2001 and the Comet Borrelly in September 2001, but the spacecraft's star tracker failed on 11 November 1999. Mission planners revised the manifest to include a flyby that would not require a star-tracker—a single flyby of Borrelly in September 2001. By the end of 1999, the ion engine of DS 1 had expended 22 kilograms of xenon to impart a total delta V of 1,300 meters per second. On its way to Borrelly, it set the record for the longest operating time for a propulsion system in space. By 17 August 2000, the engine had been operating for 162 days as part of an eight-month run. On 22 September 2001, DS 1 flew past the coma of Comet Borrelly at 16.5 kilometers per second to obtain pictures and infrared spectra of the nucleus. NASA terminated contact with DS 1 on 18 December 2001, signaling the end to one of the more successful deep space missions in recent history.

191)
Mars Climate Orbiter
Nation: U.S. (74)
Objective(s): Mars orbit
Spacecraft: MCO
Spacecraft Mass: 629 kg
Mission Design and Management: NASA JPL
Launch Vehicle: Delta 7427-9.5 (no. D264)
Launch Date and Time: 11 December 1998 / 18:45:51 UT
Launch Site: ESMC / launch complex 17A
Scientific Instruments:
1) PMIRR pressure modulated infrared radiometer
2) MARCI Mars color imaging system (two cameras)
3) UHF communications system

Results: Mars Climate Orbiter was the second probe in NASA's Mars Surveyor program, which also included the Mars Global Surveyor (launched in November 1996) and Mars Polar Lander (launched in January 1999). Mars Climate Orbiter was designed to arrive at roughly the same time as Mars Polar Lander and conduct simultaneous investigations of Mars's atmosphere, climate, and surface. Mars Climate Orbiter was also designed to serve as a communications relay for the latter. After the lander's three-month mission, MCO would have performed a two-year independent mission to monitor atmospheric dust and water vapor and take daily pictures of the planet's surface to construct an evolutionary map of climatic changes. Scientists hoped that such information would aid in reconstructing Mars' climatic history and provide evidence of buried water reserves. The spacecraft was scheduled to arrive in Mars orbit on 23 September 1999 and attain its operational near-circular Sun-synchronous orbit at 421 kilometers by 1 December 1999. After the end of its main mapping mission on 15 January 2001, Mars Climate Orbiter would have acted as a communications relay for future NASA missions to Mars. After launch, the spacecraft performed four midcourse corrections on 21 December 1998, 4 March, 25 July, and 15 September 1999. At 09:01 UT (received time) on 23 September 1999, the orbiter began its Mars orbit insertion burn as planned. The spacecraft was scheduled to reestablish contact after passing behind Mars, but no further signals were received from the spacecraft. An investigation indicated that the failure resulted from a navigational error due to commands from Earth being sent in English units without being converted into the metric standard. The error caused the orbiter to miss its intended 140- to 150-kilometer altitude orbit and instead fall into the Martian atmosphere at approximately 57 kilometers altitude and burn up.

1999

192)
Mars Polar Lander/Deep Space 2
Nation: U.S. (75)
Objective(s): Mars landing
Spacecraft: MPL
Spacecraft Mass: 583 kg
Mission Design and Management: NASA JPL
Launch Vehicle: Delta 7425-9.5 (no. D265)
Launch Date and Time: 3 January 1999 / 20:21:10 UT
Launch Site: ESMC / launch complex 17B
Scientific Instruments:
1) MVACS Mars volatile and climate surveyor instrument package
    a) SSI stereo surface imager
    b) RA robotic arm
    c) MET meteorology package
    d) TEGA thermal and evolved gas analyzer
    e) RAC robotic arm camera
2) MARDI Mars descent imager
3) LIDAR light detection and ranging instrument

Results: The Mars Polar Lander (MPL) was one of NASA's Mars Surveyor missions that called for a series of small, low-cost spacecraft for sustained exploration of Mars. MPL's primary goal was to deploy a lander and two penetrators (known as Deep Space 2) on the surface of Mars to extend our knowledge on the planet's past and present water resources. The objective was to explore the never-before-studied carbon dioxide icecap about 1,000 kilometers from the south pole. The mission called for recording local meteorological conditions, analyzing samples of polar deposits, and taking multispectral images of local areas. MPL was to have performed its mission simultaneously with that of the Mars Climate Orbiter, which would have acted as a communications relay during its surface operations. MPL itself comprised a bus section (for power, propulsion, and communications during the outbound voyage) and a 290-kilogram lander that stood 1.06 meters tall on the ground. The lander was equipped with a 2-meter-long remote arm to dig into the terrain and investigate the properties of Martian soil (using the thermal and evolved gas analyzer). MPL was supposed to arrive at Mars on 3 December 1999. After atmospheric entry, about 10 minutes prior to landing, the spacecraft was to jettison its cruise stage and solar panels and then release the two 3.572-kilogram (each) Deep Space 2 microprobes. Unlike Mars Pathfinder, MPL was scheduled to make a completely controlled landing using retro-rockets all the way to the surface. Landing was scheduled for 21:03 UT on 3 December 1999, with two-way communications planned to begin 20 minutes later. The two Deep Space 2 microprobes (renamed Amundsen and Scott on 15 November 1999), meanwhile, would impact the ground at a speed of 200 meters per second at about 50 to 85 seconds prior to the lander's touchdown about 100 kilometers away. Each penetrator was designed to obtain a small sample of subsurface soil using an electric drill for analysis. The microprobes' mission was expected to last about 36 hours, while the lander mission would continue until 1 March 2000. In the event, contact with MPL was lost at 20:00 UT on 3 December, about 6 minutes prior to atmospheric entry. With no communications for over two weeks, on 16 December 1999, NASA used the Mars Global Surveyor orbiting Mars to look for signs of the lander on the Martian surface, but the search proved fruitless. On 17 January 2000, NASA finally terminated all attempts to establish contact with the lost lander. An independent investigation into the failure, whose results were released publicly on 28 March 2000, indicated that the most probable cause of the failure was the generation of spurious signals when the lander's legs deployed during the descent. These signals falsely indicated that the spacecraft had touched down on Mars when in fact it was still descending. The main engines prematurely shut down, and the lander fell to the Martian landscape.

193)
Stardust
Nation: U.S. (76)
Objective(s): comet sample return
Spacecraft: Stardust
Spacecraft Mass: 385 kg
Mission Design and Management:
Launch Vehicle: Delta 7426-9.5 (no. D266)
Launch Date and Time: 7 February 1999 / 21:04:15 UT
Launch Site: ESMC / launch complex 17A
Scientific Instruments:
1) aerogel dust collectors
2) CIDA cometary and interstellar dust analyzer
3) NavCam navigation camera
4) DFM Whipple shield flux monitors

Results: Stardust is an ambitious mission, the fourth of NASA's Discovery program of low-cost exploration missions (after NEAR, Mars Pathfinder, and Lunar Prospector). Its primary goal was to fly by the Comet Wild-2, collect samples of dust from the coma of the comet, and then return the samples to Earth. During flight, Stardust was to collect samples of interstellar dust grains. Scientists on Earth expect to perform detailed analyses of these samples, which represent primitive substances from the time the solar system was formed. Stardust collected the samples using a low-density microporous silica-based substance known as aerogel attached to panels on the spacecraft to "soft-catch" and preserve the cometary materials. The spacecraft was launched into heliocentric orbit and performed midcourse corrections on 28 December 1999 and 18 January, 20 January, and 22 January 2000. Its first interstellar dust collection operation was carried out between 22 February and 1 May 2000. After approximately a year in heliocentric orbit, Stardust flew by Earth for a gravity-assist (closest approach to Earth was at 11:13 UT on 15 January 2001 at a range of 6,012 kilometers) to send it on a second sample-collection exercise between July and December 2002. Stardust is expected to encounter Comet Wild-2 on 2 January 2004, when the spacecraft will pass as close as 150 kilometers while flying at a relative speed of 6.1 kilometers per second. Apart from collecting samples, Stardust will also take photographs of the comet's nucleus with a resolution of 30 meters. On 15 January 2006, Stardust will release its spin-stabilized Sample Return Capsule (SRC), which is expected to descend by parachute over the U.S. Air Force Test and Training Range in Utah at approximately 03:00 local time. The sample will be recovered by a chase aircraft.

Deep Space Chronicle

Master Table of All Deep Space, Lunar, and Planetary Probes, 1958–2000

Official Name	Spacecraft / No.	Mass	Launch Date / Time	Launch Place / Pad	Launch Vehicle / No.	Nation / Organization	Design & Operation	Objective	Outcome*
1958									
"Pioneer"	Able 1	38 kg	08-17-58 / 12:18	ETR / 17A	Thor-Able I / 127	U.S.	AFBMD	lunar orbit	U
[Luna]	Ye-1 / 1	c. 360 kg	09-23-58 / 09:03:23	NIIP-5 / 1	Luna / B1-3	USSR	OKB-1	lunar impact	U
Pioneer	Able 2	38.3 kg	10-11-58 / 08:42:13	ETR / 17A	Thor-Able I / 130	U.S.	NASA / AFBMD	lunar orbit	U
[Luna]	Ye-1 / 2	c. 360 kg	10-11-58 / 23:41:58	NIIP-5 / 1	Luna / B1-4	USSR	OKB-1	lunar impact	U
Pioneer 2	Able 3	39.6 kg	11-08-58 / 07:30	ETR / 17A	Thor-Able I / 129	U.S.	NASA / AFBMD	lunar orbit	U
[Luna]	Ye-1 / 3	c. 360 kg	12-04-58 / 18:18:44	NIIP-5 / 1	Luna / B1-5	USSR	OKB-1	lunar impact	U
Pioneer 3	-	5.87 kg	12-06-58 / 05:44:52	ETR / 5	Juno II / AM-11	U.S.	NASA / ABMA	lunar flyby	U
1959									
Luna 1	Ye-1 / 4	361.3 kg	01-02-59 / 16:41:21	NIIP-5 / 1	Luna / B1-6	USSR	OKB-1	lunar impact	P
Pioneer 4	-	6.1 kg	03-03-59 / 05:10:45	ETR / 5	Juno II / AM-14	U.S.	NASA / ABMA	lunar flyby	P
[Luna]	Ye-1A / 5	c. 390 kg	06-18-59 / 08:08	NIIP-5 / 1	Luna / I1-7	USSR	OKB-1	lunar impact	U
Luna 2	Ye-1A / 7	390.2 kg	09-12-59 / 06:39:42	NIIP-5 / 1	Luna / I1-7b	USSR	OKB-1	lunar impact	S
Luna 3	Ye-2A / 1	278.5 kg	10-04-59 / 00:43:40	NIIP-5 / 1	Luna / I1-8	USSR	OKB-1	lunar flyby	S
"Pioneer"	P-3 / Able IVB	169 kg	11-26-59 / 07:26	ETR / 14	Atlas-Able / 1	U.S.	NASA / AFBMD	lunar orbit	U
1960									
Pioneer 5	P-2 / Able 6	43.2 kg	03-11-60 / 13:00:07	ETR / 17A	Thor-Able IV / 4	U.S.	NASA GSFC	solar orbit	S
[Luna]	Ye-3 / 1	N/A	04-15-60 / 15:06:44	NIIP-5 / 1	Luna / I1-9	USSR	OKB-1	lunar flyby	U
[Luna]	Ye-3 / 2	N/A	04-19-60 / 16:07:43	NIIP-5 / 1	Luna / I1-9a	USSR	OKB-1	lunar flyby	U
"Pioneer"	P-30 / Able VA	175.5 kg	09-25-60 / 15:13	ETR / 12	Atlas-Able / 2	U.S.	NASA / AFBMD	lunar orbit	U
[Mars]	1M / 1	480 kg	10-10-60 / 14:27:49	NIIP-5 / 1	Molniya / L1-4M	USSR	OKB-1	Mars flyby	U
[Mars]	1M / 2	480 kg	10-14-60 / 13:51:03	NIIP-5 / 1	Molniya / L1-5M	USSR	OKB-1	Mars flyby	U
"Pioneer"	P-31 / Able VB	176 kg	12-15-60 / 09:10	ETR / 12	Atlas-Able / 3	U.S.	NASA / AFBMD	lunar orbit	U

* Key
U = Unsuccessful
P = Partial success
S = Successful

Official Name	Spacecraft / No.	Mass	Launch Date / Time	Launch Place / Pad	Launch Vehicle / No.	Nation / Organization	Design & Operation	Objective	Outcome
1961									
[Venera]	1VA / 1	c. 645 kg	02-04-61 / 01:18:04	NIIP-5 / 1	Molniya / L1-7	USSR	OKB-1	Venus impact	U
[Venera]	1VA / 2	643.5 kg	02-12-61 / 00:34:37	NIIP-5 / 1	Molniya / L1-6	USSR	OKB-1	Venus impact	U
Ranger 1	P-32	306.18 kg	08-23-61 / 10:04	ETR / 12	Atlas-Agena B / 1	U.S.	NASA JPL	deep space orbit	U
Ranger 2	P-33	306.18 kg	11-18-61 / 08:12	ETR / 12	Atlas-Agena B / 2	U.S.	NASA JPL	deep space orbit	U
1962									
Ranger 3	P-34	330 kg	01-26-62 / 20:30	ETR / 12	Atlas-Agena B / 3	U.S.	NASA JPL	lunar impact	U
Ranger 4	P-35	331.12 kg	04-23-62 / 20:50	ETR / 12	Atlas-Agena B / 4	U.S.	NASA JPL	lunar impact	P
Mariner 1	P-37	202.8 kg	07-22-62 / 09:21:23	ETR / 12	Atlas-Agena B / 5	U.S.	NASA JPL	Venus flyby	U
[Venera]	2MV-1 / 1	1,097 kg	08-25-62 / 02:18:45	NIIP-5 / 1	Molniya / T103-12	USSR	OKB-1	Venus impact	U
Mariner 2	P-38	203.6 kg	08-27-62 / 06:53:14	ETR / 12	Atlas-Agena B / 6	U.S.	NASA JPL	Venus flyby	S
[Venera]	2MV-1 / 2	c. 1,100 kg	09-01-62 / 02:12:30	NIIP-5 / 1	Molniya / T103-13	USSR	OKB-1	Venus impact	U
[Venera]	2MV-2 / 1	N/A	09-12-62 / 00:59:13	NIIP-5 / 1	Molniya / T103-14	USSR	OKB-1	Venus flyby	U
Ranger 5	P-36	342.46 kg	10-18-62 / 16:59:00	ETR / 12	Atlas-Agena B / 7	U.S.	NASA JPL	lunar impact	P
[Mars]	2MV-4 / 1	c. 900 kg	10-24-62 / 17:55:04	NIIP-5 / 1	Molniya / T103-15	USSR	OKB-1	Mars flyby	U
Mars 1	2MV-4 / 4	893.5 kg	11-01-62 / 16:14:16	NIIP-5 / 1	Molniya / T103-16	USSR	OKB-1	Mars flyby	P
[Mars]	2MV-3 / 1	N/A	11-04-62 / 15:35:15	NIIP-5 / 1	Molniya / T103-17	USSR	OKB-1	Mars impact	U
1963									
[Luna]	Ye-6 / 2	1,420 kg	01-04-63 / 08:49	NIIP-5 / 1	Molniya / T103-09	USSR	OKB-1	lunar landing	U
[Luna]	Ye-6 / 3	1,420 kg	02-03-63 / 09:29:14	NIIP-5 / 1	Molniya / G103-10	USSR	OKB-1	lunar landing	U
Luna 4	Ye-6 / 4	1,422 kg	04-02-63 / 08:16:37	NIIP-5 / 1	Molniya / G103-11	USSR	OKB-1	lunar landing	U
Kosmos 21	3MV-1A / 2	c. 800 kg	11-11-63 / 06:23:35	NIIP-5 / 2	Molniya / G103-18	USSR	OKB-1	lunar flyby	U

Official Name	Spacecraft / No.	Mass	Launch Date / Time	Launch Place / Pad	Launch Vehicle / No.	Nation / Organization	Design & Operation	Objective	Outcome
1964									
Ranger 6	Ranger-A / P-53	364.69 kg	01-30-64 / 15:49:09	ETR / 12	Atlas-Agena B / 8	U.S.	NASA JPL	lunar impact	P
[Zond]	3MV-1A / 4A	c. 800 kg	02-19-64 / 05:47:40	NIIP-5 / 1	Molniya / T15000-19	USSR	OKB-1	Venus flyby	U
[Luna]	Ye-6 / 6	c. 1,420 kg	03-21-64 / 08:15:35	NIIP-5 / 1	Molniya / T15000-20	USSR	OKB-1	lunar landing	U
Kosmos 27	3MV-1 / 5	948 kg	03-27-64 / 03:24:42	NIIP-5 / 1	Molniya / T15000-22	USSR	OKB-1	Venus impact	U
Zond 1	3MV-1 / 4	948 kg	04-02-64 / 02:42:40	NIIP-5 / 1	Molniya / T15000-23	USSR	OKB-1	Venus impact	U
[Luna]	Ye-6 / 5	c. 1,420 kg	04-20-64 / 08:08:28	NIIP-5 / 1	Molniya / T15000-21	USSR	OKB-1	lunar landing	U
Ranger 7	Ranger-B / P-54	365.6 kg	07-28-64 / 16:50:07	ETR / 12	Atlas-Agena B / 9	U.S.	NASA JPL	lunar impact	S
Mariner 3	Mariner-64C	260.8 kg	11-05-64 / 19:22:05	ETR / 13	Atlas-Agena D / 11	U.S.	NASA JPL	Mars flyby	U
Mariner 4	Mariner-64D	260.8 kg	11-28-64 / 14:22:01	ETR / 12	Atlas-Agena D / 12	U.S.	NASA JPL	Mars flyby	S
Zond 2	3MV-4A / 2	996 kg	11-30-64 / 13:12	NIIP-5 / 1	Molniya	USSR	OKB-1	Mars flyby	P
1965									
Ranger 8	Ranger-C	366.87 kg	02-17-65 / 17:05:00	ETR / 12	Atlas-Agena B / 13	U.S.	NASA JPL	lunar impact	S
[Surveyor Model]	SD-1	951 kg	03-02-65 / 13:25	ETR / 36A	Atlas-Centaur / 5	U.S.	NASA JPL	deep space orbit	U
Kosmos 60	Ye-6 / 9	c. 1,470 kg	03-12-65 / 09:30	NIIP-5 /	Molniya / R103-25	USSR	OKB-1	lunar landing	U
Ranger 9	Ranger-D	366.87 kg	03-21-65 / 21:37:02	ETR / 12	Atlas-Agena B / 14	U.S.	NASA JPL	lunar impact	S
[Luna]	Ye-6 / 8	c. 1,470 kg	04-10-65/ N/A	NIIP-5 / 1	Molniya / R103-26	USSR	OKB-1	lunar landing	U
Luna 5	Ye-6 / 10	1,476 kg	05-09-65 / 07:49:37	NIIP-5 / 1	Molniya / U103-30	USSR	OKB-1	lunar landing	U
Luna 6	Ye-6 / 7	1,442 kg	06-08-65 / 07:40	NIIP-5 / 1	Molniya / U103-31	USSR	OKB-1	lunar landing	U
Zond 3	3MV-4A / 3	950 kg	07-18-65/ N/A	NIIP-5 / 1	Molniya	USSR	OKB-1	lunar flyby	S
Surveyor Model 1	SD-2	950 kg	08-11-65 / 14:31:04	ETR / 36B	Atlas-Centaur / 6	U.S.	NASA JPL	deep space orbit	S
Luna 7	Ye-6 / 11	1,506 kg	10-04-65 / 07:56:40	NIIP-5 / 1	Molniya / U103-27	USSR	OKB-1	lunar landing	U
Venera 2	3MV-4 / 4	963 kg	11-12-65/ N/A	NIIP-5 / 31	Molniya-M	USSR	OKB-1	Venus flyby	S
Venera 3	3MV-3 / 1	958 kg	11-16-65/ N/A	NIIP-5 / 31	Molniya-M	USSR	OKB-1	Venus impact	S
Kosmos 96	3MV-4 / 6	c. 950 kg	11-23-65/ N/A	NIIP-5 / 31	Molniya-M	USSR	OKB-1	Venus flyby	U
Luna 8	Ye-6 / 12	1,552 kg	12-03-65 / 10:46:14	NIIP-5 / 31	Molniya / U103-28	USSR	OKB-1	lunar landing	U
Pioneer 6	Pioneer-A	62.14 kg	12-16-65 / 07:31:21	ETR / 17A	Thor-Delta E / 35	U.S.	NASA ARC	solar orbit	S

Official Name	Spacecraft / No.	Mass	Launch Date / Time	Launch Place / Pad	Launch Vehicle / No.	Nation / Organization	Design & Operation	Objective	Outcome
1966									
Luna 9	Ye-6M / 202	1,538 kg	01-31-66 / 11:41:37	NIIP-5 / 31	Molniya-M / U103-32	USSR	Lavochkin	lunar landing	S
Kosmos 111	Ye-6S / 204	c. 1,580 kg	03-01-66 / 11:03:49	NIIP-5 / 31	Molniya-M / N103-41	USSR	Lavochkin	lunar orbit	U
Luna 10	Ye-6S / 206	1,582 kg	03-31-66 / 10:47	NIIP-5 / 31	Molniya-M / N103-42	USSR	Lavochkin	lunar orbit	S
Surveyor Model 2	SD-3	784 kg	04-08-66 / 01:00:02	ETR / 36B	Atlas-Centaur / 8	U.S.	NASA JPL	deep space orbit	U
Surveyor 1	Surveyor-A	995.2 kg	05-30-66 / 14:41:01	ETR / 36A	Atlas-Centaur / 10	U.S.	NASA JPL	lunar landing	S
Explorer 33	IMP-D	93.4 kg	07-01-66 / 16:02:25	ETR / 17A	Thor-Delta E1 / 39	U.S.	NASA GSFC	lunar orbit	P
Lunar Orbiter 1	LO-A	385.6 kg	08-10-66 / 19:26:00	ETR / 13	Atlas-Agena D / 17	U.S.	NASA LaRC	lunar orbit	S
Pioneer 7	Pioneer-B	62.75 kg	08-17-66 / 15:20:17	ETR / 17A	Thor-Delta E1 / 40	U.S.	NASA ARC	solar orbit	S
Luna 11	Ye-6LF / 101	1,640 kg	08-24-66 / 08:03	NIIP-5 /	Molniya-M / N103-43	USSR	Lavochkin	lunar orbit	S
Surveyor 2	Surveyor-B	995.2 kg	09-20-66 / 12:32:00	ETR / 36A	Atlas-Centaur / 7	U.S.	NASA JPL	lunar landing	U
Luna 12	Ye-6LF / 102	1,620 kg	10-22-66 / 08:42	NIIP-5 / 31	Molniya-M / N103-44	USSR	Lavochkin	lunar orbit	S
Lunar Orbiter 2	LO-B	385.6 kg	11-06-66 / 23:21:00	ETR / 13	Atlas Agena D / 18	U.S.	NASA LaRC	lunar orbit	S
Luna 13	Ye-6M / 205	1,620 kg	12-21-66 / 10:17	NIIP-5 / 1	Molniya-M / N103-45	USSR	Lavochkin	lunar landing	S
1967									
Lunar Orbiter 3	LO-C	385.6 kg	02-05-67 / 01:17:01	ETR / 13	Atlas-Agena D / 20	U.S.	NASA LaRC	lunar orbit	S
Surveyor 3	Surveyor-C	997.9 kg	04-17-67 / 07:05:01	ETR / 36B	Atlas-Centaur / 12	U.S.	NASA JPL	lunar landing	S
Lunar Orbiter 4	LO-D	385.6 kg	05-04-67 / 22:25:00	ETR / 13	Atlas-Agena D / 22	U.S.	NASA LaRC	lunar orbit	S
Kosmos 159	Ye-6LS / 111	N/A	05-17-67 / 21:43:57	NIIP-5 / 1	Molniya-M / Ya716-56	USSR	Lavochkin	lunar orbit	P
Venera 4	1V / 310	1,106 kg	06-12-67 / 02:39:45	NIIP-5 / 1	Molniya-M	USSR	Lavochkin	Venus impact	S
Mariner 5	Mariner-67E	244.9 kg	06-14-67 / 06:01:00	ETR / 12	Atlas-Agena D / 23	U.S.	NASA JPL	Venus flyby	S
Kosmos 167	1V / 311	c. 1,100 kg	06-17-67 / 02:36:38	NIIP-5 / 1	Molniya-M	USSR	Lavochkin	Venus impact	U
Surveyor-D	Surveyor-D	1,037.4 kg	07-14-67 / 11:53:29	ETR / 36A	Atlas-Centaur / 11	U.S.	NASA JPL	lunar landing	U
Explorer 35	IMP-E	104.3 kg	07-19-67 / 14:19:02	ETR / 17B	Thor-Delta E1 / 50	U.S.	NASA GSFC	lunar orbit	S

Official Name	Spacecraft / No.	Mass	Launch Date / Time	Launch Place / Pad	Launch Vehicle / No.	Nation / Organization	Design & Operation	Objective	Outcome
1967 (continued)									
Lunar Orbiter 5	LO-E	390 kg	08-01-67 / 22:33:00	ETR / 13	Atlas-Agena D / 24	U.S.	NASA LaRC	lunar orbit	S
Surveyor 5	Surveyor-E	1,006 kg	09-08-67 / 07:57:01	ETR / 36B	Atlas-Centaur / 13	U.S.	NASA JPL	lunar landing	S
[Zond]	7K-L1 / 4L	c. 5,375 kg	09-27-67 / 22:11:54	NIIP-5 / 81L	Proton-K / 229-01	USSR	TsKBEM	circumlunar	U
Surveyor 6	Surveyor-F	1,008.3 kg	11-07-67 / 07:39:01	ETR / 36B	Atlas-Centaur / 14	U.S.	NASA JPL	lunar landing	S
[Zond]	7K-L1 / 5L	c. 5,375 kg	11-22-67 / 19:07:59	NIIP-5 / 81P	Proton-K / 230-01	USSR	TsKBEM	circumlunar	U
Pioneer 8	Pioneer-C	65.36 kg	12-13-67 / 14:08	ETR / 17B	Thor-Delta E-1 / 55	U.S.	NASA ARC	solar orbit	S
1968									
Surveyor 7	Surveyor-G	1,040.1 kg	01-07-68 / 06:30:00	ETR / 36A	Atlas-Centaur / 15	U.S.	NASA JPL	lunar landing	S
[Luna]	Ye-6LS / 112	N/A	02-07-68 / 10:43:54	NIIP-5 / 1	Molniya-M / Ya716-57	USSR	Lavochkin	lunar orbit	U
Zond 4	7K-L1 / 6L	c. 5,375 kg	03-02-68 / 18:29:23	NIIP-5 / 81L	Proton-K / 231-01	USSR	TsKBEM	deep space	P
Luna 14	Ye-6LS / 113	N/A	04-07-68 / 10:09:32	NIIP-5 / 1	Molniya-M / Ya716-58	USSR	Lavochkin	lunar orbit	S
[Zond]	7K-L1 / 7L	c. 5,375 kg	04-22-68 / 23:01:57	NIIP-5 / 81P	Proton-K / 232-01	USSR	TsKBEM	circumlunar	U
Zond 5	7K-L1 / 9L	c. 5,375 kg	09-14-68 / 21:42:11	NIIP-5 / 81L	Proton-K / 234-01	USSR	TsKBEM	circumlunar	S
Pioneer 9	Pioneer-D	65.36	11-08-68 / 09:46:29	ETR / 17B	Thor-Delta E1 / 60	U.S.	NASA ARC	solar orbit	S
Zond 6	7K-L1 / 12L	c. 5,375 kg	11-10-68 / 19:11:31	NIIP-5 / 81L	Proton-K / 235-01	USSR	TsKBEM	circumlunar	S

Official Name	Spacecraft / No.	Mass	Launch Date / Time	Launch Place / Pad	Launch Vehicle / No.	Nation / Organization	Design & Operation	Objective	Outcome
1969									
Venera 5	2V / 330	1,130 kg	01-05-69 / 06:28:08	NIIP-5 / 1	Molniya-M	USSR	Lavochkin	Venus landing	S
Venera 6	2V / 331	1,130 kg	01-10-69 / 05:51:52	NIIP-5 / 1	Molniya-M	USSR	Lavochkin	Venus landing	S
[Zond]	7K-L1 / 13L	c. 5,375 kg	01-20-69 / 04:14:36	NIIP-5 / 81L	Proton-K / 237-01	USSR	TsKBEM	circumlunar	U
[Luna]	Ye-8 / 201	c. 5,700 kg	02-19-69 / 06:48:15	NIIP-5 / 81P	Proton-K / 239-01	USSR	Lavochkin	lunar rover	U
[N1 launch test]	7K-L1S / 3S	6,900 kg	02-21-69 / 09:18:07	NIIP-5 / 110P	N1 / 3L	USSR	TsKBEM	lunar orbit	U
Mariner 6	Mariner-69F	381 kg	02-25-69 / 01:29:02	ETR / 36B	Atlas-Centaur / 20	U.S.	NASA JPL	Mars flyby	S
[Mars]	M-69 / 521	c. 3,800 kg	03-27-69 / 10:40:45	NIIP-5 / 81L	Proton-K / 240-01	USSR	Lavochkin	Mars orbit	U
Mariner 7	Mariner-69G	381 kg	03-27-69 / 22:22:01	ETR / 36A	Atlas-Centaur / 19	U.S.	NASA JPL	Mars flyby	S
[Mars]	M-69 / 522	c. 3,800 kg	04-02-69 / 10:33:00	NIIP-5 / 81P	Proton-K / 233-01	USSR	Lavochkin	Mars orbit	U
[Luna]	Ye-8-5 / 402	c. 5,700 kg	06-14-69 / 04:00:47	NIIP-5 / 81P	Proton-K / 238-01	USSR	Lavochkin	lunar sample	U
[N1 test flight]	7K-L1S / 5L	c. 6,900 kg	07-03-69 / 20:18:32	NIIP-5 / 110P	N1 / 5L	USSR	TsKBEM	lunar orbit	U
Luna 15	Ye-8-5 / 401	5,700 kg	07-13-69 / 02:54:42	NIIP-5 / 81P	Proton-K / 242-01	USSR	Lavochkin	lunar sample	U
Zond 7	7K-L1 / 11	c. 5,375 kg	08-07-69 / 23:48:06	NIIP-5 / 81L	Proton-K / 243-01	USSR	TsKBEM	circumlunar	S
Pioneer	Pioneer-E	65.4 kg	08-27-69 / 21:59	ETR / 17A	Thor-Delta L / 73	U.S.	NASA ARC	solar orbit	U
Kosmos 300	Ye-8-5 / 403	c. 5,700 kg	09-23-69 / 14:07:36	NIIP-5 / 81P	Proton-K / 244-01	USSR	Lavochkin	lunar sample	U
Kosmos 305	Ye-8-5 / 404	c. 5,700 kg	10-22-69 / 14:09:59	NIIP-5 / 81P	Proton-K / 241-01	USSR	Lavochkin	lunar sample	U
1970									
[Luna]	Ye-8-5 / 405	c. 5,700 kg	02-06-70 / 04:16:06	NIIP-5 / 81	Proton-K / 247-01	USSR	Lavochkin	lunar sample	U
Venera 7	3V / 630	1,180 kg	08-17-70 / 05:38:22	NIIP-5 / 31	Molniya-M	USSR	Lavochkin	Venus landing	S
Kosmos 359	3V / 631	c. 1,200 kg	08-22-70 / 05:06:09	NIIP-5 / 31	Molniya-M	USSR	Lavochkin	Venus landing	U
Luna 16	Ye-8-5 / 406	5,727 kg	09-12-70 / 13:25:53	NIIP-5 / 81L	Proton-K / 248-01	USSR	Lavochkin	lunar sample	S
Zond 8	7K-L1 / 14	c. 5,375 kg	10-20-70 / 19:55:39	NIIP-5 / 81L	Proton-K / 250-01	USSR	TsKBEM	circumlunar	S
Luna 17	Ye-8 / 203	5,700 kg	11-10-70 / 14:44:01	NIIP-5 / 81L	Proton-K / 251-01	USSR	Lavochkin	lunar rover	S

Official Name	Spacecraft / No.	Mass	Launch Date / Time	Launch Place / Pad	Launch Vehicle / No.	Nation / Organization	Design & Operation	Objective	Outcome
1971									
Mariner 8	Mariner-71H	997.9 kg	05-09-71 / 01:11:02	ETR / 36A	Atlas-Centaur / 24	U.S.	NASA JPL	Mars orbit	U
Kosmos 419	M-71 / 170	4,549 kg	05-10-71 / 16:58:42	NIIP-5 / 81L	Proton-K / 253-01	USSR	Lavochkin	Mars orbit	U
Mars 2	M-71 / 171	4,650 kg	05-19-71 / 16:22:44	NIIP-5 / 81P	Proton-K / 255-01	USSR	Lavochkin	Mars orbit / landing	P
Mars 3	M-71 / 172	4,650 kg	05-28-71 / 15:26:30	NIIP-5 / 81L	Proton-K / 249-01	USSR	Lavochkin	Mars orbit / landing	P
Mariner 9	Mariner-71I	997.9 kg	05-30-71 / 22:23:04	ETR / 36B	Atlas-Centaur / 23	U.S.	NASA JPL	Mars orbit	S
Apollo 15 Particle & Fields Sat		35.6 kg	08-04-71 / 20:13:19	Apollo 15 CSM 112	Saturn V / 510	U.S.	NASA MSC	lunar orbit	S
Luna 18	Ye-8-5 / 407	c. 5,750 kg	09-02-71 / 13:40:40	NIIP-5 / 81P	Proton-K / 256-01	USSR	Lavochkin	lunar sample	U
Luna 19	Ye-8LS / 202	c. 5,700 kg	09-28-71 / 10:00:22	NIIP-5 / 81P	Proton-K / 257-01	USSR	Lavochkin	lunar orbit	S
1972									
Luna 20	Ye-8-5 / 408	c. 5,750 kg	02-14-72 / 03:27:59	NIIP-5 / 81P	Proton-K / 258-01	USSR	Lavochkin	lunar sample	S
Pioneer 10	Pioneer-F	258 kg	03-02-72 / 01:49:04	ETR / 36A	Atlas-Centaur / 27	U.S.	NASA ARC	Jupiter flyby	S
Venera 8	3V / 670	1,184 kg	03-27-72 / 04:15:01	NIIP-5 / 31	Molniya-M	USSR	Lavochkin	Venus landing	S
Kosmos 482	3V / 671	c. 1,180 kg	03-31-72 / 04:02:33	NIIP-5 / 31	Molniya-M	USSR	Lavochkin	Venus landing	U
Apollo 16 Particle & Fields Sat		42 kg	04-24-72 / 09:56:09	Apollo 16 CSM 113	Saturn V / 511	U.S.	NASA MSC	lunar orbit	S
[N1 launch test]	7K-LOK / 6A	c.7,500 kg	11-23-72 / 06:11:55	NIIP-5 / 100L	N1 / 7L	USSR	TsKBEM	lunar orbit	U

Official Name	Spacecraft / No.	Mass	Launch Date / Time	Launch Place / Pad	Launch Vehicle / No.	Nation / Organization	Design & Operation	Objective	Outcome
1973									
Luna 21	Ye-8 / 204	c. 5,950 kg	01-08-73 / 06:55:38	NIIP-5 / 81L	Proton-K / 259-01	USSR	Lavochkin	lunar rover	S
Pioneer 11	Pioneer-G	258.5 kg	04-05-73 / 02:11	ETR / 36B	Atlas-Centaur / 30	U.S.	NASA ARC	Jupiter, Saturn flyby	S
Explorer 49	RAE-B	330.2 kg	06-10-73 / 14:13:00	ETR / 17B	Delta 1913 / 95	U.S.	NASA GSFC	lunar orbit	S
Mars 4	M-73 / 52S	3,440 kg	07-21-73 / 19:30:59	NIIP-5 / 81L	Proton-K / 261-01	USSR	Lavochkin	Mars orbit	U
Mars 5	M-73 / 53S	3,440 kg	07-25-73 / 18:55:48	NIIP-5 / 81P	Proton-K / 262-01	USSR	Lavochkin	Mars orbit	S
Mars 6	M-73 / 50P	3,260 kg	08-05-73 / 17:45:48	NIIP-5 / 81L	Proton-K / 281-01	USSR	Lavochkin	Mars landing	P
Mars 7	M-73 / 51P	3,260 kg	08-09-73 / 17:00:17	NIIP-5 / 81P	Proton-K / 281-01	USSR	Lavochkin	Mars landing	U
Mariner 10	Mariner-73J	502.9 kg	11-03-73 / 05:45:00	ETR / 36B	Atlas-Centaur / 34	U.S.	NASA JPL	Mercury, Venus flyby	S
1974									
Luna 22	Ye-8LS / 220	5,700 kg	05-29-74 / 08:56:51	NIIP-5 / 81P	Proton-K / 282-02	USSR	Lavochkin	lunar orbit	S
Luna 23	Ye-8-5M / 410	c. 5,800 kg	10-28-74 / 14:30:32	NIIP-5 / 81P	Proton-K / 285-01	USSR	Lavochkin	lunar sample	U
Helios 1	Helios-A	370 kg	12-10-74 / 07:11:02	ETR / 41	Titan IIIE-Centaur / 2	FRG	DFVLR	solar orbit	S
1975									
Venera 9	4V-1 / 660	4,936 kg	06-08-75 / 02:38:00	NIIP-5 / 81P	Proton-K / 286-01	USSR	Lavochkin	Venus orbit / landing	S
Venera 10	4V-1 / 661	5,033 kg	06-14-75 / 03:00:31	NIIP-5 / 81P	Proton-K / 285-02	USSR	Lavochkin	Venus orbit / landing	S
Viking 1	Viking-B	3,527 kg	08-20-75 / 21:22:00	ETR / 41	Titan IIIE-Centaur / 4	U.S.	NASA JPL	Mars orbit / landing	S
Viking 2	Viking-A	3,527 kg	09-09-75 / 18:39:00	ETR / 41	Titan IIIE-Centaur / 3	U.S.	NASA JPL	Mars orbit / landing	S
[Luna]	Ye-8-5M / 412	c. 5,800 kg	10-16-75 / 04:04:56	NIIP-5 / 81L	Proton-K / 287-02	USSR	Lavochkin	lunar sample	U
1976									
Helios 2	Helios-B	370 kg	01-15-76 / 05:34:00	ETR / 41	Titan IIIE-Centaur / 5	FRG	DFVLR	solar orbit	S
Luna 24	Ye-8-5M / 413	c. 5,800 kg	08-09-76 / 15:04:12	NIIP-5 / 81L	Proton-K / 288-02	USSR	Lavochkin	lunar sample	S

Official Name	Spacecraft / No.	Mass	Launch Date / Time	Launch Place / Pad	Launch Vehicle / No.	Nation / Organization	Design & Operation	Objective	Outcome
1977									
Voyager 2	Voyager-2	2,020 kg	08-20-77 / 14:29:44	ETR / 41	Titan IIIE-Centaur / 7	U.S.	NASA JPL	Jupiter, Saturn, Uranus, Neptune flyby	S
Voyager 1	Voyager-1	2,080 kg	09-05-77 / 12:56:01	ETR / 41	Titan IIIE-Centaur / 6	U.S.	NASA JPL	Jupiter, Saturn flyby	S
1978									
Pioneer Venus 1	Pioneer Venus Orbiter	582 kg	05-20-78 / 13:13:00	ETR / 36A	Atlas Centaur / 50	U.S.	NASA ARC	Venus orbit	S
Pioneer Venus 2	Pioneer Venus Multiprobe	904 kg	08-08-78 / 07:33	ETR / 36A	Atlas Centaur / 51	U.S.	NASA ARC	Venus landings	S
ISEE-3		479 kg	08-12-78 / 15:12	ETR / 17B	Delta 2914 / 144	U.S.	NASA GSFC	L1	S
Venera 11	4V-1 / 360	4,450 kg	09-09-78 / 03:25:39	NIIP-5 / 81L	Proton-K / 296-01	USSR	Lavochkin	Venus landing	S
Venera 12	4V-1 / 361	4,461 kg	09-14-78 / 02:25:13	NIIP-5 / 81P	Proton-K / 296-02	USSR	Lavochkin	Venus landing	S
1981									
Venera 13	4V-1M / 760	4,363 kg	10-30-81 / 06:04	NIIP-5 / 200P	Proton-K / 311-01	USSR	Lavochkin	Venus landing	S
Venera 14	4V-1M / 761	4,363.5 kg	11-04-81 / 05:31	NIIP-5 / 200L	Proton-K / 311-02	USSR	Lavochkin	Venus landing	S
1983									
Venera 15	4V-2 / 860	5,250 kg	06-02-83 / 02:38:39	NIIP-5 / 200L	Proton-K / 321-01	USSR	Lavochkin	Venus orbit	S
Venera 16	4V-2 / 861	5,300 kg	06-07-83 / 02:32	NIIP-5 / 200P	Proton-K / 321-02	USSR	Lavochkin	Venus orbit	S
1984									
Vega 1	5VK / 901	c. 4,920 kg	12-15-84 / 09:16:24	NIIP-5 / 200L	Proton-K / 329-01	USSR	Lavochkin	Venus landing, Halley flyby	S
Vega 2	5VK / 902	c. 4,920 kg	12-21-84 / 09:13:52	NIIP-5 / 200P	Proton-K / 325-02	USSR	Lavochkin	Venus landing, Halley flyby	S

Official Name	Spacecraft / No.	Mass	Launch Date / Time	Launch Place / Pad	Launch Vehicle / No.	Nation / Organization	Design & Operation	Objective	Outcome
1985									
Sakigake	MS-T5	138.1 kg	01-07-85 / 19:26	Kagoshima / M1	Mu-3S-II / 1	Japan	ISAS	Halley flyby	S
Giotto	Giotto	960 kg	07-02-85 / 11:23:16	Kourou / ELA 1	Ariane 1 / V14	ESA	ESA	Halley flyby	S
Suisei	Planet-A	139.5 kg	08-18-85 / 23:33	Kagoshima / M1	Mu-3S-II / 2	Japan	ISAS	Halley flyby	S
1988									
Fobos 1	1F / 101	6,220 kg	07-07-88 / 17:38:04	NIIP-5 / 200L	Proton-K / 356-02	USSR	Lavochkin	Mars orbit / Phobos flyby / landings	U
Fobos 2	1F / 102	6,220 kg	07-12-88 / 17:01:43	NIIP-5 / 200P	Proton-K / 356-01	USSR	Lavochkin	Mars orbit / Phobos flyby / landings	P
1989									
Magellan	Magellan	3,445 kg	05-04-89 / 18:47:00	KSC / 39B	STS-30R / IUS	U.S.	NASA JPL	Venus orbit	S
Galileo	Galileo	2,561 kg	10-18-89 / 16:53:40	KSC / 39B	STS-34R / IUS	U.S.	NASA JPL	Jupiter orbit / entry	S
1990									
Hiten / Hagoromo	MUSES-A / MUSES-A subsat	197.4 kg	01-24-90 / 11:46	Kagoshima / M1	Mu-3S-II / 5	Japan	ISAS	lunar flyby / orbit	S
Ulysses	Ulysses	371 kg	10-06-90 / 11:47:16	KSC / 39B	STS-41 / IUS	ESA / U.S.	ESA / NASA JPL	solar orbit	S
1992									
Mars Observer	Mars Observer	2,573 kg	09-25-92 / 17:05:01	ESMC / 40	Titan III / 4	U.S.	NASA JPL	Mars orbit	U
1994									
Clementine	Clementine	424 kg	01-25-94 / 16:34	WSMC / SLC-4W	Titan IIG / 11	U.S.	BMDO	lunar orbit	S
Wind	Wind	1,250 kg	11-01-94 / 09:31:00	ESMC / 17B	Delta 7925-10 / 227	U.S.	NASA GSFC	L1	S

Official Name	Spacecraft / No.	Mass	Launch Date / Time	Launch Place / Pad	Launch Vehicle / No.	Nation / Organization	Design & Operation	Objective	Outcome
1995									
SOHO	SOHO	1,864 kg	12-02-95 / 08:08:01	ESMC / 36B	Atlas-Centaur IIAS / 121	ESA / U.S.	ESA / NASA	L1	S
1996									
NEAR	NEAR	805 kg	02-17-96 / 20:43:27	ESMC / 17B	Delta 7925-8 / 232	U.S.	NASA GSFC	asteroid orbit	S
Mars Global Surveyor	MGS	1,062.1 kg	11-07-96 / 17:00:49	ESMC / 17A	Delta 7925 / 239	U.S.	NASA JPL	Mars orbit	S
Mars 8	M1 / 520	6,200 kg	11-16-96 / 20:48:53	GIIK-5 / 200L	Proton-K / 392-02	Russia	Lavochkin	Mars landing	U
Mars Pathfinder	Mars Pathfinder	870 kg	12-04-96 / 06:58:07	ESMC / 17B	Delta 7925 / 240	U.S.	NASA JPL	Mars landing	S
1997									
ACE	ACE	752 kg	08-25-97 / 14:39	ESMC / 17A	Delta 7920-8 / 247	U.S.	NASA GSFC	L1	S
Cassini / Huygens	Cassini / Huygens	5,655 kg	10-15-97 / 08:43	ESMC / 40	Titan 401B-Centaur / 21	U.S. / ESA	NASA JPL / ESA	Saturn, Titan	in progress
Asiasat 3	HGS 1	3,465 kg	12-24-97 / 23:19	GIIK-5 / 81L	Proton-K / 394-01	Asiasat	Asiasat / Hughes	lunar flyby	S
1998									
Lunar Prospector	Lunar Prospector	300 kg	01-07-98 / 02:28:44	WSMC / SLC-46	Athena 2 / LM-004	U.S.	NASA ARC	lunar orbit	S
Nozomi	Planet-B	536 kg	07-03-98 / 18:12	Kagoshima / M-5	M-5 / 3	Japan	ISAS	Mars orbit	in progress
Deep Space 1	DS-1	489 kg	10-24-98 / 12:08:00	ESMC / 17A	Delta 7326-9.5 / 261	U.S.	NASA JPL	solar orbit	S
Mars Climate Orbiter	MCO	629 kg	12-11-98 / 18:45:51	ESMC / 17A	Delta 7425-9.5 / 264	U.S.	NASA JPL	Mars orbit	U

Official Name	Spacecraft / No.	Mass	Launch Date / Time	Launch Place / Pad	Launch Vehicle / No.	Nation / Organization	Design & Operation	Objective	Outcome
1999									
Mars Polar Lander / Deep Space 2	MPL / DS-2	583 kg	01-03-99 / 20:21:10	ESMC / 17B	Delta 7425-9.5 / 265	U.S.	NASA JPL	Mars landing	U
Stardust	Stardust	385 kg	02-07-99 / 21:04:15	ESMC / 17A	Delta 7426-9.5 / 266	U.S.	NASA JPL	comet sample return	in progress

Deep Space Chronicle:
Program Tables

UNITED STATES

PIONEER

Official Name	Spacecraft / No.	Mass	Launch Date / Time	Launch Place / Pad	Launch Vehicle / No.	Nation / Organization	Design & Operation	Objective	Outcome
"Pioneer"	Able 1	38 kg	08-17-58 / 12:18	ETR / 17A	Thor-Able I / 127	U.S.	AFBMD	lunar orbit	U
Pioneer	Able 2	38.3 kg	10-11-58 / 08:42:13	ETR / 17A	Thor-Able I / 130	U.S.	NASA / AFBMD	lunar orbit	U
Pioneer 2	Able 3	39.6 kg	11-08-58 / 07:30	ETR / 17A	Thor-Able I / 129	U.S.	NASA / AFBMD	lunar orbit	U
Pioneer 3	–	5.87 kg	12-06-58 / 05:44:52	ETR / 5	Juno II / AM-11	U.S.	NASA / ABMA	lunar flyby	U
Pioneer 4	–	6.1 kg	03-03-59 / 05:10:45	ETR / 5	Juno II / AM-14	U.S.	NASA / ABMA	lunar flyby	P
"Pioneer"	P-3 / Able IVB	169 kg	11-26-59 / 07:26	ETR / 14	Atlas-Able / 1	U.S.	NASA / AFBMD	lunar orbit	U
Pioneer 5	P-2 / Able 6	43.2 kg	03-11-60 / 13:00:07	ETR / 17A	Thor-Able IV / 4	U.S.	NASA GSFC	solar orbit	S
"Pioneer"	P-30 / Able VA	175.5 kg	09-25-60 / 15:13	ETR / 12	Atlas-Able / 2	U.S.	NASA / AFBMD	lunar orbit	U
"Pioneer"	P-31 / Able VB	176 kg	12-15-60 / 09:10	ETR / 12	Atlas-Able / 3	U.S.	NASA / AFBMD	lunar orbit	U
Pioneer 6	Pioneer-A	62.14 kg	12-16-65 / 07:31:21	ETR / 17A	Thor-Delta E / 35	U.S.	NASA ARC	solar orbit	S
Pioneer 7	Pioneer-B	62.75 kg	08-17-66 / 15:20:17	ETR / 17A	Thor-Delta E1 / 40	U.S.	NASA ARC	solar orbit	S
Pioneer 8	Pioneer-C	65.36 kg	12-13-67 / 14:08	ETR / 17B	Thor-Delta E-1 / 55	U.S.	NASA ARC	solar orbit	S
Pioneer 9	Pioneer-D	65.36	11-08-68 / 09:46:29	ETR / 17B	Thor-Delta E1 / 60	U.S.	NASA ARC	solar orbit	S
Pioneer	Pioneer-E	65.4 kg	08-27-69 / 21:59	ETR / 17A	Thor-Delta L / 73	U.S.	NASA ARC	solar orbit	U
Pioneer 10	Pioneer-F	258 kg	03-02-72 / 01:49:04	ETR / 36A	Atlas-Centaur / 27	U.S.	NASA ARC	Jupiter flyby	S
Pioneer 11	Pioneer-G	258.5 kg	04-05-73 / 02:11	ETR / 36B	Atlas-Centaur / 30	U.S.	NASA ARC	Jupiter, Saturn flyby	S
Pioneer Venus 1	Pioneer Venus Orbiter	582 kg	05-20-78 / 13:13:00	ETR / 36A	Atlas-Centaur / 50	U.S.	NASA ARC	Venus orbiter	S
Pioneer Venus 2	Pioneer Venus Multiprobe	904 kg	08-08-78 / 07:33	ETR / 36A	Atlas-Centaur / 51	U.S.	NASA ARC	Venus landings	S

RANGER

Official Name	Spacecraft / No.	Mass	Launch Date / Time	Launch Place / Pad	Launch Vehicle / No.	Nation / Organization	Design & Operation	Objective	Outcome
Ranger 1	P-32	306.18 kg	08-23-61 / 10:04	ETR / 12	Atlas-Agena B / 1	U.S.	NASA JPL	deep space orbit	U
Ranger 2	P-33	306.18 kg	11-18-61 / 08:12	ETR / 12	Atlas-Agena B / 2	U.S.	NASA JPL	deep space orbit	U
Ranger 3	P-34	330 kg	01-26-62 / 20:30	ETR / 12	Atlas-Agena B / 3	U.S.	NASA JPL	lunar impact	U
Ranger 4	P-35	331.12 kg	04-23-62 / 20:50	ETR / 12	Atlas-Agena B / 4	U.S.	NASA JPL	lunar impact	P
Ranger 5	P-36	342.46 kg	10-18-62 / 16:59:00	ETR / 12	Atlas-Agena B / 7	U.S.	NASA JPL	lunar impact	P
Ranger 6	Ranger-A / P-53	364.69 kg	01-30-64 / 15:49:09	ETR / 12	Atlas-Agena B / 8	U.S.	NASA JPL	lunar impact	P

Official Name	Spacecraft / No.	Mass	Launch Date / Time	Launch Place / Pad	Launch Vehicle / No.	Nation / Organization	Design & Operation	Objective	Outcome
RANGER (continued)									
Ranger 7	Ranger-B / P-54	365.6 kg	07-28-64 / 16:50:07	ETR / 12	Atlas-Agena B / 9	U.S.	NASA JPL	lunar impact	S
Ranger 8	Ranger-C	366.87 kg	02-17-65 / 17:05:00	ETR / 12	Atlas-Agena B / 13	U.S.	NASA JPL	lunar impact	S
Ranger 9	Ranger-D	366.87 kg	03-21-65 / 21:37:02	ETR / 12	Atlas-Agena B / 14	U.S.	NASA JPL	lunar impact	S
MARINER									
Mariner 1	P-37	202.8 kg	07-22-62 / 09:21:23	ETR / 12	Atlas-Agena B / 5	U.S.	NASA JPL	Venus flyby	U
Mariner 2	P-38	203.6 kg	08-27-62 / 06:53:14	ETR / 12	Atlas-Agena B / 6	U.S.	NASA JPL	Venus flyby	S
Mariner 3	Mariner-64C	260.8 kg	11-05-64 / 19:22:05	ETR / 13	Atlas-Agena D / 11	U.S.	NASA JPL	Mars flyby	U
Mariner 4	Mariner-64D	260.8 kg	11-28-64 / 14:22:01	ETR / 12	Atlas-Agena D / 12	U.S.	NASA JPL	Mars flyby	S
Mariner 5	Mariner-67E	244.9 kg	06-14-67 / 06:01:00	ETR / 12	Atlas-Agena D / 23	U.S.	NASA JPL	Venus flyby	S
Mariner 6	Mariner-69F	381 kg	02-25-69 / 01:29:02	ETR / 36B	Atlas-Centaur / 20	U.S.	NASA JPL	Mars flyby	S
Mariner 7	Mariner-69G	381 kg	03-27-69 / 22:22:01	ETR / 36A	Atlas-Centaur / 19	U.S.	NASA JPL	Mars flyby	S
Mariner 8	Mariner-71H	997.9 kg	05-09-71 / 01:11:02	ETR / 36A	Atlas-Centaur / 24	U.S.	NASA JPL	Mars orbit	U
Mariner 9	Mariner-71I	997.9 kg	05-30-71 / 22:23:04	ETR / 36B	Atlas-Centaur / 23	U.S.	NASA JPL	Mars orbit	S
Mariner 10	Mariner-73J	502.9 kg	11-03-73 / 05:45:00	ETR / 36B	Atlas-Centaur / 34	U.S.	NASA JPL	Mercury, Venus flyby	S
SURVEYOR									
"Atlas Centaur 5"	SD-1	951 kg	03-02-65 / 13:25	ETR / 36A	Atlas-Centaur / 5	U.S.	NASA JPL	deep space orbit	U
Surveyor Model 1	SD-2	950 kg	08-11-65 / 14:31:04	ETR / 36B	Atlas-Centaur / 6	U.S.	NASA JPL	deep space orbit	S
Surveyor Model 2	SD-3	784 kg	04-08-66 / 01:00:02	ETR / 36B	Atlas-Centaur / 8	U.S.	NASA JPL	deep space orbit	U
Surveyor 1	Surveyor-A	995.2 kg	05-30-66 / 14:41:01	ETR / 36A	Atlas-Centaur / 10	U.S.	NASA JPL	lunar landing	S
Surveyor 2	Surveyor-B	995.2 kg	09-20-66 / 12:32:00	ETR / 36A	Atlas-Centaur / 7	U.S.	NASA JPL	lunar landing	U
Surveyor 3	Surveyor-C	997.9 kg	04-17-67 / 07:05:01	ETR / 36B	Atlas-Centaur / 12	U.S.	NASA JPL	lunar landing	S
Surveyor 4	Surveyor-D	1,037.4 kg	07-14-67 / 11:53:29	ETR / 36A	Atlas-Centaur / 11	U.S.	NASA JPL	lunar landing	U
Surveyor 5	Surveyor-E	1,006 kg	09-08-67 / 07:57:01	ETR / 36B	Atlas-Centaur / 13	U.S.	NASA JPL	lunar landing	S
Surveyor 6	Surveyor-F	1,008.3 kg	11-07-67 / 07:39:01	ETR / 36B	Atlas-Centaur / 14	U.S.	NASA JPL	lunar landing	S
Surveyor 7	Surveyor-G	1,040.1 kg	01-07-68 / 06:30:00	ETR / 36A	Atlas-Centaur / 15	U.S.	NASA JPL	lunar landing	S

Official Name	Spacecraft / No.	Mass	Launch Date / Time	Launch Place / Pad	Launch Vehicle / No.	Nation / Organization	Design & Operation	Objective	Outcome
EXPLORER									
Explorer 33	IMP-D	93.4 kg	07-01-66 / 16:02:25	ETR / 17A	Thor-Delta E1 / 39	U.S.	NASA GSFC	lunar orbit	P
Explorer 35	IMP-E	104.3 kg	07-19-67 / 14:19:02	ETR / 17B	Thor-Delta E1 / 50	U.S.	NASA GSFC	lunar orbit	S
Explorer 49	RAE-B	330.2 kg	06-10-73 / 14:13:00	ETR / 17B	Delta 1913 / 95	U.S.	NASA GSFC	lunar orbit	S
LUNAR ORBITER									
Lunar Orbiter 1	LO-A	385.6 kg	08-10-66 / 19:26:00	ETR / 13	Atlas-Agena D / 17	U.S.	NASA LaRC	lunar orbit	S
Lunar Orbiter 2	LO-B	385.6 kg	11-06-66 / 23:21:00	ETR / 13	Atlas-Agena D / 18	U.S.	NASA LaRC	lunar orbit	S
Lunar Orbiter 3	LO-C	385.6 kg	02-05-67 / 01:17:01	ETR / 13	Atlas-Agena D / 20	U.S.	NASA LaRC	lunar orbit	S
Lunar Orbiter 4	LO-D	385.6 kg	05-04-67 / 22:25:00	ETR / 13	Atlas-Agena D / 22	U.S.	NASA LaRC	lunar orbit	S
Lunar Orbiter 5	LO-E	390 kg	08-01-67 / 22:33:00	ETR / 13	Atlas-Agena D / 24	U.S.	NASA LaRC	lunar orbit	S
APOLLO PARTICLE AND FIELDS SUBSATELLITE									
Apollo 15 Particle & Fields Sat		35.6 kg	08-04-71 / 20:13:19	Apollo 15 CSM 112	Saturn V / 510	U.S.	NASA MSC	lunar orbit	S
Apollo 16 Particle & Fields Sat		42 kg	04-24-72 / 09:56:09	Apollo 16 CSM 113	Saturn V / 511	U.S.	NASA MSC	lunar orbit	S
VIKING									
Viking 1	Viking-B	3,527 kg	08-20-75 / 21:22:00	ETR / 41	Titan IIIE-Centaur / 4	U.S.	NASA JPL	Mars orbit / landing	S
Viking 2	Viking-A	3,527 kg	09-09-75 / 18:39:00	ETR / 41	Titan IIIE-Centaur / 3	U.S.	NASA JPL	Mars orbit / landing	S

Official Name	Spacecraft / No.	Mass	Launch Date / Time	Launch Place / Pad	Launch Vehicle / No.	Nation / Organization	Design & Operation	Objective	Outcome
VOYAGER									
Voyager 2	Voyager-2	2,020 kg	08-20-77 / 14:29:44	ETR / 41	Titan IIIE-Centaur / 7	U.S.	NASA JPL	Jupiter, Saturn, Uranus, Neptune flyby	S
Voyager 1	Voyager-1	2,080 kg	09-05-77 / 12:56:01	ETR / 41	Titan IIIE-Centaur / 6	U.S.	NASA JPL	Jupiter, Saturn flyby	S
ISEE									
ISEE-3	ISEE-C	479 kg	08-12-78 / 15:12	ETR / 17B	Delta 2914 / 144	U.S.	NASA GSFC	L1	S
MAGELLAN									
Magellan	Magellan	3,445 kg	05-04-89 / 18:47:00	KSC / 39B	STS-30R / IUS	U.S.	NASA JPL	Venus orbit	S
GALILEO									
Galileo	Galileo	2,561 kg	10-18-89 / 16:53:40	KSC / 39B	STS-34R / IUS	U.S.	NASA JPL	Jupiter orbit / entry	S
MARS OBSERVER									
Mars Observer	Mars Observer	2,573 kg	09-25-92 / 17:05:01	ESMC / 40	Titan III / 4	U.S.	NASA JPL	Mars orbit	U
CLEMENTINE									
Clementine	Clementine	424 kg	01-25-94 / 16:34	WSMC / SLC-4W	Titan IIG / 11	U.S.	BMDO	lunar orbit	S
WIND									
Wind	Wind	1,250 kg	11-01-94 / 09:31:00	ESMC / 17B	Delta 7925-10 / 227	U.S.	NASA GSFC	L1	S
NEAR									
NEAR	NEAR	805 kg	02-17-96 / 20:43:27	ESMC / 17B	Delta 7925-8 / 232	U.S.	NASA GSFC	asteroid orbit	S
MARS GLOBAL SURVEYOR									
Mars Global Surveyor	MGS	1,062.1 kg	11-07-96 / 17:00:49	ESMC / 17A	Delta 7925 / 239	U.S.	NASA JPL	Mars orbit	S

Official Name	Spacecraft / No.	Mass	Launch Date / Time	Launch Place / Pad	Launch Vehicle / No.	Nation / Organization	Design & Operation	Objective	Outcome
MARS PATHFINDER									
Mars Pathfinder	Mars Pathfinder	870 kg	12-04-96 / 06:58:07	ESMC / 17B	Delta 7925 / 240	U.S.	NASA JPL	Mars landing	S
ACE									
ACE	ACE	752 kg	08-25-97 / 14:39	ESMC / 17A	Delta 7920-8 / 247	U.S.	NASA GSFC	L1	S
LUNAR PROSPECTOR									
Lunar Prospector	Lunar Prospector	300 kg	01-07-98 / 02:28:44	WSMC / SLC-46	Athena 2 / LM-004	U.S.	NASA ARC	lunar orbit	S
DEEP SPACE									
Deep Space 1	DS-1	489 kg	10-24-98 / 12:08:00	ESMC / 17A	Delta 7326-9.5 / 261	U.S.	NASA JPL	solar orbit	S
MARS CLIMATE ORBITER									
Mars Climate Orbiter	MCO	629 kg	12-11-98 / 18:45:51	ESMC / 17A	Delta 7425-9.5 / 264	U.S.	NASA JPL	Mars orbit	U
MARS POLAR LANDER									
Mars Polar Lander / Deep Space 2	MPL / DS-2	583 kg	01-03-99 / 20:21:10	ESMC / 17B	Delta 7425-9.5 / 265	U.S.	NASA JPL	Mars landing	U
STARDUST									
Stardust	Stardust	385 kg	02-07-99 / 21:04:15	ESMC / 17A	Delta 7426-9.5 / 266	U.S.	NASA JPL	comet sample return	in progress

Official Name	Spacecraft / No.	Mass	Launch Date / Time	Launch Place / Pad	Launch Vehicle / No.	Nation / Organization	Design & Operation	Objective	Outcome
SOVIET UNION / RUSSIA									
LUNA									
[Luna]	Ye-1 / 1	c. 360 kg	09-23-58 / 09:03:23	NIIP-5 / 1	Luna / B1-3	USSR	OKB-1	lunar impact	U
[Luna]	Ye-1 / 2	c. 360 kg	10-11-58 / 23:41:58	NIIP-5 / 1	Luna / B1-4	USSR	OKB-1	lunar impact	U
[Luna]	Ye-1 / 3	c. 360 kg	12-04-58 / 18:18:44	NIIP-5 / 1	Luna / B1-5	USSR	OKB-1	lunar impact	U
Luna 1	Ye-1 / 4	361.3 kg	01-02-59 / 16:41:21	NIIP-5 / 1	Luna / B1-6	USSR	OKB-1	lunar impact	P
[Luna]	Ye-1A / 5	c. 390 kg	06-18-59 / 08:08	NIIP-5 / 1	Luna / I1-7	USSR	OKB-1	lunar impact	U
Luna 2	Ye-1A / 7	390.2 kg	09-12-59 / 06:39:42	NIIP-5 / 1	Luna / I1-7b	USSR	OKB-1	lunar impact	S
Luna 3	Ye-2A / 1	278.5 kg	10-04-59 / 00:43:40	NIIP-5 / 1	Luna / I1-8	USSR	OKB-1	lunar flyby	S
[Luna]	Ye-3 / 1	N/A	04-15-60 / 15:06:44	NIIP-5 / 1	Luna / I1-9	USSR	OKB-1	lunar flyby	U
[Luna]	Ye-3 / 2	N/A	04-19-60 / 16:07:43	NIIP-5 / 1	Luna / I1-9a	USSR	OKB-1	lunar flyby	U
[Luna]	Ye-6 / 2	1,420 kg	01-04-63 / 08:49	NIIP-5 / 1	Molniya / T103-09	USSR	OKB-1	lunar landing	U
[Luna]	Ye-6 / 3	1,420 kg	02-03-63 / 09:29:14	NIIP-5 / 1	Molniya / G103-10	USSR	OKB-1	lunar landing	U
Luna 4	Ye-6 / 4	1,422 kg	04-02-63 / 08:16:37	NIIP-5 / 1	Molniya / G103-11	USSR	OKB-1	lunar landing	U
[Luna]	Ye-6 / 6	c. 1,420 kg	03-21-64 / 08:15:35	NIIP-5 / 1	Molniya / T15000-20	USSR	OKB-1	lunar landing	U
[Luna]	Ye-6 / 5	c. 1,420 kg	04-20-64 / 08:08:28	NIIP-5 / 1	Molniya / T15000-21	USSR	OKB-1	lunar landing	U
Kosmos 60	Ye-6 / 9	c. 1,470 kg	03-12-65 / 09:30	NIIP-5 /	Molniya / R103-25	USSR	OKB-1	lunar landing	U
[Luna]	Ye-6 / 8	c. 1,470 kg	04-10-65/ N/A	NIIP-5 / 1	Molniya / R103-26	USSR	OKB-1	lunar landing	U
Luna 5	Ye-6 / 10	1,476 kg	05-09-65 / 07:49:37	NIIP-5 / 1	Molniya / U103-30	USSR	OKB-1	lunar landing	U
Luna 6	Ye-6 / 7	1,442 kg	06-08-65 / 07:40	NIIP-5 / 1	Molniya / U103-31	USSR	OKB-1	lunar landing	U
Luna 7	Ye-6 / 11	1,506 kg	10-04-65 / 07:56:40	NIIP-5 / 1	Molniya / U103-27	USSR	OKB-1	lunar landing	U
Luna 8	Ye-6 / 12	1,552 kg	12-03-65 / 10:46:14	NIIP-5 / 31	Molniya / U103-28	USSR	OKB-1	lunar landing	U
Luna 9	Ye-6M / 202	1,538 kg	01-31-66 / 11:41:37	NIIP-5 / 31	Molniya-M / U103-32	USSR	Lavochkin	lunar landing	S
Kosmos 111	Ye-6S / 204	c. 1,580 kg	03-01-66 / 11:03:49	NIIP-5 / 31	Molniya-M / N103-41	USSR	Lavochkin	lunar orbit	U
Luna 10	Ye-6S / 206	1,582 kg	03-31-66 / 10:47	NIIP-5 / 31	Molniya-M / N103-42	USSR	Lavochkin	lunar orbit	S
Luna 11	Ye-6LF / 101	1,640 kg	08-24-66 / 08:03	NIIP-5 /	Molniya-M / N103-43	USSR	Lavochkin	lunar orbit	S
Luna 12	Ye-6LF / 102	1,620 kg	10-22-66 / 08:42	NIIP-5 / 31	Molniya-M / N103-44	USSR	Lavochkin	lunar orbit	S
Luna 13	Ye-6M / 205	1,620 kg	12-21-66 / 10:17	NIIP-5 / 1	Molniya-M / N103-45	USSR	Lavochkin	lunar landing	S
Kosmos 159	Ye-6LS / 111	N/A	05-17-67 / 21:43:57	NIIP-5 / 1	Molniya-M / Ya716-56	USSR	Lavochkin	lunar orbit	P
[Luna]	Ye-6LS / 112	N/A	02-07-68 / 10:43:54	NIIP-5 / 1	Molniya-M / Ya716-57	USSR	Lavochkin	lunar orbit	U

Official Name	Spacecraft / No.	Mass	Launch Date / Time	Launch Place / Pad	Launch Vehicle / No.	Nation / Organization	Design & Operation	Objective	Outcome
LUNA (continued)									
Luna 14	Ye-6LS / 113	N/A	04-07-68 / 10:09:32	NIIP-5 / 1	Molniya-M / Ya716-58	USSR	Lavochkin	lunar orbit	S
[Luna]	Ye-8 / 201	c. 5,700 kg	02-19-69 / 06:48:15	NIIP-5 / 81P	Proton-K / 239-01	USSR	Lavochkin	lunar rover	U
[Luna]	Ye-8-5 / 402	c. 5,700 kg	06-14-69 / 04:00:47	NIIP-5 / 81P	Proton-K / 238-01	USSR	Lavochkin	lunar sample	U
Luna 15	Ye-8-5 / 401	5,700 kg	07-13-69 / 02:54:42	NIIP-5 / 81P	Proton-K / 242-01	USSR	Lavochkin	lunar sample	U
Kosmos 300	Ye-8-5 / 403	c. 5,700 kg	09-23-69 / 14:07:36	NIIP-5 / 81P	Proton-K / 244-01	USSR	Lavochkin	lunar sample	U
Kosmos 305	Ye-8-5 / 404	c. 5,700 kg	10-22-69 / 14:09:59	NIIP-5 / 81P	Proton-K / 241-01	USSR	Lavochkin	lunar sample	U
[Luna]	Ye-8-5 / 405	c. 5,700 kg	02-06-70 / 04:16:06	NIIP-5 / 81	Proton-K / 247-01	USSR	Lavochkin	lunar sample	U
Luna 16	Ye-8-5 / 406	5,727 kg	09-12-70 / 13:25:53	NIIP-5 / 81L	Proton-K / 248-01	USSR	Lavochkin	lunar sample	S
Luna 17	Ye-8 / 203	5,700 kg	11-10-70 / 14:44:01	NIIP-5 / 81L	Proton-K / 251-01	USSR	Lavochkin	lunar rover	S
Luna 18	Ye-8-5 / 407	c. 5,750 kg	09-02-71 / 13:40:40	NIIP-5 / 81P	Proton-K / 256-01	USSR	Lavochkin	lunar sample	U
Luna 19	Ye-8LS / 202	c. 5,700 kg	09-28-71 / 10:00:22	NIIP-5 / 81P	Proton-K / 257-01	USSR	Lavochkin	lunar orbit	S
Luna 20	Ye-8-5 / 408	c. 5,750 kg	02-14-72 / 03:27:59	NIIP-5 / 81P	Proton-K / 258-01	USSR	Lavochkin	lunar sample	S
Luna 21	Ye-8 / 204	c. 5,950 kg	01-08-73 / 06:55:38	NIIP-5 / 81L	Proton-K / 259-01	USSR	Lavochkin	lunar rover	S
Luna 22	Ye-8LS / 220	5,700 kg	05-29-74 / 08:56:51	NIIP-5 / 81P	Proton-K / 282-02	USSR	Lavochkin	lunar orbit	S
Luna 23	Ye-8-5M / 410	c. 5,800 kg	10-28-74 / 14:30:32	NIIP-5 / 81P	Proton-K / 285-01	USSR	Lavochkin	lunar sample	U
[Luna]	Ye-8-5M / 412	c. 5,800 kg	10-16-75 / 04:04:56	NIIP-5 / 81L	Proton-K / 287-02	USSR	Lavochkin	lunar sample	U
Luna 24	Ye-8-5M / 413	c. 5,800 kg	08-09-76 / 15:04:12	NIIP-5 / 81L	Proton-K / 288-02	USSR	Lavochkin	lunar sample	S
MARS									
[Mars]	1M / 1	480 kg	10-10-60 / 14:27:49	NIIP-5 / 1	Molniya / L1-4M	USSR	OKB-1	Mars flyby	U
[Mars]	1M / 2	480 kg	10-14-60 / 13:51:03	NIIP-5 / 1	Molniya / L1-5M	USSR	OKB-1	Mars flyby	U
[Mars]	2MV-4 / 1	c. 900 kg	10-24-62 / 17:55:04	NIIP-5 / 1	Molniya / T103-15	USSR	OKB-1	Mars flyby	U
Mars 1	2MV-4 / 4	893.5 kg	11-01-62 / 16:14:16	NIIP-5 / 1	Molniya / T103-16	USSR	OKB-1	Mars flyby	P
[Mars]	2MV-3 / 1	N/A	11-04-62 / 15:35:15	NIIP-5 / 1	Molniya / T103-17	USSR	OKB-1	Mars impact	U
[Mars]	M-69 / 521	c. 3,800 kg	03-27-69 / 10:40:45	NIIP-5 / 81L	Proton-K / 240-01	USSR	Lavochkin	Mars orbit	U
[Mars]	M-69 / 522	c. 3,800 kg	04-02-69 / 10:33:00	NIIP-5 / 81P	Proton-K / 233-01	USSR	Lavochkin	Mars orbit	U
Kosmos 419	M-71 / 170	4,549 kg	05-10-71 / 16:58:42	NIIP-5 / 81L	Proton-K / 253-01	USSR	Lavochkin	Mars orbit	U
Mars 2	M-71 / 171	4,650 kg	05-19-71 / 16:22:44	NIIP-5 / 81P	Proton-K / 255-01	USSR	Lavochkin	Mars orbit / landing	P
Mars 3	M-71 / 172	4,650 kg	05-28-71 / 15:26:30	NIIP-5 / 81L	Proton-K / 249-01	USSR	Lavochkin	Mars orbit / landing	P
Mars 4	M-73 / 52S	3,440 kg	07-21-73 / 19:30:59	NIIP-5 / 81L	Proton-K / 261-01	USSR	Lavochkin	Mars orbit	U

Official Name	Spacecraft / No.	Mass	Launch Date / Time	Launch Place / Pad	Launch Vehicle / No.	Nation / Organization	Design & Operation	Objective	Outcome
MARS (continued)									
Mars 5	M-73 / 53S	3,440 kg	07-25-73 / 18:55:48	NIIP-5 / 81P	Proton-K / 262-01	USSR	Lavochkin	Mars orbit	S
Mars 6	M-73 / 50P	3,260 kg	08-05-73 / 17:45:48	NIIP-5 / 81L	Proton-K / 281-01	USSR	Lavochkin	Mars landing	P
Mars 7	M-73 / 51P	3,260 kg	08-09-73 / 17:00:17	NIIP-5 / 81P	Proton-K / 281-01	USSR	Lavochkin	Mars landing	U
Mars 8	M1 / 520	6,200 kg	11-16-96 / 20:48:53	GIIK-5 / 200L	Proton-K / 392-02	Russia	Lavochkin	Mars landing	U
VENERA									
[Venera]	1VA / 1	c. 645 kg	02-04-61 / 01:18:04	NIIP-5 / 1	Molniya / L1-7	USSR	OKB-1	Venus impact	U
[Venera]	1VA / 2	643.5 kg	02-12-61 / 00:34:37	NIIP-5 / 1	Molniya / L1-6	USSR	OKB-1	Venus impact	U
[Venera]	2MV-1 / 1	1,097 kg	08-25-62 / 02:18:45	NIIP-5 / 1	Molniya / T103-12	USSR	OKB-1	Venus impact	U
[Venera]	2MV-1 / 2	c. 1,100 kg	09-01-62 / 02:12:30	NIIP-5 / 1	Molniya / T103-13	USSR	OKB-1	Venus impact	U
[Venera]	2MV-2 / 1	N/A	09-12-62 / 00:59:13	NIIP-5 / 1	Molniya / T103-14	USSR	OKB-1	Venus flyby	U
Venera 2	3MV-4 / 4	963 kg	11-12-65 / N/A	NIIP-5 / 31	Molniya-M	USSR	OKB-1	Venus flyby	S
Venera 3	3MV-3 / 1	958 kg	11-16-65 / N/A	NIIP-5 / 31	Molniya-M	USSR	OKB-1	Venus impact	S
Kosmos 96	3MV-4 / 6	c. 950 kg	11-23-65 / N/A	NIIP-5 / 31	Molniya-M	USSR	OKB-1	Venus flyby	U
Venera 4	1V / 310	1,106 kg	06-12-67 / 02:39:45	NIIP-5 / 1	Molniya-M	USSR	Lavochkin	Venus impact	S
Kosmos 167	1V / 311	c. 1,100 kg	06-17-67 / 02:36:38	NIIP-5 / 1	Molniya-M	USSR	Lavochkin	Venus impact	U
Venera 5	2V / 330	1,130 kg	01-05-69 / 06:28:08	NIIP-5 / 1	Molniya-M	USSR	Lavochkin	Venus landing	S
Venera 6	2V / 331	1,130 kg	01-10-69 / 05:51:52	NIIP-5 / 1	Molniya-M	USSR	Lavochkin	Venus landing	S
Venera 7	3V / 630	1,180 kg	08-17-70 / 05:38:22	NIIP-5 / 31	Molniya-M	USSR	Lavochkin	Venus landing	S
Kosmos 359	3V / 631	c. 1,200 kg	08-22-70 / 05:06:09	NIIP-5 / 31	Molniya-M	USSR	Lavochkin	Venus landing	U
Venera 8	3V / 670	1,184 kg	03-27-72 / 04:15:01	NIIP-5 / 31	Molniya-M	USSR	Lavochkin	Venus landing	S
Kosmos 482	3V / 671	c. 1,180 kg	03-31-72 / 04:02:33	NIIP-5 / 31	Molniya-M	USSR	Lavochkin	Venus landing	U
Venera 9	4V-1 / 660	4,936 kg	06-08-75 / 02:38:00	NIIP-5 / 81P	Proton-K / 286-01	USSR	Lavochkin	Venus orbit / landing	S
Venera 10	4V-1 / 661	5,033 kg	06-14-75 / 03:00:31	NIIP-5 / 81P	Proton-K / 285-02	USSR	Lavochkin	Venus orbit / landing	S
Venera 11	4V-1 / 360	4,450 kg	09-09-78 / 03:25:39	NIIP-5 / 81L	Proton-K / 296-01	USSR	Lavochkin	Venus landing	S
Venera 12	4V-1 / 361	4,461 kg	09-14-78 / 02:25:13	NIIP-5 / 81P	Proton-K / 296-02	USSR	Lavochkin	Venus landing	S
Venera 13	4V-1M / 760	4,363 kg	10-30-81 / 06:04	NIIP-5 / 200P	Proton-K / 311-01	USSR	Lavochkin	Venus landing	S
Venera 14	4V-1M / 761	4,363.5 kg	11-04-81 / 05:31	NIIP-5 / 200L	Proton-K / 311-02	USSR	Lavochkin	Venus landing	S
Venera 15	4V-2 / 860	5,250 kg	06-02-83 / 02:38:39	NIIP-5 / 200L	Proton-K / 321-01	USSR	Lavochkin	Venus orbit	S
Venera 16	4V-2 / 861	5,300 kg	06-07-83 / 02:32	NIIP-5 / 200P	Proton-K / 321-02	USSR	Lavochkin	Venus orbit	S

Official Name	Spacecraft / No.	Mass	Launch Date / Time	Launch Place / Pad	Launch Vehicle / No.	Nation / Organization	Design & Operation	Objective	Outcome
ZOND (early)									
Kosmos 21	3MV-1A / 2	c. 800 kg	11-11-63 / 06:23:35	NIIP-5 / 2	Molniya / G103-18	USSR	OKB-1	lunar flyby	U
[Zond]	3MV-1A / 4A	c. 800 kg	02-19-64 / 05:47:40	NIIP-5 / 1	Molniya / T15000-19	USSR	OKB-1	Venus flyby	U
Kosmos 27	3MV-1 / 5	948 kg	03-27-64 / 03:24:42	NIIP-5 / 1	Molniya / T15000-22	USSR	OKB-1	Venus impact	U
Zond 1	3MV-1 / 4	948 kg	04-02-64 / 02:42:40	NIIP-5 / 1	Molniya / T15000-23	USSR	OKB-1	Venus impact	U
Zond 2	3MV-4A / 2	996 kg	11-30-64 / 13:12	NIIP-5 / 1	Molniya	USSR	OKB-1	Mars flyby	P
Zond 3	3MV-4A / 3	950 kg	07-18-65 / N/A	NIIP-5 / 1	Molniya	USSR	OKB-1	lunar flyby	S
ZOND (later)									
[Zond]	7K-L1 / 4L	c. 5,375 kg	09-27-67 / 22:11:54	NIIP-5 / 81L	Proton-K / 229-01	USSR	TsKBEM	circumlunar	U
[Zond]	7K-L1 / 5L	c. 5,375 kg	11-22-67 / 19:07:59	NIIP-5 / 81P	Proton-K / 230-01	USSR	TsKBEM	circumlunar	U
Zond 4	7K-L1 / 6L	c. 5,375 kg	03-02-68 / 18:29:23	NIIP-5 / 81L	Proton-K / 231-01	USSR	TsKBEM	deep space	P
[Zond]	7K-L1 / 7L	c. 5,375 kg	04-22-68 / 23:01:57	NIIP-5 / 81P	Proton-K / 232-01	USSR	TsKBEM	circumlunar	U
Zond 5	7K-L1 / 9L	c. 5,375 kg	09-14-68 / 21:42:11	NIIP-5 / 81L	Proton-K / 234-01	USSR	TsKBEM	circumlunar	S
Zond 6	7K-L1 / 12L	c. 5,375 kg	11-10-68 / 19:11:31	NIIP-5 / 81L	Proton-K / 235-01	USSR	TsKBEM	circumlunar	S
[Zond]	7K-L1 / 13L	c. 5,375 kg	01-20-69 / 04:14:36	NIIP-5 / 81L	Proton-K / 237-01	USSR	TsKBEM	circumlunar	U
Zond 7	7K-L1 / 11	c. 5,375 kg	08-07-69 / 23:48:06	NIIP-5 / 81L	Proton-K / 243-01	USSR	TsKBEM	circumlunar	S
Zond 8	7K-L1 / 14	c. 5,375 kg	10-20-70 / 19:55:39	NIIP-5 / 81L	Proton-K / 250-01	USSR	TsKBEM	circumlunar	S
N1 LUNAR TESTS									
[N1 launch test]	7K-L1S / 3S	6,900 kg	02-21-69 / 09:18:07	NIIP-5 / 110P	N1 / 3L	USSR	TsKBEM	lunar orbit	U
[N1 test flight]	7K-L1S / 5L	c. 6,900 kg	07-03-69 / 20:18:32	NIIP-5 / 110P	N1 / 5L	USSR	TsKBEM	lunar orbit	U
[N1 launch test]	7K-LOK / 6A	N/A	11-23-72 / 06:11:55	NIIP-5 / 100L	N1 / 7L	USSR	TsKBEM	lunar orbit	U

Official Name	Spacecraft / No.	Mass	Launch Date / Time	Launch Place / Pad	Launch Vehicle / No.	Nation / Organization	Design & Operation	Objective	Outcome
VEGA									
Vega 1	5VK / 901	c. 4,920 kg	12-15-84 / 09:16:24	NIIP-5 / 200L	Proton-K / 329-01	USSR	Lavochkin	Venus landing, Halley flyby	S
Vega 2	5VK / 902	c. 4,920 kg	12-21-84 / 09:13:52	NIIP-5 / 200P	Proton-K / 325-02	USSR	Lavochkin	Venus landing, Halley flyby	S
FOBOS									
Fobos 1	1F / 101	6,220 kg	07-07-88 / 17:38:04	NIIP-5 / 200L	Proton-K / 356-02	USSR	Lavochkin	Mars orbit / Phobos flyby / landings	U
Fobos 2	1F / 102	6,220 kg	07-12-88 / 17:01:43	NIIP-5 / 200P	Proton-K / 356-01	USSR	Lavochkin	Mars orbit / Phobos flyby / landings	P
INTERNATIONAL									
HELIOS									
Helios 1	Helios-A	370 kg	12-10-74 / 07:11:02	ETR / 41	Titan IIIE-Centaur / 2	FRG	DFVLR	solar orbit	S
Helios 2	Helios-B	370 kg	01-15-76 / 05:34:00	ETR / 41	Titan IIIE-Centaur / 5	FRG	DFVLR	solar orbit	S
PLANET									
Sakigake	MS-T5	138.1 kg	01-07-85 / 19:26	Kagoshima / M1	Mu-3S-II / 1	Japan	ISAS	Halley flyby	S
Suisei	Planet-A	139.5 kg	08-18-85 / 23:33	Kagoshima / M1	Mu-3S-II / 2	Japan	ISAS	Halley flyby	S
Nozomi	Planet-B	536 kg	07-03-98 / 18:12	Kagoshima / M-5	M-5 / 3	Japan	ISAS	Mars orbit	in progress
GIOTTO									
Giotto	Giotto	960 kg	07-02-85 / 11:23:16	Kourou / ELA 1	Ariane 1 / V14	ESA	ESA	Halley flyby	S

Official Name	Spacecraft / No.	Mass	Launch Date / Time	Launch Place / Pad	Launch Vehicle / No.	Nation / Organization	Design & Operation	Objective	Outcome
MUSES									
Hiten/ Hagoromo	MUSES-A / MUSES-A subsat	197.4 kg	01-24-90 / 11:46	Kagoshima / M1	Mu-3S-II / 5	Japan	ISAS	lunar flyby / orbit	S
ULYSSES									
Ulysses	Ulysses	371 kg	10-06-90 / 11:47:16	KSC / 39B	STS-41 / IUS	ESA / U.S.	ESA / NASA JPL	solar orbit	S
SOHO									
SOHO	SOHO	1,864 kg	12-02-95 / 08:08:01	ESMC / 36B	Atlas-Centaur IIAS / 121	ESA / U.S.	ESA / NASA	L1	S
CASSINI/HUYGENS									
Cassini/ Huygens	Cassini/ Huygens	5,655 kg	10-15-97 / 08:43	ESMC / 40	Titan 401B-Centaur / 21	U.S. / ESA	NASA JPL / ESA	Saturn, Titan	in progress
ASIASAT									
Asiasat 3	HGS 1	3,465 kg	12-24-97 / 23:19	GIIK-5 / 81L	Proton-K / 394-01	Asiasat	Asiasat / Hughes	lunar flyby	S

Program Tables 205

Deep Space Chronicle:
Appendices

Appendix 1

Abbreviations

AFBMD	Air Force Ballistic Missile Division
ARC	Ames Research Center
ASI	Italian Space Agency
AU	astronomical unit
DoD	Department of Defense
DSPSE	Deep Space Program Science Experiment
ESA	European Space Agency
ESMC	Eastern Space and Missile Center
ETR	Eastern Test Range
GSFC	Goddard Space Flight Center
GSMZ Lavochkin	Lavochkin State Union Machine Building Plant
IASTP	Inter-Agency Solar-Terrestrial Physics (Program)
ISAS	Institute of Space and Astronautical Science
JPL	Jet Propulsion Laboratory
KSC	Kennedy Space Center
LaRC	Langley Research Center
NASA	National Aeronautics and Space Administration
NEAR	Near Earth Asteroid Rendezvous
NIIP-5	Scientific-Research and Testing Range No. 5 (Baykonur)
NPO Lavochkin	Lavochkin Scientific-Production Association
OKB-1	Experimental Design Bureau No. 1

SETI	Search for Extraterrestrial Intelligence
SOHO	Solar and Heliospheric Observatory
SSI	Solid State Imaging (system)
STL	Space Technology Laboratories
STSP	Solar Terrestrial Science Programme
TETR-B	Test and Training Satellite
TsKBEM	Central Design Bureau of Experimental Machine Building (formerly OKB-1)
U.S.	United States (of America)
USAF	U.S. Air Force
USSR	Union of Soviet Socialist Republics (Soviet Union)
UT	Universal Time
WSMC	Western Space and Missile Center

Appendix 2

Lunar, Planetary, and Deep Space "Firsts"

Overall

First lunar probe attempt:
    U.S. / **Able 1** / 17 August 1958

First probe to reach escape velocity:
    USSR / **Luna 1** / 2 January 1959

First probe to heliocentric orbit:
    USSR / **Luna 1** / 2 January 1959

First spacecraft to impact on another celestial body (Moon):
    USSR / **Luna 2** / 14 September 1959

First spacecraft to fly by the Moon:
    USSR / **Luna 3** / 6 October 1959

First photographs of the far side of the Moon:
    USSR / **Luna 3** / 6 October 1959

First Mars probe attempt:
    USSR / **[Mars]** / 10 October 1960

First spacecraft to fly past Venus successfully:
    U.S. / **Mariner 2** / 14 December 1962

First spacecraft to fly past Mars successfully:
    U.S. / **Mariner 4** / 15 July 1965

First spacecraft to impact another planet (Venus):
    USSR / **Venera 3** / 1 March 1966

First spacecraft to make a survivable landing on the Moon:
    USSR / **Luna 9** / 3 February 1966

First spacecraft to orbit the Moon:
    USSR / **Luna 10** / 2 April 1966

First spacecraft to take pictures of Earth from the Moon:
    U.S. / **Lunar Orbiter 2** / 23 August 1966

First successful planetary atmospheric entry probe (Venus):
    USSR / **Venera 4** / 18 October 1967

First liftoff from the Moon:
    U.S. / **Surveyor 6** / 17 November 1967

First successful circumlunar mission:
    USSR / **Zond 5** / 14–21 September 1968

First transmission from the surface of another planet (Venus):
    USSR / **Venera 7** / 15 December 1970

First robotic spacecraft to recover and return lunar samples:
    USSR / **Luna 16** / 12–21 September 1970

First wheeled vehicle on the Moon:
    USSR / **Lunokhod 1** / 17 November 1970

First spacecraft to impact on Mars:
    USSR / **Mars 2** / 27 November 1971

First spacecraft to enter orbit around a planet (Mars):
    U.S. / **Mariner 9** / 14 November 1971

First spacecraft to fly through the asteroid belts:
    U.S. / **Pioneer 10** / out in February 1973

First spacecraft to fly past Jupiter:
    U.S. / **Pioneer 10** / 4 December 1973

First spacecraft to use gravity-assist to change its trajectory:
    U.S. / **Mariner 10** / 5 February 1974 (at Venus)

First spacecraft to fly past Mercury:
    U.S. / **Mariner 10** / 29 March 1974

First spacecraft to transmit photos from the surface of another planet (Venus):
    USSR / **Venera 9** / 22 October 1975

First spacecraft to orbit Venus:
    USSR / **Venera 9** / 22 October 1975

First spacecraft to take photos on the surface of Mars:
U.S. / **Viking 1** / 20 July 1976

First spacecraft to orbit a libration point:
U.S. / **ISEE-3** / 20 November 1978

First spacecraft to fly past Saturn:
U.S. / **Pioneer 11** / 1 September 1979

First spacecraft to leave the solar system:
U.S. / **Pioneer 10** / 13 June 1983

First spacecraft to fly past a comet (Comet Giacobini-Zinner):
U.S. / **ISEE-3** / 11 September 1985

First spacecraft to fly past Uranus:
U.S. / **Voyager 2** / 24 January 1986

First spacecraft to fly past Neptune:
U.S. / **Voyager 2** / 25 August 1989

First spacecraft to use Earth for a gravity-assist:
ESA / **Giotto** / 2 July 1990

First spacecraft to use aerobraking to reduce velocity:
Japan / **Hiten** / 19 March 1991

First spacecraft to fly past an asteroid (Gaspra):
U.S. / **Galileo** / 29 October 1991

First spacecraft to enter Jupiter's atmosphere:
U.S. / **Galileo Probe** / 7 December 1995

First spacecraft to orbit Jupiter:
U.S. / **Galileo Orbiter** / 8 December 1995

First wheeled vehicle on another planet (Mars):
U.S. / **Sojourner** / 5 July 1997

First spacecraft to orbit an asteroid (Eros):
U.S. / **NEAR** / 14 February 2000

First spacecraft to land on an asteroid (Eros):
U.S. / **NEAR Shoemaker** / 12 February 2001

Mercury

First flyby:
U.S. / **Mariner 10** / 29 March 1974

Venus

First probe attempt:
   USSR / **[Venera]** / 4 February 1961

First successful flyby:
   U.S. / **Mariner 2** / 14 December 1962

First impact:
   USSR / **Venera 3** / 1 March 1966

First successful atmospheric entry:
   USSR / **Venera 4** / 18 October 1967

First soft-landing:
   USSR / **Venera 7** / 15 December 1970

First surface photos:
   USSR / **Venera 9** / 22 October 1975

First orbiter:
   USSR / **Venera 9** / 22 October 1975

Moon

First lunar probe attempt:
   U.S. / **Able 1** / 17 August 1958

First impact:
   USSR / **Luna 2** / 14 September 1959

First flyby:
   USSR / **Luna 3** / 6 October 1959

First photos of the far side:
   USSR / **Luna 3** / 6 October 1959

First survivable landing:
   USSR / **Luna 9** / 3 February 1966

First orbiter:
   USSR / **Luna 10** / 2 April 1966

First liftoff from the Moon:
   U.S. / **Surveyor 6** / 17 November 1967

First successful circumlunar mission:
   USSR / **Zond 5** / 14–21 September 1968

First robotic soil sample:
   USSR / **Luna 16** / 12–21 September 1970

First wheeled vehicle on the Moon:
    USSR / **Lunokhod 1** / 17 November 1970

Mars

First probe attempt:
    USSR / **[Mars]** / 10 October 1960

First successful flyby:
    U.S. / **Mariner 4** / 15 July 1965

First spacecraft to orbit:
    U.S. / **Mariner 9** / 14 November 1971

First impact:
    USSR / **Mars 2** / 27 November 1971

First surface photos:
    U.S. / **Viking 1** / 20 July 1976

First wheeled vehicle:
    U.S. / **Sojourner** / 5 July 1997

Jupiter

First flyby:
    U.S. / **Pioneer 10** / 4 December 1973

First atmospheric entry:
    U.S. / **Galileo Probe** / 7 December 1995

First orbiter:
    U.S. / **Galileo Orbiter** / 8 December 1995

Saturn

First flyby:
    U.S. / **Pioneer 11** / 1 September 1979

Uranus

First flyby:
    U.S. / **Voyager 2** / 24 January 1986

Neptune

First flyby:
    U.S. / **Voyager 2** / 25 August 1989

Deep Space Chronicle:
Bibliography

Bibliography

United States

Baker, David, ed. *Jane's Space Directory, 1999–2000*. Coulsdon, UK: Jane's Information Group Limited, 1999.

Carr, M. H., et al. *Viking Orbiter Views of Mars*. Washington, DC: NASA SP-441, 1980.

Dunne, James A., and Eric Burgess. *The Voyage of Mariner 10: Mission to Venus and Mercury*. Washington, DC: NASA SP-424, 1978.

Ezell, Linda Neumann. *NASA Historical Data Book, Volume II: Programs and Projects 1958–1968*. Washington, DC: NASA SP-4012, 1988.

Ezell, Linda Neumann. *NASA Historical Data Book, Volume III: Programs and Projects 1969–1978*. Washington, DC: NASA SP-4012, 1988.

Fimmel, Richard O., et al. *Pioneer Odyssey*. Washington, DC: NASA SP-396, 1977.

Gatland, Kenneth. *Robot Explorers*. London: Blanford Press, 1972.

Hall, R. Cargill. *Lunar Impact: A History of Project Ranger*. Washington, DC: NASA SP-4210, 1977.

Major NASA Launches, Total Major ETR and WTR Launches. Kennedy Space Center, FL: NASA Information Summaries, PMS 031 (KSC), December 1989.

Powell, Joel W. "Thor-Able and Atlas-Able," *Journal of the British Interplanetary Society* 37 (1984): 219–25.

Rumerman, Judy A. *NASA Historical Data Book, Volume V: NASA Launch Systems, Space Transportation, Human Spaceflight, and Space Science 1979–1988*. Washington, DC: NASA SP-4012, 1999.

A Summary of Major NASA Launches, October 1, 1958–December 31, 1989. Kennedy Space Center, FL: KSC Historical Report No. (KHR-1), June 1992.

Wilson, Andrew. *The Eagle Has Wings: The Story of American Space Exploration, 1945–1975.* London: British Interplanetary Society, 1982.

Wilson, Andrew. *Solar System Log.* London: Jane's Publishing Company Limited, 1987.

Soviet Union/Russia

Chertok, B. Ye. *Rakety i luidi: Fili Podlipki Tyuratam.* Moscow: Mashinostroyeniye, 1996.

Chertok, B. Ye. *Rakety i luidi: goryachiye dni kholodnoy voyny.* Moscow: Mashinostroyeniye, 1997.

Glushko, V. P., ed. *Kosmonavtika entsiklopediya.* Moscow: Sovetskaya entsiklopediya, 1985.

Johnson, Nicholas L. *Handbook of Soviet Lunar and Planetary Exploration.* San Diego, CA: American Astronautical Society, 1979.

Lantratov, K. "25 Years From Lunokhod-1" (in Russian), *Novosti kosmonavtiki* no. 23 (5–18 November 1995): 79–83.

Lantratov, K. "25 Years From Lunokhod-1" (in Russian), *Novosti kosmonavtiki* no. 24 (19 November–2 December 1995): 70–79.

Lantratov, K. "Russia. To Mars!" (in Russian), *Novosti kosmonavtiki* no. 20 (23 September –6 October 1996): 53–72.

Lantratov, K. "To Mars!" (in Russian), *Novosti kosmonavtiki* no. 21 (7–20 October 1996): 41–51.

Maksimov, G. Yu. "Construction and Testing of the First Soviet Automatic Interplanetary Stations," in J. D. Hunley, ed., *History of Rocketry and Astronautics, Vol. 20.* San Diego: American Astronautical Society, 1997, pp. 233–46.

Perminov, V. G. *A Difficult Road to Mars: A Brief History of Mars Exploration in the Soviet Union.* Washington, DC : NASA, 1999.

Sagdeev, R. Z., and A. V. Zakharov. "Brief History of the Phobos Mission," *Nature* 341 (10 October 1989): 581–85.

Siddiqi, Asif A. "First To The Moon," *The Journal of the British Interplanetary Society* 51 (May 1998): 231–38.

Siddiqi, Asif A., Bart Hendrickx, and Timothy Varfolomeyev. "The Tough Road Travelled: A New Look at the Second Generation Luna Probes," *Journal of the British Interplanetary Society*, 53 (2000): 319–56.

Varfolomeyev, Timothy. "Soviet Rocketry That Conquered Space: Part 3: Lunar Launchings for Impact and Photography," *Spaceflight* 38 (June 1996): 206–08.

Varfolomeyev, Timothy. "Soviet Rocketry That Conquered Space: Part 5: The First Planetary Probe Attempts, 1960–1964," *Spaceflight* 40 (March 1998): 85–88.

Varfolomeyev, Timothy. "Soviet Rocketry That Conquered Space: Part 6: The Improved Four-Stage Launch Vehicle, 1964–1972," *Spaceflight* 40 (May 1998): 181–84.

Vladimirov, A. "Table of Launches of the 'Proton' and 'Proton-K' RN" (in Russian), *Novosti kosmonavtiki* no. 10 (18 April–1 May 1998): 25–30.

Project Web Sites on the World Wide Web

"Cassini-Huygens Mission to Saturn and Titan." Jet Propulsion Laboratory. *http://www.jpl.nasa.gov/cassini/*

Christian, Eric R. "Advanced Composition Explorer (ACE) Project Page." Goddard Space Flight Center. 16 February 2001. *http://helios.gsfc.nasa.gov/ace/ace.html*

"Clementine-DSPSE." Naval Research Laboratory. *http://www.nrl.navy.mil/clementine/clementine.html*

"Deep Space 1." Jet Propulsion Laboratory. *http://nmp.jpl.nasa.gov/ds1/*

"Deep Space 2." Jet Propulsion Laboratory. *http://nmp.jpl.nasa.gov/ds2/*

"ESA Science: Giotto." European Space Agency. *http://spdext.estec.esa.nl/home/giotto/*

"ESA Science: Huygens." European Space Agency. *http://sci.esa.int/huygens/*

"ESA Science: SOHO." European Space Agency. *http://spdext.estec.esa.nl/home/soho/*

"ESA Science: Ulysses." European Space Agency. *http://spdext.estec.esa.nl/home/ulysses/*

"ISAS: Missions." *http://www.isas.ac.jp/e/enterp/missions/index.html*

"Galileo: Journey to Jupiter." Jet Propulsion Laboratory. *http://www.jpl.nasa.gov/galileo/*

"Lunar Prospector." Ames Research Center. *http://lunar.arc.nasa.gov/*

"MARS 96: Robotic Spacecraft Mission to Mars." Space Research Institute. 1996. *http://www.iki.rssi.ru/mars96/mars96hp.html*

"Mars Climate Orbiter." Jet Propulsion Laboratory. *http://mpfwww.jpl.nasa.gov/msp98/orbiter/*

"Mars Global Surveyor." Jet Propulsion Laboratory. *http://mpfwww.jpl.nasa.gov/mgs/index.html*

"Mars Polar Lander." Jet Propulsion Laboratory. *http://mars.jpl.nasa.gov/msp98/lander/*

"Near Earth Asteroid Rendezvous: Discovery is NEAR." Johns Hopkins University. *http://near.jhuapl.edu/*

"Pioneer." Ames Research Center.
http://spaceprojects.arc.nasa.gov/Space_Projects/pioneer/PNhome.html

"STARDUST." Jet Propulsion Laboratory. *http://stardust.jpl.nasa.gov/top.html*

"Voyager: Celebrating 25 Years of Discovery." Jet Propulsion Laboratory. 27 March 2002. *http://voyager.jpl.nasa.gov*

"Wind." Goddard Space Flight Center. *http://www-istp.gsfc.nasa.gov/istp/wind/*

Unofficial Sources on the World Wide Web

"Launch Log." *http://hea-www.harvard.edu/~jcm/space/log/launch.html*

"Planetary Sciences at the National Space Science Data Center." National Space Science Data Center, Goddard Space Flight Center.
http://nssdc.gsfc.nasa.gov/planetary/planetary_home.html

Deep Space Chronicle:
About the Author

About the Author

Asif A. Siddiqi was born in Dhaka, Bangladesh, and educated in Bangladesh, the United Kingdom, and the United States.

His award-winning book *Challenge to Apollo: The Soviet Union and the Space Race, 1945–1974* (NASA SP-2000-4408) was published in 2000. An earlier book of poems, *Politics*, was published in Dhaka, Bangladesh in 1991.

He is currently a Ph.D. candidate in the History Department at Carnegie Mellon University.

The NASA History Series

Reference Works, NASA SP-4000:

Grimwood, James M. *Project Mercury: A Chronology*. NASA SP-4001, 1963.

Grimwood, James M., and C. Barton Hacker, with Peter J. Vorzimmer. *Project Gemini Technology and Operations: A Chronology*. NASA SP-4002, 1969.

Link, Mae Mills. *Space Medicine in Project Mercury*. NASA SP-4003, 1965.

Astronautics and Aeronautics, 1963: Chronology of Science, Technology, and Policy. NASA SP-4004, 1964.

Astronautics and Aeronautics, 1964: Chronology of Science, Technology, and Policy. NASA SP-4005, 1965.

Astronautics and Aeronautics, 1965: Chronology of Science, Technology, and Policy. NASA SP-4006, 1966.

Astronautics and Aeronautics, 1966: Chronology of Science, Technology, and Policy. NASA SP-4007, 1967.

Astronautics and Aeronautics, 1967: Chronology of Science, Technology, and Policy. NASA SP-4008, 1968.

Ertel, Ivan D., and Mary Louise Morse. *The Apollo Spacecraft: A Chronology, Volume I, Through November 7, 1962*. NASA SP-4009, 1969.

Morse, Mary Louise, and Jean Kernahan Bays. *The Apollo Spacecraft: A Chronology, Volume II, November 8, 1962–September 30, 1964*. NASA SP-4009, 1973.

Brooks, Courtney G., and Ivan D. Ertel. *The Apollo Spacecraft: A Chronology, Volume III, October 1, 1964–January 20, 1966*. NASA SP-4009, 1973.

Ertel, Ivan D., and Roland W. Newkirk, with Courtney G. Brooks. *The Apollo Spacecraft: A Chronology, Volume IV, January 21, 1966–July 13, 1974*. NASA SP-4009, 1978.

Astronautics and Aeronautics, 1968: Chronology of Science, Technology, and Policy. NASA SP-4010, 1969.

Newkirk, Roland W., and Ivan D. Ertel, with Courtney G. Brooks. *Skylab: A Chronology*. NASA SP-4011, 1977.

Van Nimmen, Jane, and Leonard C. Bruno, with Robert L. Rosholt. *NASA Historical Data Book, Volume I: NASA Resources, 1958–1968*. NASA SP-4012, 1976, rep. ed. 1988.

Ezell, Linda Neuman. *NASA Historical Data Book, Volume II: Programs and Projects, 1958–1968*. NASA SP-4012, 1988.

Ezell, Linda Neuman. *NASA Historical Data Book, Volume III: Programs and Projects, 1969–1978*. NASA SP-4012, 1988.

Gawdiak, Ihor Y., with Helen Fedor, compilers. *NASA Historical Data Book, Volume IV: NASA Resources, 1969–1978*. NASA SP-4012, 1994.

Rumerman, Judy A., compiler. *NASA Historical Data Book, 1979-1988: Volume V, NASA Launch Systems, Space Transportation, Human Spaceflight, and Space Science*. NASA SP-4012, 1999.

Rumerman, Judy A., compiler. *NASA Historical Data Book, Volume VI: NASA Space Applications, Aeronautics and Space Research and Technology, Tracking and Data Acquisition/Space Operations, Commercial Programs, and Resources, 1979–1988*. NASA SP-2000-4012, 2000.

Astronautics and Aeronautics, 1969: Chronology of Science, Technology, and Policy. NASA SP-4014, 1970.

Astronautics and Aeronautics, 1970: Chronology of Science, Technology, and Policy. NASA SP-4015, 1972.

Astronautics and Aeronautics, 1971: Chronology of Science, Technology, and Policy. NASA SP-4016, 1972.

Astronautics and Aeronautics, 1972: Chronology of Science, Technology, and Policy. NASA SP-4017, 1974.

Astronautics and Aeronautics, 1973: Chronology of Science, Technology, and Policy. NASA SP-4018, 1975.

Astronautics and Aeronautics, 1974: Chronology of Science, Technology, and Policy. NASA SP-4019, 1977.

Astronautics and Aeronautics, 1975: Chronology of Science, Technology, and Policy. NASA SP-4020, 1979.

Astronautics and Aeronautics, 1976: Chronology of Science, Technology, and Policy. NASA SP-4021, 1984.

Astronautics and Aeronautics, 1977: Chronology of Science, Technology, and Policy. NASA SP-4022, 1986.

Astronautics and Aeronautics, 1978: Chronology of Science, Technology, and Policy. NASA SP-4023, 1986.

Astronautics and Aeronautics, 1979-1984: Chronology of Science, Technology, and Policy. NASA SP-4024, 1988.

Astronautics and Aeronautics, 1985: Chronology of Science, Technology, and Policy. NASA SP-4025, 1990.

Noordung, Hermann. *The Problem of Space Travel: The Rocket Motor.* Edited by Ernst Stuhlinger and J. D. Hunley, with Jennifer Garland. NASA SP-4026, 1995.

Astronautics and Aeronautics, 1986–1990: A Chronology. NASA SP-4027, 1997.

Astronautics and Aeronautics, 1990–1995: A Chronology. NASA SP-2000-4028, 2000.

Management Histories, NASA SP-4100:

Rosholt, Robert L. *An Administrative History of NASA, 1958–1963.* NASA SP-4101, 1966.

Levine, Arnold S. *Managing NASA in the Apollo Era.* NASA SP-4102, 1982.

Roland, Alex. *Model Research: The National Advisory Committee for Aeronautics, 1915–1958.* NASA SP-4103, 1985.

Fries, Sylvia D. *NASA Engineers and the Age of Apollo.* NASA SP-4104, 1992.

Glennan, T. Keith. *The Birth of NASA: The Diary of T. Keith Glennan.* J. D. Hunley, editor. NASA SP-4105, 1993.

Seamans, Robert C., Jr. *Aiming at Targets: The Autobiography of Robert C. Seamans, Jr.* NASA SP-4106, 1996.

Project Histories, NASA SP-4200:

Swenson, Loyd S., Jr., James M. Grimwood, and Charles C. Alexander. *This New Ocean: A History of Project Mercury.* NASA SP-4201, 1966; rep. ed. 1998.

Green, Constance McLaughlin, and Milton Lomask. *Vanguard: A History.* NASA SP-4202, 1970; rep. ed. Smithsonian Institution Press, 1971.

Hacker, Barton C., and James M. Grimwood. *On Shoulders of Titans: A History of Project Gemini.* NASA SP-4203, 1977.

Benson, Charles D., and William Barnaby Faherty. *Moonport: A History of Apollo Launch Facilities and Operations.* NASA SP-4204, 1978.

Brooks, Courtney G., James M. Grimwood, and Loyd S. Swenson, Jr. *Chariots for Apollo: A History of Manned Lunar Spacecraft.* NASA SP-4205, 1979.

Bilstein, Roger E. *Stages to Saturn: A Technological History of the Apollo/Saturn Launch Vehicles.* NASA SP-4206, 1980, rep. ed. 1997.

SP-4207 not published.

Compton, W. David, and Charles D. Benson. *Living and Working in Space: A History of Skylab.* NASA SP-4208, 1983.

Ezell, Edward Clinton, and Linda Neuman Ezell. *The Partnership: A History of the Apollo-Soyuz Test Project.* NASA SP-4209, 1978.

Hall, R. Cargill. *Lunar Impact: A History of Project Ranger.* NASA SP-4210, 1977.

Newell, Homer E. *Beyond the Atmosphere: Early Years of Space Science.* NASA SP-4211, 1980.

Ezell, Edward Clinton, and Linda Neuman Ezell. *On Mars: Exploration of the Red Planet, 1958–1978.* NASA SP-4212, 1984.

Pitts, John A. *The Human Factor: Biomedicine in the Manned Space Program to 1980.* NASA SP-4213, 1985.

Compton, W. David. *Where No Man Has Gone Before: A History of Apollo Lunar Exploration Missions.* NASA SP-4214, 1989.

Naugle, John E. *First Among Equals: The Selection of NASA Space Science Experiments.* NASA SP-4215, 1991.

Wallace, Lane E. *Airborne Trailblazer: Two Decades with NASA Langley's Boeing 737 Flying Laboratory.* NASA SP-4216, 1994.

Butrica, Andrew J., ed. *Beyond the Ionosphere: Fifty Years of Satellite Communication.* NASA SP-4217, 1997.

Butrica, Andrew J. *To See the Unseen: A History of Planetary Radar Astronomy.* NASA SP-4218, 1996.

Mack, Pamela E., ed. *From Engineering Science to Big Science: The NACA and NASA Collier Trophy Research Project Winners.* NASA SP-4219, 1998.

Reed, R. Dale, with Darlene Lister. *Wingless Flight: The Lifting Body Story.* NASA SP-4220, 1997.

Heppenheimer, T. A. *The Space Shuttle Decision: NASA's Search for a Reusable Space Vehicle.* NASA SP-4221, 1999.

Hunley, J. D., ed. *Toward Mach 2: The Douglas D-558 Program.* NASA SP-4222, 1999.

Swanson, Glen E., ed. *"Before this Decade is Out . . .": Personal Reflections on the Apollo Program.* NASA SP-4223, 1999.

Tomayko, James E. *Computers Take Flight: A History of NASA's Pioneering Digital Fly-by-Wire Project.* NASA SP-2000-4224, 2000.

Morgan, Clay. *Shuttle-Mir: The U.S. and Russia Share History's Highest Stage.* NASA SP-2001-4225, 2001.

Mudgway, Douglas J. *Uplink-Downlink: A History of the Deep Space Network, 1957–1997.* NASA SP-2001-4227, 2002.

Center Histories, NASA SP-4300:

Rosenthal, Alfred. *Venture into Space: Early Years of Goddard Space Flight Center.* NASA SP-4301, 1985.

Hartman, Edwin P. *Adventures in Research: A History of Ames Research Center, 1940–1965.* NASA SP-4302, 1970.

Hallion, Richard P. *On the Frontier: Flight Research at Dryden, 1946-1981.* NASA SP-4303, 1984.

Muenger, Elizabeth A. *Searching the Horizon: A History of Ames Research Center, 1940–1976.* NASA SP-4304, 1985.

Hansen, James R. *Engineer in Charge: A History of the Langley Aeronautical Laboratory, 1917–1958.* NASA SP-4305, 1987.

Dawson, Virginia P. *Engines and Innovation: Lewis Laboratory and American Propulsion Technology.* NASA SP-4306, 1991.

Dethloff, Henry C. *"Suddenly Tomorrow Came . . .": A History of the Johnson Space Center.* NASA SP-4307, 1993.

Hansen, James R. *Spaceflight Revolution: NASA Langley Research Center from Sputnik to Apollo.* NASA SP-4308, 1995.

Wallace, Lane E. *Flights of Discovery: 50 Years at the NASA Dryden Flight Research Center.* NASA SP-4309, 1996.

Herring, Mack R. *Way Station to Space: A History of the John C. Stennis Space Center.* NASA SP-4310, 1997.

Wallace, Harold D., Jr. *Wallops Station and the Creation of the American Space Program.* NASA SP-4311, 1997.

Wallace, Lane E. *Dreams, Hopes, Realities: NASA's Goddard Space Flight Center, The First Forty Years.* NASA SP-4312, 1999.

Dunar, Andrew J., and Stephen P. Waring. *Power to Explore: A History of the Marshall Space Flight Center.* NASA SP-4313, 1999.

Bugos, Glenn E. *Atmosphere of Freedom: Sixty Years at the NASA Ames Research Center.* NASA SP-2000-4314, 2000.

General Histories, NASA SP-4400:

Corliss, William R. *NASA Sounding Rockets, 1958–1968: A Historical Summary*. NASA SP-4401, 1971.

Wells, Helen T., Susan H. Whiteley, and Carrie Karegeannes. *Origins of NASA Names*. NASA SP-4402, 1976.

Anderson, Frank W., Jr. *Orders of Magnitude: A History of NACA and NASA, 1915–1980*. NASA SP-4403, 1981.

Sloop, John L. *Liquid Hydrogen as a Propulsion Fuel, 1945–1959*. NASA SP-4404, 1978.

Roland, Alex. *A Spacefaring People: Perspectives on Early Spaceflight*. NASA SP-4405, 1985.

Bilstein, Roger E. *Orders of Magnitude: A History of the NACA and NASA, 1915–1990*. NASA SP-4406, 1989.

Logsdon, John M., ed., with Linda J. Lear, Jannelle Warren-Findley, Ray A. Williamson, and Dwayne A. Day. *Exploring the Unknown: Selected Documents in the History of the U.S. Civil Space Program, Volume I, Organizing for Exploration*. NASA SP-4407, 1995.

Logsdon, John M., ed., with Dwayne A. Day and Roger D. Launius. *Exploring the Unknown: Selected Documents in the History of the U.S. Civil Space Program, Volume II, Relations with Other Organizations*. NASA SP-4407, 1996.

Logsdon, John M., ed., with Roger D. Launius, David H. Onkst, and Stephen J. Garber. *Exploring the Unknown: Selected Documents in the History of the U.S. Civil Space Program, Volume III, Using Space*. NASA SP-4407, 1998.

Logsdon, John M., gen. ed., with Ray A. Williamson, Roger D. Launius, Russell J. Acker, Stephen J. Garber, and Jonathan L. Friedman. *Exploring the Unknown: Selected Documents in the History of the U.S. Civil Space Program, Volume IV, Accessing Space*. NASA SP-4407, 1999.

Logsdon, John M., gen. ed., with Amy Paige Snyder, Roger D. Launius, Stephen J. Garber, and Regan Anne Newport. *Exploring the Unknown: Selected Documents in the History of the U.S. Civil Space Program, Volume V, Exploring the Cosmos*. NASA SP-2001-4407, 2001.

Siddiqi, Asif A. *Challenge to Apollo: The Soviet Union and the Space Race, 1945–1974*. NASA SP-2000-4408, 2000.

Monographs in Aerospace History, NASA SP-4500:

Maisel, Martin D., Demo J. Giulianetti, and Daniel C. Dugan. *The History of the XV-15 Tilt Rotor Research Aircraft: From Concept to Flight*. NASA SP-2000-4517, 2000.

Jenkins, Dennis R. *Hypersonics Before the Shuttle: A Concise History of the X-15 Research Airplane*. NASA SP-2000-4518, 2000.

Chambers, Joseph R. *Partners in Freedom: Contributions of the Langley Research Center to U.S. Military Aircraft in the 1990s*. NASA SP-2000-4519, 2000.

Waltman, Gene L. *Black Magic and Gremlins: Analog Flight Simulations at NASA's Flight Research Center.* NASA SP-2000-4520, 2000.

Portree, David S. F. *Humans to Mars: Fifty Years of Mission Planning, 1950–2000.* NASA SP-2001-4521, 2001.

Thompson, Milton O., with J. D. Hunley. *Flight Research: Problems Encountered and What They Should Teach Us.* NASA SP-2000-4522, 2000.

Tucker, Tom. *The Eclipse Project.* NASA SP-2000-4523, 2000.

Index

Able 1, 9
Able IVB, 23, 26
Able VA, 26
Able VB, 27
accelerometer, 104, 109, 110, 129, 130
ACP, aerosol collector/pyrolyser, 170
Advanced Composition Explorer, ACE, 169
Agena, B, D, 31, 32, 44, 47, 66
Air Force, U.S., Test and Training Range, 17, 178
Aldebaran, Taurus constellation, 97
Aldrin, Buzz, 78
ALPHA, alpha/proton spectrometer, 165
alpha-scattering instrument, 67, 69
Alphonsus, crater, 48
Amalthea, Jupiter moon, 117, 121, 147
Ames Research Center, NASA ARC, 102
aneroid barometer, 64, 65, 73, 74, 82, 87, 104, 109, 110, 126
ANGSTREM, x-ray spectrometer, 165
Apollo, 4, 55, 56, 58, 61, 66, 71, 101
Apollo 8, 74
Apollo 11, 61, 78
Apollo 12, 61, 62, 63, 83
Apollo 15, 90
Apollo 16, 98
Apollo 17, 102

APXS, alpha particle proton and x-ray spectrometer, 165
Ariel, Uranus moon, 120
ARGUS, imaging system, 165
Aristarchus, crater, 58
Armstrong, Neil, 78
Asiasat 1, 170
Asiasat 3, 171
ASPERA, energy mass experiment, 164
Atlantis, Space Shuttle, 143, 145, 149
Atlas, 24, 47
Atlas-Able, 26, 27
Atlas-Agena B, 33, 34, 41, 47, 48, 58
Atlas-Agena D, 58, 61, 63
Atlas-Centaur, 47, 61, 67, 69, 75, 76, 88, 93, 94, 105, 123
atomic hydrogen detector, 40, 41
Austria, 133
Automatic Interplanetary Station, AMS, 23

Bean, Alan L., 62, 63
Bulgaria, 133

Callisto, Jupiter moon, 97, 117, 121, 146, 147
Cape Canaveral, Florida, 7, 55
Cassini-Huygens, 169, 9, 169, 170
CDS, coronal diagnostic spectrometer, 159

CELIAS, charge, element/isotope analysis experiment, 159
Centaur, 54, 63, 85
Centaur-Surveyor, 54
Challenge to Apollo: The Soviet Union and the Space Race, 1945–1974, 9
charged-particle traps, detector, 29, 40, 41, 45, 54, 64, 94, 98, 102, 123
Cherenkov Effect, 19
Chryse Planitia, 111
CIDA, cometary and interstellar dust analyzer, 178
Clementine, 103, 116, 155, 157, 173
Comet Borrelly, 176
Comet Wild-2, 178
Control Computer and Sequencer, CC&S, 76
Conrad, Charles, Jr., 62, 63
Copernicus, crater, 57, 58
cosmic dust detector, 43, 44, 68, 79, 103, 138, 149, 174
cosmic radio emission receivers, 51
cosmic-ray-anisotropy detector, 52, 68, 71, 79, 81, 82, 85, 87, 91, 97, 102, 104, 107, 108, 115, 117, 129, 130, 131
cosmic-ray gas-discharge counters, 50, 53, 54, 65
cosmic-ray telescope, 43, 44, 52, 68, 79, 94, 120
Cosmic Rocket, Luna 1, 21, 22
CRIS, cosmic-ray isotope spectrometer, 169
Czechoslovakia, 133, 157

Deep Space Program Science Experiment, DSPSE, 155
Deep Space 1, 174
Deep Space 2, 177
Delta 2, 169
Department of Defense, DOD, 155
DesCam, descent phase camera, 165
Dione, Saturn moon, 122, 170
DWE, Doppler wind experiment, 170
DPI, three component accelerometer, 165
DYMIO, omni ionosphere energy mass spectrometer, 164

Earth, 8, 13, 18, 19, 21, 23, 25, 26, 27, 29, 30, 35, 36, 39, 40, 42, 43, 44, 48, 49, 50, 51, 54, 55, 56, 58, 62, 63, 64, 65, 66, 67, 68, 70, 73, 74, 76, 78, 79, 80, 81, 82, 84, 85, 86, 90, 93, 96, 97, 98, 102, 104, 106, 108, 109, 110, 112, 113, 116, 119, 122, 123, 124, 134, 137, 146, 147, 155, 157, 161, 162, 165, 169, 170, 174, 178
Eastman-Kodak, 56
EIT, extreme ultraviolet imaging telescope, 159
electric field detector, 68, 79
ELISMA, wave complex experiment, 164
Enceladus, Saturn moon, 117, 170
EPAM, electron, proton, and alpha particle monitor, 169
ER, electron reflectometer, 173
ERNE, energetic-particle analyzer, 159
Eros, 8, 161, 163
Europa, Jupiter moon, 8, 97, 117, 121, 146, 147
European Space Agency, ESA, 124, 138, 149, 150, 151, 157, 160, 170
EVRIS, stellar oscillations photometer, 164
Explorer 33, 56, 66
Explorer 35, 65, 90
Explorer 49, 103

Faraday-cup plasma probe, 56, 65
Federal Aviation Administration, FAA, 52
Fobos 1, 141, 142
Fobos 2, 141, 142
FONEMA, omni non-scanning energy-mass ion analyzer, 164

Galileo, 7, 8, 9, 145, 146, 147, 156, 170
Galileo Europa Mission, GEM, 146
Ganymede, Jupiter moon, 8, 97, 117, 121, 146, 147
gas-analyzer cartridges, 64, 65, 73, 97, 102
gas chromatograph, 129, 130
Gaspra, 8
GCMS, gas chromatograph neutral mass spectrometer, 170
Geiger-Mueller tube, photon, counter, 25, 50, 51, 65, 94, 102
Germany, Federal Republic, West, 133, 149, 174
Giacobini-Zinner, comet, 125, 138, 139
Giotto, comet, 137, 138

Goddard Space Flight Center, NASA GSFC, 124

GOLF, global oscillations at low frequencies experiment, 159

Grand Tour, 6, 7, 120

Grigg-Skjellerup, comet, 138

GRUNT, accelerometers, 165

Hagomoro, 149

Halley's Comet, 57, 125, 130, 133, 134, 135, 137, 138

HASI, Huygens atmospheric structure instrument, 170

Helios 1, 108, 115

Helios 2, 115

Helios-B, 115

Hiten, Muses-A, 149

Hughes Aircraft Company, 67

Hughes Global Systems, 171

Hyperion, Saturn moon, 117, 170

Iapetus, 117, 170

IMAP-6, magnetometer, 165

Inertial Upper Stage, IUS, 143, 145

infrared camera, 17, 155

infrared radiometer, 57, 58, 76, 86, 88, 103, 107, 110, 153, 176

infrared spectrometer, 131

infrared thermal mapper, 110

Institute of Microbiology, National Academy of Sciences, 34

Institute of Space and Astronautical Sciences, ISAS, 137, 138

Inter-Agency Solar-Terrestrial Physics Program, IASTP, Wind, 157

wind speed recorder, 98

International Cometary Explorer, ICE, 125

International Solar Polar Mission, ISPM, 150

International Sun-Earth Explorers, ISEE, 124

Interplanetary Monitoring Platform, IMP, 108

Intrepid, 62, 63

Io, Jupiter moon, 117, 121, 146, 147

ionization chamber, traps, thrusters, densitometer, 21, 25, 43, 44, 49, 50, 51, 54, 64, 73, 74, 109, 110

ISA, energetic ions experiment, 174

ISS, imaging system, 170

Japan, 149, 157, 174

Jet Propulsion Laboratory, JPL, 4, 5, 34, 36, 43, 144, 163, 169

Jupiter, 3, 7, 8, 9, 13, 93, 95, 97, 102, 103, 117, 120, 121, 122, 145, 146, 147, 150, 156, 170

Kamerton seismometer, 165

Kennedy Space Center, John F., NASA KSC, 5

Kepler, crater, 50

Kohoutek, Comet 52

Kosmos, 159, 13, 51, 54

Kosmos 300, 79, 80

Kosmos 305, 80

Kosmos 359, 82

Kosmos 419, 86

Kosmos 482, 98

LASCO, white light/spectrometric coronograph, 159

Lavochkin, design bureau, 53, 64, 76, 77, 87

LIDAR, light detection and ranging instrument, 177

LILAS-2, cosmic and solar gamma-burst spectrometer, 164

Luna, 14,

Luna 3, 23, 24

Luna 5, 49

Luna 6, 49

Luna 7, 50

Luna 8, 52

Luna 9, 53

Luna 10, 54

Luna 11, 57

Luna 12, 58

Luna 13, 59

Luna 14, 70

Luna 15, 78

Luna 16, 82, 83, 90, 93, 108

Luna 17, 83, 84

Luna 18, 90, 93

Luna 19, 91

Luna 20, 93

Luna 21, 101, 107

Luna 22, 107

Luna 23, 108, 113, 116

Luna 24, 116

Lunar Module, LM, 62

Lunar Orbiter, 4

Lunar Prospector, 173, 178

Lunokhod 1, 83, 84, 91, 101

Lunokhod 2, 101, 102, 107

LWR, longwave radar, 165

MAG, magnetometer, 17, 21, 25, 29, 40, 41, 43, 44, 45, 49, 50, 51, 52, 53, 54, 56, 57, 58, 63, 64, 65, 66, 71, 86, 87, 91, 93, 98, 101, 102, 103, 104, 105, 107, 109, 115, 117, 123, 126, 129, 130, 133, 137, 138, 145, 153, 157, 161, 169, 173, 174

Magellan, 4, 5, 143, 144, 145, 147

MAK, quadruple mass spectrometer, 165

MARCI, Mars color imaging system, 176

Mare Crisium, crater, 78, 108, 115

Mare Serenitatis, crater, 23, 101

Mare Sirenum, crater, 88

Mariner 1, 4, 35

Mariner 2, 4, 25, 35

Mariner 3, 44

Mariner 4, 5, 34, 44, 64

Mariner 5, 45, 64, 65

Mariner 6, 76, 77, 89

Mariner 7, 76, 89

Mariner 8, 88

Mariner 9, 5, 88, 89, 90, 104

Mariner 10, 96, 106

Mariner 71H, Mariner H, 85, 86

Mariner R, 34, 35

MARIPROB, ionosphere plasma spectrometer, 164

Marius, crater, 53

Mars, U.S.S.R., 2, 9, 14, 86, 87, 88, 91, 103, 104, 105

Mars, Red Planet, 3, 4, 5, 6, 8, 9, 13, 34, 26, 27, 36, 37, 40, 44, 45, 49, 50, 51, 75, 76, 77, 85, 86, 87, 88, 89, 93, 103, 104, 105, 111, 112, 141, 142, 153, 164, 165, 166, 174, 176, 177, 178

Mars Climate Orbiter, MCO, 176

Mars descent imager, MARDI, 177

Mars Global Surveyor, MGS, 6, 47, 50, 111, 163, 164, 167, 176, 177, 178

Mars Observer, 153, 164

Mars Pathfinder, Sagan Memorial Station, 6, 165, 166, 167, 178

Mars Polar Lander, MPL, 176

Maxwell Montes, Venus, 123, 147

MDI, Michelson Doppler imager, 159

MECOM, meteorological unit, 165

Mercury, 13, 96, 106

MET, meteorology package, 177

meteoroid detectors, 49, 57, 58, 61, 91, 94, 102, 104, 107

Metis, Jupiter moon, 121

MIC, visible camera, 174

Milky Way, 7, 169

micrometeoroid detector, spectrometer, 17, 25, 56, 57, 58, 61, 63, 65, 66

Mimas, Saturn moon, 122, 170

Miranda, Uranus moon, 120

MIS, meteorology instrument system, 165

Moon, 5, 13, 17, 18, 19, 21, 22, 23, 26, 27, 33, 34, 36, 40, 41, 42, 43, 48, 49, 50, 53, 54, 55, 58, 62, 63, 65, 66, 69, 70, 71, 75, 76, 78, 79, 81, 83, 84, 90, 91, 93, 98, 101, 102, 103, 106, 108, 113, 116, 122, 149, 157, 171

MORION-S, science data acquisition instrument, 165

MSI, multispectral imager, 161

Muses-A, Hiten, 149

MVACS, Mars volatile and climate surveyor, 177

National Academy of Sciences, NAS, 147

National Aeronautics and Space Administration, NASA, 3, 4, 5, 6, 7, 8, 14, 18, 26, 27, 34, 35, 44, 45, 55, 61, 64, 65, 67, 68, 94, 97, 102, 103, 108, 111, 116, 122, 125, 129, 137, 143, 144, 145, 146, 151, 156, 157, 159, 160, 163, 164, 167, 169, 170, 174, 176, 177, 178,

National Research Council, NRC, NAS, 147

NavCam, navigation camera, 178

Near Earth Asteroid Rendezvous, NEAR, NEAR-Shoemaker, 8, 161, 162, 163, 178

nephelometer, 109, 126, 129, 130, 134, 145

Neptune, 7, 9, 13, 97, 102, 119, 120

neutral mass spectrometer, 138, 170, 174

NEUTRON-S, neutron spectrometer, 165, 173

NIS, near infrared mapping spectrometer, 145, 161
Nix Olympia, 5, 89
NLR, laser rangefinder, 161
Nozomi, 174

Ocean of Storms, 55, 61, 62
Oceanus Procellarum, 63
Olympus Mons, 5, 88, 90
OPTIMIZM, seismometer/magnetometer/inclinometer, 165

PanCam, panoramic camera, 165
PEGAS, gamma-ray spectrometer, 165
penetrometer, 58, 83, 87, 101
PFS, infrared Fourier spectrometer, 165
Phoebe, Saturn moon, 117
Phobos, 77, 141
photoelectric cell aspect indicator, 25, 73, 74
photo-emulsion camera, 71
PHOTON, gamma spectrometer, 165
piezoelectric detector, 21, 40, 41, 45, 50, 51, 54
Pioneer 0, 14, 150
Pioneer 3, 19
Pioneer 4, 22
Pioneer 5, 25
Pioneer 6, 52, 57, 68
Pioneer 7, 52, 57, 68
Pioneer 8, 52, 57, 68
Pioneer 9, 52, 71, 95
Pioneer 10, 7, 94, 95, 97, 102, 108, 120
Pioneer 11, 7, 102, 108, 120
Pioneer Venus 1, 4, 18, 123, 124, 131, 144
Pioneer Venus 2, 4, 124
plasma analyzer, 52, 56, 68, 71, 94, 105, 108, 115, 123, 124, 125, 133, 137, 138, 145, 157
Pluto, 6, 7, 13
proportional counter, 25
Pwyll, crater, 146

radiation densitometer, 59, 87
radiation detector, 39, 40, 41, 43, 44, 45, 48, 49, 50, 51, 53, 56 (dosimeters), 57, 58, 59, 61, 63, 64, 66, 71, 75, 76, 77, 79, 80, 81, 83, 91, 93, 101, 107, 115

radio altimeter, 64, 73, 74, 91, 93, 97, 104, 107, 109, 113, 115, 153, 155
radio propagation detector, 79
radiotelescope, 40, 41, 45, 49, 75, 86, 87, 103
radioisotope thermoelectric generators, RTGs, 121
radiometer, 76, 77, 87, 102, 123
RADIUS-MD, dosimeter, 164
Ranger, Block II, 4, 30, 33, 34, 36, 43, 48
Ranger 1, 31, 32
Ranger 2, 31, 32
Ranger 4, 34
Ranger 5, 36
Ranger 6, 41
Ranger 7, 43, 47, 48
Ranger 8, 47, 48
Ranger 9, 48
Reiner, crater, 53
resistance thermometer, 64, 73, 74, 81, 82, 97, 104, 105, 109, 110
Rhea, Saturn moon, 122, 170
robotic arm, RA, 177
robotic arm camera, RAC, 177
RTSW, real-time solar wind experiment, 169
Russia, Soviet Union, 3, 4, 5, 13, 14, 17, 19, 21, 23, 24, 25, 34, 36, 37, 39, 40, 41, 42, 43, 45, 48, 49, 64, 65, 68, 71, 78, 82, 83, 86, 90, 93, 98, 105, 109, 110, 113, 129, 133, 137, 142, 149, 157

Sagan, Carl, 167
Sakigake, 137
Sample Return Capsule, SRC, 178
Saturn, 7, 8, 9, 13, 97, 102, 117, 120, 122, 170
scintillation counter, 21
Sea of Fertility, crater, 90
Sea of Rains, crater, 58, 84
Sea of Tranquillity, 47, 61
Search for Extraterrestrial Intelligence, SETI, 71
seismometer, single-axis, 33, 130
SEPICA, solar energetic particle ionic charge analyzer, 169
Shoemaker, Eugene, 163, 173
SIS, solar isotope spectrometer, 16
SLED-2, low-energy charged particle spectrometer, 164

Sojourner, 6, 9, 166, 167

Solar and Heliospehric Observatory, SOHO, 159, 160

solar plasma probe, 64

Solar System Log, 9, 14

solar wind detector, 81, 83, 97, 129, 131, 137

Solid State Imaging, 33, 39, 44, 45, 47, 48, 49, 50, 51, 53, 55, 56, 57, 58, 61, 65, 66, 67, 69, 71, 75, 76, 79, 83, 85, 86, 87, 91, 93, 101, 102, 103, 107, 109, 110, 113, 115, 117, 120, 129, 130, 134, 145, 153

Soyuz, 98

Space Shuttle, 8, 143, 145, 150

Space Technology Laboratories, 24

SPICAM, multichannel spectrometer, 165

Sputnik, 13, 18

SSP, surface science package, 170

Stardust, 178

stereo surface imager, SSI, 77, 78, 79, 80, 177

SUMER, solar-ultraviolet emitted radiation experiment, 159

Sun, 6, 7, 8, 13, 21, 36, 53, 68, 103, 106, 108, 115, 122, 147, 150, 151, 156, 159, 164, 169

Surveyor 2, 57, 70

Surveyor 3, 61, 62, 63, 65, 69

Surveyor 4, 13, 54, 55, 65

Surveyor 5, 67, 69

Surveyor 6, 68, 69

Surveyor 7, 69

Susei, 138

SVET, mapping spectrometer, 165

SWAN, solar wind anisotropies experiment, 159

Sweden, 174

SWEPAM, solar wind electron, proton, and alpha monitor, 169

SWICS, solar wind ion composition spectrometer, 169

SWIMS, solar wind ion mass spectrometer, 169

synthetic aperture radar, SAR, 143,

Taurus, 97

Taurus Mountains, 101

temperature sensors, 17

TERMOSCAN, mapping radiometer, 165

Tethys, Saturn moon, 117, 122, 170

Thebe, Jupiter moon, 121

thermal and evolved gas analyzer, TEGA, 177

Thor-Able, 19

Thor-Able 1, 17, 18,

Thor-Delta E, 52, 56, 65, 66, 68, 71

Thor-Delta L, 79

Titan, Saturn moon, 8, 117, 122, 170

Titania, Uranus moon, 120

Transfer Orbit Stage, TOS, 153

Transvaal, South Africa, 26

Triton, 7, 120

Tycho, crater, 69

ULEIS, ultra-low-energy isotope spectrometer, 169

ultraviolet and infrared spectrophotometer, 49, 64, 65, 75, 86, 87, 103, 129, 130

ultraviolet photometer, 85, 94, 101, 102, 103, 110, 138, 155

ultraviolet spectrograph, spectrometer, 49, 76, 77, 85, 88, 91, 97, 101, 104, 109, 117, 120, 124, 125, 133, 134, 145, 153, 174

Ulysses, 150, 151

Umbriel, Uranus moon, 120

United States, U.S., 3, 4, 6, 14, 33, 34, 43, 115, 137, 143, 155, 157

Uranus, 7, 9, 13, 119, 120, 122

UVCS, ultraviolet coronograph spectrometer, 159

UVS-M, ultraviolet spectrometer, 165

Valles Marineris, 5

Van Allen, 18

variometer, 29

Vega, 133

Vega 1, 134, 135, 138

Vega 2, 134, 135, 138

Venera, 14, 39, 50, 51, 64, 65, 131, 135

Venera 4, 74, 81

Venera 5, 74, 81

Venera 6, 74, 81

Venera 7, 81, 91, 97

Venera 8, 91, 97, 98

Venera 9, 109, 110, 126

Venera 10, 110, 126

Venera 11, 126, 127, 130

Venera 12, 126, 130

Venera 13, 129, 130

Venera 14, 129

Venera 15, 131

Venera 16, 131

Venus, 3, 4, 5, 8, 24, 25, 29, 34, 35, 40, 42, 43, 45, 50, 51, 64, 73, 74, 81, 82, 97, 98, 106, 109, 123, 124, 125, 126, 129, 130, 131, 132, 133, 134, 143, 144, 145, 147, 147, 170

Viking 1, 5, 85, 103, 111, 112

Viking 2, 5, 85, 103, 111

Viking A, 111

Viking B, 111

VIMS, visual infrared mapping spectrometer, 170

VIRGO, variability of solar irradiance experiment, 159

Voyager, 7, 118, 147

Voyager Interstellar Mission, VIM, 120, 122

Voyager 1, 7, 97, 102, 117, 121, 122, 150

Voyager 2, 7, 102, 117, 119, 120, 121, 150

Webb, crater, 82

Weiler, Edward, 6

Wilson, Andrew, 9, 14

Wilson-Harrington Comet, 176

XRS-GRS, x-ray/gamma-ray spectrometer, 33, 53, 54, 57, 75, 77, 83, 87, 103, 109, 110, 133, 134, 153, 161

Ye-1, 22

Ye-1A, 22

Ye-2A, 25

Ye-6, 39, 40, 41, 48, 49, 50, 53, 54, 69, 107

Ye-8, 74, 75, 77, 78, 81, 90, 91, 93, 101, 107, 115

Zond, 14, 42, 70, 78, 98

Zond 1, 43

Zond 2, 45

Zond 3, 49, 57

Zond 6, 71, 72

Zond 7, 79

Zond 8, 83

www.ingramcontent.com/pod-product-compliance
Lightning Source LLC
Chambersburg PA
CBHW082114230426
43671CB00015B/2700